A Thousand Hills
to Heaven

A Thousand Hills to Heaven

Love, Hope, and a
Restaurant in Rwanda

JOSH RUXIN

LITTLE, BROWN AND COMPANY
New York   Boston   London

Little, Brown and Company
Hachette Book Group
237 Park Avenue, New York, NY 10017
littlebrown.com

First Edition: November 2013

Little, Brown and Company is a division of Hachette Book Group, Inc. The Little, Brown name and logo are trademarks of Hachette Book Group, Inc.

The publisher is not responsible for websites (or their content) that are not owned by the publisher.

The Hachette Speakers Bureau provides a wide range of authors for speaking events. To find out more, go to hachettespeakersbureau.com or call (866) 376-6591.

Photographs by Josh and Alissa Ruxin, unless otherwise noted

Title page photograph by Ian Christmann

Map by Jeffrey L. Ward

Library of Congress Cataloging-in-Publication Data
Ruxin, Josh
    A thousand hills to heaven : love, hope, and a restaurant in Rwanda / Josh Ruxin. — First edition.
        pages cm
    Includes index.
    ISBN 978-0-316-23291-3
    1. Ruxin, Josh. 2. Ruxin, Alissa. 3. Rwanda—Description and travel. 4. Americans—Rwanda—Biography. 5. Restaurateurs—Rwanda. I. Title.
    CT275.R8955A3 2013
    967.57104'3092—dc23   2013026116

10 9 8 7 6 5 4 3 2 1

RRD-C

Printed in the United States of America

For Alissa

Contents

Contents

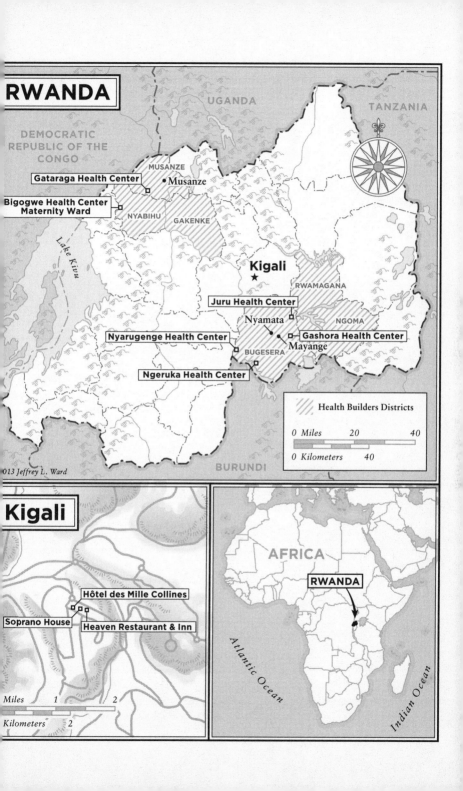

A Thousand Hills
to Heaven

Preface

This is not a book about the Rwandan genocide, nor is it a book about politics. It is not a cookbook (exactly). It's a book about our marriage, our adventures together in the Heart of Darkness, and about Heaven, our hillside restaurant and bar in Rwanda, where, from the outdoor dining deck, there is a very good evening view of the end of poverty.

CHAPTER 1

~~~

Getting There

Our plane drifts up over the Atlantic at dusk. We watch a film or two, then doze off. The sun comes up as we float down to Brussels. A cup of coffee there, then we rise over the morning Alps, and then the blue Mediterranean, and finally the torn, brown edge of Africa. There is a thick brown haze below—a midday sandstorm in the Sahara. It takes time to cross the Sahara, as it is about the size of the United States. Africa is big enough to hold all of the United States, including Alaska, plus all of Mexico, all of China, India, France, Spain, Germany, Italy, Greece, Turkey, Pakistan, Afghanistan, and the United Kingdom. Even then, you'd have enough land left over for two States of Texas—but Africa has enough trouble. When economists describe Africa as the next China, or the next New World, you have to keep in mind how impossibly big it is, but also how filled it is with energetic, ambitious young people and unmeasured resources. It is too violent, yes, but so was North America once.

In a few hours we are high above the pain and beauty of Darfur, where horrific atrocities are still playing out, and then over oil-rich and therefore troubled South Sudan. Then over

Uganda with its booming economy and new construction—its traffic jams are glowing jewelry below, as night has fallen. Beyond that, only a few slash-and-burn fires below relieve the incredible darkness in the heart of Africa. Finally we slide down along the swampy, reed-lined shores of Lake Victoria, which is as large as Lake Michigan, and into Rwanda. The nation of Rwanda is two-thirds the size of Switzerland, or about the size of Massachusetts, but round like a fist and tucked just under the Equator.

On approach to the little nation's capital, Kigali, we fly over the spot where the plane carrying the presidents of Rwanda and Burundi was shot down on April 6, 1994, triggering perhaps the cruelest one hundred days in human history. Roughly a million men, women, and children were killed, mostly by machete. Then, east of Rwanda, across the Congo border—the darkest spot on the continent—millions more died in the years following 1994, and fighting continues there even now, driven by a lack of government and an excess of militias, gold, diamonds, oil, and memories of murder. It is the nation next door and a constant worry.

But we do not go quite that far. As our plane lands and finally rolls to a stop, four men push a stairway to the door. We hundred people pull down our bags, fumble for business cards for seatmates, relocate passports and yellow fever vaccination cards, and shuffle out. Most passengers seem to be Rwandans or other Africans, coming home or on business. Maybe a quarter of the people are Europeans and Americans, some no doubt coming to work with a charity or church group. A few look like tourists: middle-agers on their way to the misty ridges of the volcanoes in the north of Rwanda, where they will sit among the mountain gorillas like the fellow primates they are. As we exit, there are some very awake people, young and old, whose eyes seem ravenous for every new sight around them and whose smiles are as fixed as if they had just taken a hit of something—Africa is indeed an altered state for those fully open to it.

If you arrived before dark, you would see a green hilly country with farming terraces cut into every slope—even terraced up the sides of the volcanoes, and terraced down into the bowls of them. Rwanda is the most crowded country in Africa, and therefore the most farmed. But one usually arrives late, as it is a long way from anywhere.

Arriving at nine o'clock in the evening seems like midnight. It feels good to walk around on the tarmac after such a lengthy flight. The airplane is massive in the darkness above you, and the miracle of flight seems more real than in a Western airport, where you slip out through a deep corridor, never really seeing the big bird for what it is, and never having that moment to just look up and marvel at it for bringing you such a long way, so quickly and safely. Travelers and explorers of the past had to suffer years of canoe paddling, diseases, and murderous jungle trekking to get here—most not arriving this far inland until well into the twentieth century.

You have used the assembled knowledge of Western civilization to get here more easily, though you are tired. You stand in the cool African air, hear the caws of night birds, smell the signature scent of Africa—a blend of the day's burning of leaves swept from the streets by ten thousand women with straw brooms and gunny sacks, plus the tropical sweetness of flowers and the dust and faint pungency of the faraway open sewers of poverty. There might be a bread bakery in the distance, is how it seems.

Not so long ago this same tarmac saw people running toward the last planes out, as artillery fired from the sides of the runway toward the rebel army perched on Parliament Hill, just over there—now with bright lights on it, and the Parliament building still with holes in it. The holes are intentionally preserved for history, like the cannonballs stuck in Virginia's fine old homes.

For me, when I stand in such a place, I can't help but visualize Rwanda's nightmare. It's not my own memory, but after years here, the memories of friends saturate my thinking.

If you met us now at the airport, you would see my wife, Alissa, our two young daughters, our toddler son, and me. It has become a milk run for us, yet always a very long way to come.

Is it right to raise children in such a place—a crime scene, really? We've lived here nearly a decade, so clearly we've voted with our feet (and frequent flier miles). And there are Abed and Apollo, waving just outside the security area. Abed is the driver for our agricultural and health projects in the rural villages, and Apollo is our family driver. They have both come knowing that we'd be returning with more than two dozen fifty-pound bags loaded with treats from Trader Joe's, wet wipes and diapers, cereal, and cooking supplies for our restaurant. We are deeply grateful for their smiles and help: we are home.

You might think that Rwanda, situated just south of the Equator, would be a constant steam bath, but it is not. The elevation of the entire country is about a mile up, which makes the weather rather like early spring in Southern California, all year long. In the morning, there is nowhere you can look and not see flowers, bananas, fiery orange blossoms in treetops, birds of paradise, lush hillsides and imposing volcanoes, and giant birds sailing overhead instead of airplanes and their jet trails. And it rains a great deal—Rwanda needs two rainy seasons just to get all that rain in. Sunrise always comes at about the same time, as does sunset, and the days are always the same length, with the dark hours equal to the light. If you were us, you might miss the four seasons of New York and Connecticut, and the long summer evenings there, but you would soon embrace this short-sleeved world of flowering landscapes and trees full of birds.

As for the people, there are no kinder in the world than Rwandans.

Kigali, the capital, consists of one hill after another, much like the rest of Rwanda. The constant hill climbing keeps everyone lean, though poverty makes a contribution. The country's nickname for itself is "the land of a thousand hills" or *le pays des mille collines*. The native language is Kinyarwanda, and Swahili is widely used as well. English is the language used lately in schools and between Rwandans and foreigners who might not know much Kinyarwanda. Further complicating communication, French is the residual language of colonial days under the Belgians and is the lingua franca of many people.

The so-called Hotel Rwanda, made famous by the movie of the same name, is on the same hill as our home and also our restaurant. Its real name is the Hôtel des Mille Collines, and it has been remodeled into a luxury hotel since the troubles. The swimming pool that saved the thousand barricaded people from dying of thirst has nice bamboo furniture around it now, and a thatch-roofed bar. Some things, some, have moved on.

CHAPTER 2

—◁◦▷—

Moisture

You want to sleep in after that long flight. But the morning birds!

We were still new to our present house in Rwanda—a home built by a Belgian architect who fled with his family during the 1994 genocide—when a strange rainstorm woke us one morning after an arduous flight. It was strange because the rains usually come in the afternoon, but it was also strange because of the women who seemed to come in with it.

Every morning, rainy or not, begins about the same here, and you never need an alarm clock. The glass louvers of your windows are open year-round, but screened to keep out the dangerous mosquitoes. (Most mosquitoes only make you itch, but the varieties with white spots can transmit malaria.) Breezes and the rich smells of ripe fruit and big flowers drift in during the day and night. Your skin enjoys the moist air. The mosquito net over your bed catches the blue dawn like a sultan's tent.

At four thirty, if you are awake, through the silence you will just barely hear the day's first call to prayer from the Muslim section of town, which is perhaps a mile away and around several hills. It is lovely. It is lovely for its own sake, and also because the Muslim section of town was protected from the genocide by the people's refusal to kill and their willingness to protect others—an untold story of the Rwandan genocide. So it is a good sound to begin the day. And then the birds.

The prayer awakens the birds. A few birds have been making simple chirps through the hours, but they are just the night watch. Now arriving, however, are the symphony's main players. They begin with a few peeps, twitters, whistles, and caws, as if tuning up. You might sleep through that, with practice. But then big leaves and pods, heavy with dew, begin to fall on the roof with leathery thumps. The guayava fruit, pecked-at for breakfast by big birds high in the trees, fall like hammer blows on your tin roof—if you have a tin roof, as most do, rich and poor. If you are yet sleeping, you will now wake to the turacos and other big-beaked, long-tailed, colorful jungle birds as they take their turns with brilliantly loud soprano ululations that rise over this million-bird overture to the new day. If you have two little daughters and a baby boy, their voices will be next.

The birds and babies are not alone in their vociferous response to the dawn: though each day is a challenge for Rwandans, whose homes, tiny and large, spread out in smoky pastels below our bedroom window's vista, it is, very simply, another day to be thankful to be alive. Rwandans are conscious of, and thankful for, the miraculous luck of their personal survival. They are proud of their country for how it has moved on from unspeakably dark times. They believe it is on its way to greatness—the Singapore of Africa, perhaps. That thought helps them get out of bed and keep at it.

On that strange morning in the house that was new to us, I

was under the great net canopy of our bed, propped on an elbow to watch Alissa sleep a little longer beside me as the lavender light came in. She sometimes wears earplugs to sleep longer—only one earplug, actually, as the other ear listens for the children.

I watch Alissa stir awake. She is brave to be here, especially after a miscarriage during her first pregnancy. This is our home now, but that is only a geographic fact. Where you grew up and came of age is always your true home. As I listen to the birds chatter, I like to think of the bigger picture, to feel that these jungles are our deeper home. Indeed, they were the planet's main genetic labs, where our human ancestors began our story a quarter-million years ago. Some humans stayed to evolve in place and some migrated across the savannahs and up the Nile, becoming the people of the Middle East, of Southern Europe, of Asia and the New World. But this jungle is our truest home. The European explorers, the Stanleys and Livingstones, who journeyed up the Nile to find its source, were salmons of a sort, coming home. And this place, where we live, is that river's source, or very near it. We fashion our fancy cultures and think we have sprung from some American story, some Irish sod, some English countryside, some Asian or European village, some Eastern European shtetl, but all that has merely been the journey. This has always been the home.

Rwanda's mornings, like the evenings, have a tranquilizing coolness that is quite comfortable. Alissa has surrendered to the weather here; she wears open-toed sandals on the evening terrace of Heaven, our restaurant, which often results in a chilly bedtime surprise for me. She is considerate, however, and sometimes runs warm water over her icy little dancer's feet before coming to bed.

At five o'clock this morning, the thunder announced an unusual morning storm on its way. The birds screamed their songs suddenly louder—no empathy for lazy creatures still abed. Then lightning struck nearby. Alissa said good morning and rolled into me as the windows were still rattling. Her toes were warm.

African rains arrive like waterfalls. It was noisily drowning the trees a few blocks away, then it rushed closer, then we were underneath it. The escaping birds warned their friends downwind. Three big kites—big black birds with five-foot wingspans and muscles enough to carry away small animals—suddenly rose up across our view through the window as the last helicopters out.

When the rain stopped suddenly, as it does—it just turns off—we could hear the beeping of horns and little motorcycles, the moto-taxis, down on the road. We could hear a dog or two barking. There are some dogs in Rwanda, but not many. They are expensive to feed, and most of them were shot in the days after the genocide, when so many bodies were on the streets and in the underbrush. The starving dogs found them and lost the affection of the nation. We have a little mutt we rescued as a newborn puppy on the street, and our neighbors have a dog, but otherwise they are rare.

Then a knock came at the gate. It was still very early.

We have a cook and helper, Joel (pronounced in the French way: *Jo-Ell*), who had already arrived for the day. I knew because I could smell his coffee—rich Rwandan coffee from beans grown and roasted by our neighbor. I heard Joel go outside to open the gate. He brought three women to the front door as I headed downstairs.

They were Rwandan women, dressed in the flowing bright

prints and headdresses of Africa. They had calm but serious expressions as they shook off their umbrellas and stood them against the long wall of the front veranda, which is accented by several banana trees. Thumb-sized bananas grace our table nearly year-round, and we use the flower of the plant in Asian-inspired salads at the restaurant.

"*Bonjour,*" said the eldest woman. "I am here to inform you that the body of my brother is buried in your backyard, and we would like to arrange a time to come with a priest and some workers to remove his bones," she said in French.

"*S'il vous plaît, entrez,*" I said, inviting them in.

"*Merci,*" she said as they came in and sat on our big blue and white couches that have hosted many gatherings of public health experts, journalists, American friends on safari, and Kigali friends from down the road. Joel disappeared to prepare African tea with ginger and milk, and a tray of cookies. The oldest in the group calmly explained that the murderer of her brother had recently confessed and had given exact information about where the bones had been buried during the hundred days of terror. She showed us the X on the map of our side yard. The grave was in a far corner against the concrete block wall. It was no doubt very shallow, and we had been lucky not to disturb it when we planted the birds of paradise, bamboo, banana, red hibiscus, acacia, frangipani, and mandarin trees to obscure the security wall.

It is a regular occurrence for bones to be discovered somewhere, almost everywhere, and then be moved to the genocide memorial tombs. You often see machete-scarred people on the street with limbs missing, and those bones must be somewhere, too—though the rest of the person hobbles on to return your morning *Mwaramutse!* with a smile. Such sights were more common when we first arrived, but even now, a savage scar or missing limb receives no more notice on the street than a bold tattoo in Manhattan, though we still feel a great heaviness when we see it.

Even now we occasionally find human bones when we walk along the dirt road that goes uphill from our house. They wash out in the rainy seasons from shallow graves dug twenty years ago.

Most of that history was something we could shut out when we closed the door and turned on our music from back home. The heavy ghosts had not come into our own house, at least until now. But, indeed, we now understood that a good young man named Epafrodite Rugengamanzi, whose sister loved him very much, died a brutal death in our yard at the age of thirty-six. Epafrodite was buried where he fell.

We agreed on a date when the body could be exhumed. The women thanked us as they left.

I heard Alissa quietly crying in the bathroom. I think we had not properly mourned a few things ourselves, and now there were these bones.

CHAPTER 3

—⁓—

The Neighbors Will Know About the Bones

I am not one for ghosts, but you want your home to be a joyful place with the atmosphere of good memories, not terror. I was curious to learn more about the killing, and I figured our neighbors might know more about what happened in our yard, as they had been here during the genocide. Also, I had not thanked them for the sack of roasted coffee beans that appeared at our door soon after we moved in. They have a small coffee plantation—a hobby really.

Olivier Costa, the son and family scion, who races sports cars and manages the family automotive and advertising businesses, is in his mid-forties, as am I. He greeted me at their gate, and we sat down for a cup with his father, Pierantonio. Their housekeeper set a table with silver for us on a lush lawn, near the family's prized orchids. The family's cook then appeared and set a French press decanter of coffee before us.

Pierantonio looks fit for his years. He has the pink, round face of prosperity and deeply sympathetic blue-green eyes. Olivier, the son, was but twenty-two when it all began. He and his sister, as his father explained, had just come home for spring break from their studies in Europe. Their ten-year-old brother was also at home that evening of April 6, 1994. The five of them, including Olivier's mother, Swiss-born Mariann, heard two explosions: the rocket hitting the president's airplane as it approached the Kigali airport, and the sound of the plane's impact, killing all aboard and triggering the meticulously planned genocide. Roadblocks were instantly erected all over the city to hold the doomed Tutsi and the politically moderate Hutus in their neighborhoods so they could be slaughtered door to door. Hutu death mobs were given long lists of family addresses.

I asked Pierantonio about the bones in our yard.

"Oui," he said as he stirred the sugar into his coffee. He looked at me a little sadly, as no one needs to hear such things about the house they call home. *"En fait, j'ai le regret de vous informer, quatre personnes ont été assassinées dans votre maison."*

Four people had been killed at our home—in the yard, he believed. Three of them, he knew, had been buried down the hill—right across the road—and the other one on our property somewhere. His description chilled me: I had noticed when we moved in that many of the doorframes in our house had been repaired. Now I knew that the doors had been kicked in. The Interahamwe—the death mobs—filled the city with so many corpses that they came back through and forced those not targeted for killing to bury them where they lay or nearby. They killed a quarter of the big city's population. That was a great deal of killing, as Kigali and its outskirts had a population of about a million. Larger percentages, up to 80 percent or more of a village's population, were killed elsewhere.

Four people had run to our house—a few hours vacant since the Belgian architect sped his family to the airport. The streets were barricaded, block by block, by men with machetes. The bodies of Tutsi men, women, and children were piling up at the barricades. The Interahamwe, blowing whistles in unison like soccer fans, were chasing people down streets, up driveways, into gardens and houses. They were burning some alive in the streets with gasoline.

It should be understood that Hutus and Tutsi were not even tribal groups, though they once had been. By the nineteenth century, the terms were used mainly as a class system: if you owned many cattle, you were considered a Tutsi. An overlay of ethnic differences remained, but there had been so much mobility up and down, and so much intermarriage, that Tutsi really meant upper class and Hutu meant laborer. They shared the same language, traditions, religions, and lands.

The Belgian colonists had marked their identity cards as Hutu or Tutsi based on almost random considerations. Narrower nose: mark her a Tutsi. Fewer than ten cattle: mark him Hutu. Whatever old divisions had once been real, after Belgium's arrival the main difference between the Rwandan people was simply ink marks on identity cards. The Belgians elevated the Tutsi to coveted government positions, leaving the Hutu a mostly unrepresented majority. If the Belgians needed a justification for the division, there was a handy theory that the Tutsi came from Ethiopia or thereabouts, where they were a lost tribe of Israelites—they were kin to whites in that way. Many Tutsi believe they are related to the Israelites and, as Alissa and I are Jews who celebrate Passover with our Rwandan friends, the subject has come up. Among the more insane parallels to the Passover story is the fact that at the beginning of the genocide, baby boys and young men were the first to be taken from their families to be killed.

When the Belgians left in 1959, the Hutu used their overwhelming numbers to rule over and massacre the Tutsi, prompting an exodus of Tutsi to neighboring countries and abroad. In the 1980s the ongoing oppression in Rwanda led a number of refugees, including future president Paul Kagame and his friend and colleague Fred Rwigema, to begin hatching one of the most elaborate military plans of all time. Incredibly, they built a secret military consisting of Rwandan refugees within the Ugandan army. Their war for Rwanda began in 1990, just as the Ugandans were about to uncover their plot. By 1994 the rebel army had pushed the Hutu government to the negotiating table, precisely when the most brutal hundred days of genocide began. Thus, in historical perspective, 1959 was the real commencement of the conflict, of which 1994 was but the insane crescendo.

On that first night, April 6, 1994, as Pierantonio explained to me, the Costa family slept in their bathroom, the only room without exposed windows. Ten-year-old Matthew slept in the bathtub. As the dawn came, they stood on their lawn and peered through their hedges, where they saw the Interahamwe shooting at and trying to break into the homes of two of their good neighbors. Fifteen people ran to Pierantonio's house and found protection in the attic.

There were twenty-five hundred United Nations peacekeepers in Rwanda, so the families under siege desperately telephoned for UN help. A white UN pickup truck arrived several times across the way, and the attackers dispersed. But then the truck went away and did not come again, and the attackers worked like zombies at the iron bars of the windows. (Many middle-class houses have iron bars. Some have safe rooms or hiding places, but they will buy only a little time under such intense attack.)

The Costas watched through their hedges and listened as the Sebulicocos, their neighbors directly across the dirt road, Rue de Progrès, were invaded and killed. Perhaps their other neighbors across the Rue, the Lando family, would be luckier. Pierantonio admired them. Mr. Lando, perhaps forty, was a professional, a minister in the government. His wife was Canadian. They had two fine boys, tall for their ages, and a teenage daughter who was beautiful and sparkling in temperament. Pierantonio admired how the girl was poised in conversation and how she took issue with the opinions of her mother, but in a charming way. The Landos' only problem this morning was that the father was a Tutsi, so his children were Tutsi, and his wife was the wife of a Tutsi. The Costas, other than make pleading phone calls on behalf of their neighbors, could do nothing against the well-armed death squad. They saw the Lando home finally overtaken by the butchers who then ravaged and killed the family.

Pierantonio's eyes welled up. He remembered the feeling of being powerless to help. It was a feeling of immense but unwarranted shame.

Pierantonio happened to hold the honorific title of Italian Consul to Kigali at the time of the genocide. Normally it meant nothing. But, as many of the professional diplomats, including the Italian ambassador to Rwanda, were back in their European homes for Easter, the fate of the nearly two hundred Italian expats in Rwanda fell to Pierantonio.

Mariann, his wife, quickly rummaged through all the shirts and trousers and towels and tablecloths and bedclothes in the house to find enough green, white, and red cloth to quickly stitch together some tricolor Italian flags. One was posted on the corner of their yard, visible from the road. Rwandans are an obedient people. Those who were killing were indeed obeying orders. With luck, they would obey the international convention of diplomatic protection—rules are rules. Other flags were rigged on the family's big Land Cruiser, as Pierantonio and Olivier would need to wade out into the killing to do what was now clearly necessary: get the Italians and as many other people as possible to the airport and out of Rwanda.

Pierantonio was not new to Africa or its horrors. He is the grandson of a planter who was perhaps the first white man to arrive at nearby Lake Tanganyika from the west, cutting through the jungles of Congo. He was only the fifth or sixth white man seen in many African places, just fifty-five years behind Stanley and Livingstone and the opening of Equatorial Africa.

When he was a young man, Pierantonio had been the sole person left defending a family plantation in Congo when an uprising overwhelmed the area. He waited for the warriors to drink themselves to sleep, then loaded his guns into his truck and sped out through the middle of them before they knew what he was doing. The thirty years since that narrow escape had been spent in neighboring Rwanda, which, until this moment, had been calmer for him. Even so, he had seen this coming. Right-wing radio programs had been demonizing the Tutsi minority, calling them cockroaches in need of extermination. Rumors were everywhere that weapons were being assembled in huge caches, and that the Interahamwe, in smaller massacres around Rwanda, were practicing to see how many people they could kill in an hour.

Pierantonio knew the value of cash in a bloody crisis. Days before, he had withdrawn the equivalent of $300,000 from his bank accounts. His coat now had pockets for each denomination of Rwandan franc. He had maps of where the Italians and others lived, prepared for this eventuality.

As if additional dangers were needed, mortar rounds were soon falling in parts of the city; a small contingent of the rebelled RPA—the Rwandan Patriotic Army—had been at the hilltop Parliament building during the peace negotiations that ended when the president's plane was shot down. The president was a Hutu, and radical elements within his own Hutu-dominant government were later accused of downing their own president's plane to scuttle the peace agreement that would have shared power with the rebels. The marooned RPA soldiers, under Rwandan Army artillery fire from the airport, were making bold excursions into the city to rescue many Tutsi and, within twenty-four hours of the commencement of the genocide, had joined with a much larger contingent of fellow soldiers. So, two things were going on in Kigali: a planned genocide, and urban warfare between two powerful armies.

Mariann watched her husband and her son drive away, the tricolor flags flapping from every quarter of the Land Cruiser and one stretched over the big hood. The sound of screaming and gunfire was now constant in the city, with big explosions coming from the district to the east, where the Parliament building still stood against the artillery barrage. There was smoke everywhere in the air.

Pierantonio rarely tells this story. He pauses and his eyes turn somber when he sees it all again in his head—the horror.

"Ce n'était pas seulement l'Afrique," he said. It was not just Africa. It was Bosnia, it was many places. But here the evil

shone its red eyes brightest, as neighbors killed the beautiful children they had seen playing the previous day.

The story of his rescues kept me for an hour more. He had pulled people from the instant of their deaths, using handfuls of cash. He had walked past groups of men with bloody machetes to find people in hiding places and escort them to safe houses. Olivier had done the same, sometimes walking over bodies to get across rooms and courtyards to find someone in hiding who had managed a phone call. They rushed people to the airport, though the artillery guns were still booming along the edges of the runway.

With his own family in the final motorcade, Pierantonio halted the vehicles to rush over to where a young girl was about to be killed. He bought her away from death and pushed her into one of their crowded vehicles. It was in such moments that Pierantonio's experience and knowledge of how much money to offer for what, how to make an offer irresistible without showing too much cash and risking your own life, came into good use. Over the incredible days to come, he would become a great master, knowing even when to smile and show complete confidence.

He ended the story, for now, with the scene of the last plane leaving Kigali. He was on it, as was his family. Olivier sat next to him and as they looked down at the smoke of Kigali, Olivier praised his father for doing an amazing job for the Italians and many others. But he asked his father if they had done enough for their Rwandan friends. This haunted Pierantonio. When they reached the safety of Nairobi, Kenya, he put Olivier and his sister on a plane back to Europe, and then he told Mariann that he must go back into Rwanda. She understood. That would be the beginning of a far greater adventure, and it would mean the difference—he would mean the difference—between life and death for thousands of people.

I asked him if anything good had come out of that horrible time. He brightened. He said that the long oppression of the Tutsi had forced them out of the country and into other countries where they got educated with important skills. When they came flowing back in 1994, the country really flowered into something new, he said.

"*Une autre fois,*" Pierantonio said—another time. He had said enough, remembered enough, for one morning. I went home to tell the story to Alissa. It is one of my favorite things, telling Alissa something that I have just learned, which now was that our neighbor could be put forth for the Nobel Peace Prize.

I am telling the story of the bones, and of our neighbor, so you can know something of the history of the place. It happened twenty years ago. For people who were there and who survived it, it was but yesterday. For us, it was a shadow over everything, but a fading shadow.

Rwandans, after all, were intent on moving ahead. Today, you see the big red Coca-Cola billboard with the smiling woman and you think that the other time was a crazy nightmare.

CHAPTER 4

———✖———

Feet on the Ground

The nightmare is indeed over. People work in shops now, as they do anywhere. They go to restaurants, as people do everywhere. They fall in love, as all people do. The men look at the women openly and the women look at the men furtively, as is the usual way. Alissa gets a lot of looks here, too. I don't mind it, as fair-skinned people are still unusual in many places here, and some of it is just that. You walk into a big open-air vegetable market and heads turn. It's not only that we are white, but that whites are considered rich, with the ability to change lives magically. Almost whatever you do here as a visitor will be met with approval: "The rich man never dances badly" is a local proverb.

But Alissa is also looked at because she is pretty. African women feel sorry for the fact that she has a small behind and a slim stature, but they have told her they think her face makes up for it.

Abed, the driver who takes me back and forth to the Millennium Village, the desperate community we came here to turn around, understands how much I care about Alissa, and he wants to support me in my taste.

"The good thing about her is that Apollo says it is no trouble for her to sit between the car seats of the children in back," he says, grasping for a silver lining. I had mentioned that she and I would be working out later that afternoon at the Serena Hotel. Perhaps he thought that working out was some kind of physical therapy to get bigger.

Abed is quick to find silver linings or to paper over our difficulties with proverbs. His ready wisdom has earned him the nickname "Op-ed," from my family.

He is shorter than Apollo, and quicker to complain as well as to comment. He wants to understand everything that is going on. If some VIPs are in the car, he later wants to know all about them.

"Hey boss, *je veux savoir*," he is always saying— "I want to know."

Abed's energy overflows into every department of his life. He is a Muslim and lives in the Muslim quarter, Nyamirambo, with a daughter and an aunt and some other kids he cares for—I have never understood the web of relationships, but I do know that his one salary provides for what seems to be a whole neighborhood. He has an old blue Peugeot, a remnant of colonial days, that sometimes comes alive in a great cloud of diesel smoke and can be driven up and down the fine stone streets of the district. He is a soccer player of some neighborhood fame. He is proud of the close-set stone streets of the Muslim district, set by imported Italian stonemasons, and he should be. And he is proud of how the Muslim quarter responded during the genocide. He should be.

—◦—

Meeting Alissa was actually the second time a pretty girl changed my life, and it is because of both of them that I'm in Rwanda.

I was finishing up a typically depressing freshman year of high school when I saw a great-looking girl go into a Global Issues Club meeting after school, so I followed her in. The group was talking about a terrible famine in Ethiopia. To impress her, I made a couple of suggestions and volunteered to help with some fundraising to finance development projects there.

The club co-president and I started organizing other schools, and began giving what then seemed state-of-the-art presentations with music and slideshows. Soon after we hooked up with some international non-governmental organizations (NGOs); what we were doing seemed cool to them. We organized high school students nationally, and, with four other students, I had the opportunity to go to Ethiopia and see things for myself. Just a year after a famine that killed a million, conditions were appalling. In a village in the North, some Ethiopian kids took me by the hand and led me up a dirt road to their mud and thatch classroom. On the wall was a poster with a picture of some American kids who were helping them. I was in the photo. It knocked me over. It was my small world moment.

The impressions made on youth at that age—I was seventeen—tend to stick with you always. I was hooked. After that trip to Ethiopia, if I wasn't in the middle of some big effort to help someone somewhere—in the States and elsewhere—I felt deeply hungry for it. And I got a case of developed country guilt: I would see people leaving food on their plates, or buying stupid stuff they didn't need, the cost of which would have fed a whole village for a month. The people around me were living to eat—fancy restaurants, banquets, holiday meals—while much of the world was eating to live. It became the filter through which I saw nearly everything around me.

When I first got back to school from that trip, students made bad jokes about starving people, just for my benefit—sometimes on the seniors' chalkboard in the cafeteria. I think now that this is what radicalized me. It was likely that time and those jokes that gave me an opportunity to make a decision about how I would spend my life. Did I want to be one of the gang, or was I willing to knock against the status quo?

In any event, my Ethiopian adventure is probably what got me into Yale, since I certainly didn't have the SAT scores or grades to go there. My degree, which was partly funded by a Truman Foundation Scholarship (in exchange for my promise to live a life of public service), led to a Fulbright Scholarship in Bolivia, then a Columbia University master's degree, then a London PhD on a Marshall Scholarship, then to positions in international consulting and a berth at Columbia. While consulting, I made frequent trips to Latin America and Africa and spent a year living in El Salvador after the war. I was there to help them pick up the economic pieces after a time of unimaginable violence. It was humbling to see how courageous people can be in the face of loss, and how they can point themselves to the future. I visited the sites of horrific massacres against the backdrop of beautiful jungles. I knew I was very, very fortunate to have found a life—steamy and dirty though it often was—that felt so emotionally meaningful. And it all started that moment I chased a pretty girl. We are simple creatures.

During these years, before I met the second (and more important) girl who changed my life, I would go into a small coffee-producing country and show them how the export of raw coffee beans would not get them anywhere, but, if they would process the coffee into products that could go right onto grocery shelves, they could double or triple or even quadruple the wealth of their nation. My international development coworkers and I would identify opportunities to boost industrial competitiveness and thereby spread prosperity through profits and increased wages. We were particularly proud when governments paid directly for our services, because that meant that they were more likely to value our advice and follow it. One of those was the government of Rwanda.

I was a development nerd, and it consumed me. Imagine my attempts at dating in Boston and New York City (not to mention San Salvador, Rio, and Warsaw): I wanted to talk about wonky international public health policy and economic development issues that just didn't compute with most of the people seated across the dinner table. I eventually gave up and just stuck with my friends. Besides, I had too many reports to read and write each evening. I decided that if Fate had a serious partner in mind for me, it would have to make the necessary introductions.

A few months before 9/11, I was at a party in Greenwich Village. By then, I was a cofounder of an international consulting group and was running all over the world like a big shot. But at that party I saw that I was getting too far away from my Ethiopian moment. Our strategic prescriptions were right, but you never know if your advice is getting through to help real people. Even if it does, you don't see it close up like you need to. The Greenwich Village party was with a bunch of college friends in a three-level apartment where the air was thick with cannabis and somebody was playing a grand piano. It struck me very dramatically—I probably was inhaling—that I had spread myself too thin, I had gotten away from contact with real people and their life and death problems. I was far from the friendly hands that had led me up the path as a teenager in

Ethiopia. I was now part of the development business, putting on conferences and meetings and writing reports. While I did all this, those kids I had met in Ethiopia were having kids, and they were being raised in the same poverty that had shocked me. Nothing was changing. Not enough, anyway.

One of my closest friends at the party, now a cardiologist, asked me whether I was truly happy doing what I did for a living—I guess he was checking my heart. I couldn't honestly say I was. So, standing in the smoke and listening to music on that pre-9/11 New York night, I decided to chuck it all and start over. Maybe it was because I had recently been diagnosed with diabetes—a strong memo reminding me that people do not live forever. Whatever the reason, I decided to just take some time off.

CHAPTER 5

—◦◦◦—

Details of the Tough Life

I knew I could make more of a difference, and the next trip I took changed my life. I had saved enough money to go to Paris for a few months to read a stack of books I had always meant to read. Paris is a deliciously hedonistic place, and I got a small but very Parisian three-hundred-square-foot apartment in a sixteenth-century building on Île Saint-Louis—the little ghetto of Americans in Paris. It was a sixth-floor walk-up attic space. From the slanting skylight of my sleeping loft I could see Notre Dame Cathedral in the distance. Every day I took in the faint aroma of the *fromagerie* just next door, which schooled me quickly in the delights of *chèvre cendré,* a goat cheese covered with ash; *reblochon,* a soft, stinky cheese made from the second milking of the cow; and *tomme de Savoie,* a gorgeously colored, nutty cheese round. Maybe my sudden affection for great food and wine and the sheer beauty of Paris was some kind of reaction to all the poverty and hardship I had seen in the world. It was my trip to food heaven even if, by night, I was often thinking about what I might do better when I got back to global development.

I enrolled in French classes, which I needed for my line of

work. It was also a good way to meet people. For my new friends, I fixed dinners on my camper-sized, two-burner stovetop. I would hit the Sunday open markets to buy fresh, cheap ingredients in the morning, and then try my best to create the dishes I loved from around the world by night. Indian food was my specialty, since it would feed a packed apartment. My guests brought copious wine—you could find good French wines in the summer of 2001 for less than five dollars a bottle.

Then 9/11 happened and I knew I had to get back, at least for a while.

Once the grounding orders were lifted after the attack, I was on the first flight back to the United States. It was September 14. Our American Airlines captain huddled all the passengers in the lounge before we boarded—everyone was so paranoid during those first few days—to tell us to take action as a group if we saw any other passengers doing anything suspicious. "And enjoy your flight," he said.

I came back to a changed America and a very changed New York City. I checked on my downtown friends. They were OK, but everyone knew someone who had not been heard from yet. Handmade posters and candles were everywhere. People were going way out of their way to be kind to each other, to strangers.

My family and friends asked me about my plans. For the first time in my adult life, my nonjudgmental father gave me the nudge: "So, Josh, when are you getting back to work?"

I assured him that my savings would hold until I was ready to make a move—I had been financially independent since my earliest days at college.

So I went back to Paris. Just before Thanksgiving, Jeffrey

Sachs, then a Harvard powerhouse, called out of the blue and implied that I was AWOL in the war against poverty. He reminded me that the war on poverty is also the war against terrorism. I don't like to use the word "war" for humanitarian efforts, but it was the right moment for that word. And, while "Make Love Not War" is the better slogan to guide one's days and nights in Paris, I knew Paris was over. It had been a dream. We had suffered our generation's Pearl Harbor, and you couldn't just sit there gobbling clafouti and drowning in latte.

I had learned something about myself in Paris. I learned that I'm an oddball mixture of poverty worker and epicure. I had taken the luxurious break I needed, relaxing into the best pleasures of the planet and learning interesting things. Everyone should do that from time to time, if the chance comes.

But for most of us, this kind of time ends, and we're ready to go back home.

In his office in Cambridge, Jeff said that despite the worldwide chaos caused by the attack and the coming US response, it was an important time for us to get busy. In fact—and with a big nudge from Jeff—global leaders had recently created the Global Fund to Fight AIDS, Tuberculosis, and Malaria, which intended to very quickly put big money into health programs that everyone knew would save lives. The established aid programs, especially those funded by USAID, the UN, and the World Bank, always took forever to do anything, so the idea of the Global Fund was to cut through the red tape and make a big effort to knock down three mass killers as quickly as possible.

Jeff and Rob Glaser, the founder of RealNetworks and a former vice president at Microsoft, wanted me to create a website that would help developing nations apply for the new dollars that were now ready to flow from the Global Fund.

I told Jeff that I didn't want to spend my time weaving web-sites. I wanted to get my feet in the mud by applying business management tools to public health. I intended to create some-thing, then called the Access Project and now called Health Builders, that I had been thinking about in Paris when not reading books or cooking.

It would be a program to help countries create business plans for massive public health investments through the Global Fund. It would also pump good American-style management into the developing world's horribly managed health clinics, so that the new dollars would actually do something. I'd finally have the chance to realize my sinister plan—to pilfer insights from the private sector and apply them in the public sector.

Jeff and Rob said to go for it. Health Builders was born. I ran it out of Harvard.

As soon as I got used to Jeff's around-the-clock work habits in Cambridge, he told me that he was moving to Columbia University, where he would head their Earth Institute, and that he wanted me to come along. New York City is certainly a bet-ter city for fundraising, and the UN would be but a cab ride away. Besides, moving into Manhattan right after 9/11 felt almost brave at the time. It was the right place to be. And the real estate market allowed me to buy a place that I never could have otherwise afforded.

Health Builders was just taking off when Jeff filled me in on another big idea. Every nation in the world had recently signed an agreement to achieve the Millennium Development Goals—a birthday present in honor of the new millennium—to attack poverty with massive new aid programs. But which aid programs and which priority areas would take priority?

Kofi Annan, Secretary-General of the UN, had asked Sachs to figure all that out. This think tank project resulted in setting up "Millennium Villages" in a dozen or so desperate places, to demonstrate what good planning and strategic donor investing could do to erase disease and poverty in any terrain or climate.

One of those desperate places was Rwanda.

CHAPTER 6

—◦◦◦—

NY ❤ Monkeys

Alissa cannot resist stuffed plush monkeys. If you know someone's weakness, you can capture and marry them. Here in Rwanda, she has made several trips up the mist-shrouded volcanoes where Dian Fossey spent her life protecting the great gorillas. Alissa has sat among the gorillas and watched the babies perform their acrobatics on bamboo stalks above her. (There was a concern years ago, by the way, that such contact might be damaging, but the opposite was found: the great gorillas are increasing in numbers perhaps because the humans are babysitting, allowing the huge parents more time for romance.)

Before she had her own children to cuddle, Alissa kept going back to babysit the little gorillas even after an attack by ants once made her strip bare and run through the other tourists on the trek. "It was just part of the adventure," she told me when she got back. She is such a good sport.

But the stuffed monkeys: She was twenty-eight when we met; I was already thirty-three and ancient. She was working for New York City's public health department, though she was soon after recruited by Goldman Sachs to help run their in-house wellness program, which keeps everyone productive, despite the stress and long hours. They even have quiet nap rooms and a pinkish room for breastfeeding between the morning's IPOs and hostile takeovers.

As the daughter of a San Francisco psychiatrist, Alissa has always looked into her own life pretty deeply. Then as now, she had a firm grip on what she wanted her life to be about. She wanted it to be about helping others, making a noticeable difference in the big, wide world. When I had surrendered my dating life to Fate, I guess that's the one thing I checked on the wish list, and that's who was literally delivered to my door.

A few years before we met, when she was working on her public health master's, Alissa had something of an emotional crash. Then, on an internship in Tanzania, bordering Rwanda to the east, she worked through a summer to improve the efficiency of health centers there. The depression she had been suffering vanished. She put her pills away. She even fell for a guy who was also volunteering there—an AIDS-educating puppeteer from South Africa whom she watched through her office window as he delighted and mesmerized the happy kids. At the end of the summer, her folks came over and they went on a two-week safari during the great annual migration of the Serengeti.

Africa colonized a part of her mind during all that—a personal refuge, a place of meaningful beauty and love. She was able to go back to the States and finish up her degree, thankfully (for me) sans puppeteer.

Just before her finals, in the dead of winter, her emotional heaviness returned. Her mother, Aurèle, whisked her away to the Kripalu Center for Yoga and Health in western Massachusetts. As long as I've known and loved Alissa, daily yoga practice has been the foolproof way to keep her happy and energetic. Her control of the moment, of her body, through yoga usually brings her smile back. Yoga is an inbred family comfort—her mother is a yoga teacher and her father a devoted practitioner (but only, he claims, because it helps his tennis). During the weekend at Kripalu, mother and daughter, after eating like monks and exercising all day, would sneak out at night for a nice dinner with wine and desserts. I love that she is like that. (You can't imagine how important it is to give in to your happier needs when things get difficult over here.)

At that same yoga retreat, Alissa and her mom made a new friend, Aura, whose daughter lived in New York City. The daughter happened to know my sister, Lisa the Matchmaker. And that is how a weekend of yoga changed our lives.

Alissa, Aurèle, and Aura move slowly in white landscapes as I picture them at that retreat—it all seems a bit heavenly, which it was, and that's where our match was made.

The chemistry we felt for each other hit even before we met in person. I had called her and left a message at my sister's insistence. I liked her voice on her recorded greeting. She called back when I was at JFK, on my way to a conference in Geneva. I was supposed to go on to Africa after the Geneva meeting, but instead I got on a plane back to New York, just for that first date. I recommend that as a dating strategy.

After that first phone call at JFK, Alissa told her sister that she "had the strangest feeling" that she had just talked to the person she would marry. I had the same reaction. It was a short call, and we didn't say much, but we somehow knew. Maybe it was the spaces of comfortable silence in that conversation, since silence always has the most to say. She struck me as the real thing: She graduated from Wellesley and then got her master's in public health at Harvard. She was very classy with a sexy and seductive demeanor, even via email. I had to up my game.

For our first date, she knew what I looked like because my public health and development work was easy to find online. I hadn't seen a picture of her yet. My sister said she was hot, but sisters will say whatever they need to say.

I waited for her on the front step of my apartment. I saw someone I hoped was her coming up the street from the subway station. The closer she came, the more I hoped. Longish dark hair, trim, a wise and kind smile on a supermodel face— I'm not kidding. She smiled even wider when she recognized me. Incredible smile. I suddenly wished I had sprung for a much better bottle of wine upstairs. She was wearing nice jeans with a sequined belt, and heels. It was a long walk for her in those heels, but worth every step.

I had roof rights above my apartment, and I had fixed up a little garden there with white lights and everything. We felt as though we already knew everything about each other, which left room only for explanations. In the Manhattan dusk we moved close and watched the city lights arrive like fireflies. Romantically, I had expected against the odds to be captivated by her, and sure enough I was.

From my sister's friend, she knew all about my high school work in the Ethiopian famine and everything since. She knew more about me than I remembered about myself. She also knew that I was working with Jeff Sachs, which she thought was particularly cool. Actually, it was for me, too. You don't think international public health would have its rock stars, but it does.

I didn't feel particularly cool about myself, though, because

I knew the truth about the mark of chance on my life's trajec-
tory: I had been lucky enough to attend a high school club
meeting one afternoon. The rest of my life had been pretty
much been dominoes falling in lucky but predictable succes-
sion, all up until now. After our glass of wine, we walked to a
restaurant across from the Museum of Natural History. We
held hands and I kissed her during dinner. Our first date! I
couldn't help it, and she didn't resist.

She was living near the Village in a tiny apartment with one
little window. I ribbed her that it happened to be upstairs from
one of the better-known strip clubs. She ribbed me for knowing it was there.

Alissa glowed when she told me about the peace that yoga
brings to her. She described that weekend with her mother
when snowflakes fell outside the window, when the music was
classical and the pose was *shavasana,* which is lying on your
back with your arms and legs out, snow angel style. She said
she had experienced something like a spiritual out-of-body
experience. She had been doing yoga for years, but that was,
she said, the first time she really got it.

I jumped headfirst. She was the one. I invited her for a
weekend in Nantucket. She accepted but, after that, said she
was uncomfortable with the intensity of the relationship during a time of her life she hoped would be her girl-in-the-city
freedom—at least that's what she said when she broke up with
me. The whole thing seemed over just a couple of weeks from
the night we met.

It was horrible. Didn't she see how perfect we were for each
other? Couldn't she see what great trouble Fate (and my sister)
had gone to?

We made up in Washington Square Park in the Village.

Perhaps the sun was just setting and there was a violinist and dance troupe—I wouldn't have noticed. The breakup lasted only forty-eight hours, though it seemed like weeks to me.

We were now a couple, though I was often in Africa and elsewhere. She was learning the ropes at Goldman (literally, at times—they have a two-story rock climbing wall). When I was in town and we were together, she didn't like the way our workday stories didn't seem to fit together. She felt out of place at Goldman. She wanted to put her public health education to better use in the world. She liked the kinds of things I was doing overseas, and we romanticized over email and expensive calls what it would be like for us to be in those countries together.

We took some more weekends together, and she eventually moved in with me, thereby allowing us many evenings on the roof at sunset. It was a familiar situation for her to be in such a tree house, as she had grown up in San Francisco's Twin Peaks neighborhood in a home that overlooks the city, the bay, and the Golden Gate Bridge.

She got me doing yoga.

I know how all this sounds. Great moments, great schools—a place in Manhattan, for God's sake. But we were not rich, had no trust funds, and we pinched ourselves daily to be living like this. We knew that luck and privilege were involved, and we were intent on earning our keep and paying it back to the world, somehow.

We had been living together for about a year, and I still hadn't proposed. She thought maybe I couldn't commit. If I ever did propose, she said it should please be romantic. I asked her what would be romantic to her.

"You know, it should be a surprise," she said.

I took the cue. One very cold and wet holiday evening—the last days of 2004—I told Alissa there was a Columbia University holiday party at a restaurant that was a good walk from our apartment. I insisted we go to the party, and I insisted we walk. She was angry that I wouldn't spring for a cab and would make her walk in the cold rain.

Sometimes Alissa thinks I am too frugal. I am pretty frugal, like my dad. I try to apply that to the programs I manage. It's not a bad thing, but it seemed like the wrong thing that night to Alissa, who simply didn't want to soak her heels. A bit miffed, she came along.

I said I wanted to walk by way of the Museum of Natural History to see if they had decorated. That was not the most direct route to the party, and they really don't decorate, so that, too, was very upsetting to her, getting her just shy of exasperated and close to irate. I was just being a selfish jerk that evening, she decided, but she sighed and hurried along beside me.

As there often is on New York sidewalks, some type of protest was happening in front of the museum. Three guys in monkey costumes were bouncing around, huffing around on their haunches. Others were holding signs about "monkey rights" and passing out flyers about the abuse of monkeys in zoos and labs. They were selling stuffed monkeys to fund their protest organization. We looked, but we walked right by.

"We have to go back," Alissa said.

She had a great, Smithsonian-sized collection of stuffed monkeys at the time. She looked at the pile on offer, covered in clear plastic to protect them from the drizzle. There was a pretty white monkey on top. She liked it and she looked at me. I asked the protesters how much it was. It was twenty bucks.

I said that seemed a little steep to me—I was intent on playing the part of the tightwad.

"But I don't have a white one," she said, squeezing my arm. "And it's for a good cause." So, grumbling like a cheapskate, I pulled out a bill and we went on our way with the monkey in a little bag.

A few blocks later, along the edge of Central Park, I stopped at a bench in the prettiest place I could find and said, "Let's stop for a minute and take a look at that monkey." She pulled it out. It had a ribbon around its neck, holding a little jeweler's box. She saw it and knew she had been had. Her engagement ring was in the box. She said yes.

I knew she would pick the white one, by the way. But if I had guessed wrong? The men in the monkey costumes were, of course, our well-masked friends, who would later be in our wedding party. My guys were prepared to somehow get the ring onto the right monkey—I would have distracted her any way I could.

In the months of our engagement I was often in Kenya, Nigeria, and Ethiopia, running and expanding the health management assistance for those countries. I spent a lot of time in Rwanda as well. Alissa was proud of my work. And she likes frequent flier miles.

I emailed her one evening from Kenya and informed her that although we weren't even married yet, we had just sort of adopted a daughter.

Her name was Melsa. I had been speaking at a Global Fund conference in Nairobi when, afterward, a big, forceful Kenyan woman in full African prints assailed me and insisted that I listen to her tell me about this amazing young woman, Melsa, whose parents and baby sister had died of AIDS.

Sometimes you give someone your business card to finally get rid of them, but by the time I got rid of this woman, I had agreed to get Melsa started at a business college. For the price of a few lattes a week, I could do it. Alissa, though she might have liked to be in on the decision, was half a world away and quite asleep when the sale was closed. But she agreed it was a good thing to do, the right thing.

There was only one big piece left in our puzzle: in what way would we orient our professions, beyond gestures? What was the right thing for us? Just what would we *do?* We couldn't have much of a marriage if we were constantly half a world apart.

On a pretty evening in 2005, a few months before our wedding, we were at a rooftop party in the Chelsea district of the city (and, coincidentally, Chelsea Clinton was in attendance). We got talking with Stephen Lewis, an advocate for Africa, about his recent visit to the new Millennium Village in Kenya. He had been thinking about it the whole way back — and it's a long flight.

"Why in the world aren't you doing a Millennium Village in Rwanda?" he asked me. "Now, there's a country that has an AIDS epidemic and could benefit from a comprehensive approach to poverty." By comprehensive, he meant integrating health, economic, and educational programs. Integrative development isn't taught in many public health schools, but it makes great sense when you think about it, because with prosperity people can afford good health and education.

He was impressed that the national government of Rwanda, unlike some in the area, wasn't hopelessly corrupt. Certainly, the human need justified action, and the lack of corruption would mean that the dollars would go to the right places. People were suffering from malnutrition in Rwanda, which is a country that should actually be one of the breadbaskets of Africa. The upside potential was tremendous, and the Rwandans had already lived through their downside. They were ready and willing to do great, new things.

Lewis has led a political party in Canada and is a big name in the global fight against AIDS, having served as the UN Special Envoy for HIV/AIDS in Africa. He has spent time all over Africa and knows the continent. He has put his personal resources to work in a foundation that bears his name and funds many projects. And he stands nicely at rooftop cocktail parties.

I was cochairing the UN Millennium Project's task force on AIDS, alongside the head of Rwanda's national AIDS program, who would later become the ambitious health minister of the country.

"I couldn't agree with you more," I said to Lewis. Rwanda was, in fact, one of the countries where I would have liked to put all the marbles because the results could have been mind-boggling—a beacon to be emulated throughout the developing world.

"Well, I'm glad to hear you say that," he replied. "So why don't you go and do it?" he pressed.

"Rwanda didn't make the cut. There's not enough money for an extra location," I said.

"Well, of course. But…" he paused. He was giving it one last thought. When you have money, the things you say at such parties can be very expensive for you.

The pause was brief. "Here's the thing. My foundation will help find the funds for it," he said.

"That's a very, very cool idea," I said. It's all I could get out.

"Yes, well, it would require someone like you, exactly like you, to go put it together on the ground. If you are interested, I would back you. I wouldn't be interested otherwise." I knew he was talking about millions of dollars.

"Such a thrilling offer," I said. Again. And then I reminded him that Alissa, who was standing beside me, had recently accepted my marriage proposal, and we would be getting married in a few months. I was saying that I really was not available for moving into the Heart of Darkness. Or, I didn't think I could be.

"And what are you doing these days with your Harvard public health degree?" he asked Alissa. I'm sure I had told him that she was not too happy to be using her training to help run a corporate health center. Before she could answer, he continued:

"Here's an adventure to start off your marriage. You'll have great stories from a great continent. Both of you should go."

She squeezed my arm. I didn't know if it was a squeeze yes or a squeeze no. I looked at her face. It was a squeeze yes.

Had I known what awaited us in Rwanda—especially for Alissa—would I have accepted his offer? I have wondered that a thousand times when things are bad, and not wondered it a thousand other times when things are wonderful.

We were a little quiet on the walk home from the subway station that night.

"So you really want to go?" I asked. I knew she would see some seriously great monkeys in Rwanda—golden monkeys and, of course, the big, big, gorillas in the mist, in northwest Rwanda.

We let the question percolate through the weekend's chores,

46

window-shopping walks, and little meals. New York City never seems so fine a city as when you are thinking of leaving it. I knew the windows of our favorite haunts were staring at Alissa like worried friends—*would you really abandon us for that place?* And there were her real friends and family to think about. There would be years of missed moments, birthdays, holidays, births, bar mitzvahs, double dates on Broadway, simple meals in terrific little restaurants, our friends' dramas, even deaths.

But the idea of moving to Africa, starting a family there, making a home and a life there, was bigger than the yearning for a particular city and missing moments with friends and family. The real question was more like: do we want to have a normal life, with all its comforts and conveniences and friends and family, or do we want to take a chance on a unique adventure? You can see how I was leaning, and Alissa was leaning the same way. It helped that she was sick of New York winters and her morning subway schlep to a job that wasn't exactly fulfilling.

But did we know of any Americans who had permanently moved to Rwanda? Could we look at their decisions and take some comfort? Well, there just weren't any that we knew of, unless you wanted to count Dian Fossey. She had a great life, indeed. However, if she had known that she would be so alone for so long, and that she might be killed in a lonely little house in the jungle by poachers, would she still have gone? You have to imagine that she would have. A great life usually has great risks, doesn't it?

"If we hate it, we can move back, right?" Alissa asked more than once. Yes, but it would be an expensive mistake, and embarrassing, both personally and professionally, so we needed to make the decision seriously. And it was not an easy choice. It was too big a decision to just say, OK, we're going. Instead, we started to be more vague in our replies to family members who worried that it would be a bad idea. And our conversations began to move to the mundane details of what we might take with us, what we could sell, what we would keep in storage. Alissa started collecting boxes from New York street corners—there was no funding to ship our belongings in a cargo container to Mombasa, Kenya, and then on to Kigali by road.

In time, logistics invaded fully and the question of whether to go silently left our presence, being so ignored.

I suppose it is logistics that helps push away a soldier's worry before battle and helps a woman prepare to give birth, leaving as little room as possible for thoughts of the event itself. There were so many thousands of things to prepare if we were to do this. Even a week after that rooftop party, it was clear we had decided to do it. Our friends could see the boxes piled high in our apartment and knew: the biggest box was marked "MONKEYS" and contained Alissa's whole collection. We wouldn't need them where we were going.

CHAPTER 7

⸺⸺

Into Africa

Even though I was an experienced African traveler, the idea of us both going there to *live* and to raise kids remained a serious eyebrow-raiser among friends and family right up to the last days before we left. Maybe they would have not worried so much if we were headed to Kenya or South Africa. But *Rwanda?* In the popular imagination, that name was but a synonym for mass murder on an inconceivable scale.

"And you want to raise children there?" our friends asked. Of course, they doubted that we really would have kids there. They were certain we'd do Africa Peace Corps–style and be back in just two years. Based on the amount of stuff that Alissa put into storage, we probably believed it, too.

I came to Rwanda before Alissa, in order to find a house and prepare things. Rwanda is a long trip from JFK. It's about eight hours across the Atlantic to Brussels, a few hours or so there, then another ten hours south through Africa. You start in the afternoon in New York, and it's late night when you finally arrive in Rwanda, but you've lived through a very long day in between.

Besides finding a place for us to live, I also needed to begin the process of getting the Millennium Villages Project approved by the Rwandan government. Assuming a green light, I would then need to start recruiting medical and agricultural experts and community organizers—a full team of great professionals who could turn a poor and sick corner of Rwanda into a global success story. There would be no point in doing this if we could not reach that goal.

After packing up our stuff and jigsaw-puzzling it into my dad's Connecticut garage, Alissa took a long look at the Manhattan skyline and got on a plane.

The nighttime final approach into Kigali reminded her, she said, of coming into San Francisco—the sparkling lights on the hills.

These lights, however, were mostly low-wattage lightbulbs shining here and there through bedroom windows. There were no streetlights then, but trash fires were plentiful. And some young students, then as now, studied by candlelight, so that must have accounted for some of the flickering of this earnestly striving city.

I knew Alissa would be very tired and a little worried about her new home, as moving to a new country, especially a place like Rwanda, is not like going on a vacation; it's a huge good-bye to everything you know. Traveling on a one-way ticket is emotionally heavy, but balanced by the thrill of uncertainty and adventure. So, yes, I wanted her arrival to be nice.

She looked beat when she came down the stairs from the customs booth, but she was very happy to see me. On our way up the hill, she gazed at the last struggles of the African day, as men and women and children moved along the roads bearing pushcarts and balanced loads of fabrics, wares, and produce on their heads.

"Where's the litter?" she asked. She couldn't get over how clean the streets were. They still are.

We pulled up to the big, white house I had leased not only for the two of us, but also for our team. A team house. It was not a frat house, exactly. It had big white columns and a curved portico and maybe it was a little much. With six bedrooms, an ample kitchen, a big, echoing front room, and a long porch, it could accommodate the constant stream of doctors, nurses, agronomists, community organizers, and managers we would need for the Millennium Village, while still having space for storing thousands of mosquito nets, doses of malaria treatment, and boxes of medical and office equipment. We would eat together there and hold our planning meetings in the front room and on the porch at all hours of the night, as we were often in the field or working the halls of Rwanda's government by day.

Alissa would soon dub it the "Soprano" house because it looked like a gangster mini-mansion from Jersey. Yes, and this woman of refined tastes would now get to call it her home. Her first impression came with one word:

"Really?"

She said that as we pulled up. She took a breath. The place was lit up like the White House, if Tony Soprano lived in the White House.

"Well, it does look very clean," she said.

The six members of my team, plus some of their friends and the housekeeper and the cook and the drivers, gathered in the living room to welcome her. Maybe it was a little much.

We had scrubbed the joint for her arrival; it was the cleanest place in Africa that day, most hospitals included. She liked the size of it, coming from a Manhattan apartment of perhaps one-fifth its size, and she was happy to learn that the electricity in our part of the city went out no more than once or twice a day. The water didn't go off much either. In fact, the house had an elevated water tank and a pump that could guarantee a good American-style shower whenever desired, assuming the power for the pump and the water did not go out at the same time. Also, I informed her, you shouldn't let too much water get into your mouth. We boiled and filtered water in the kitchen for drinking.

In her first days she organized the kitchen, brought order to the rest of the house, and sent patrols to the sprawling Kimisagara and Kimironko markets on impossible missions for household essentials.

"You might have told me they don't have Purell. I could have brought some, like maybe a fifty-five-gallon drum."

"It's mostly alcohol, and maybe lanolin. They have that here. I'll make you some," I said. She stared at me and smiled. "I'll add some DEET for the mosquitoes," I chimed in.

Then I said goodbye. I had to be in Kenya for the first few days of her new life in Africa, but it couldn't be helped. The very best people I could find now surrounded her: the six team members and a staff of five workers to help with the kitchen, the house, and the vehicles. Everyone looked to her as sort of the housemother. The staff, while helpful, still was a lot to manage, especially if you don't speak the local language.

I didn't know until I got back into town that her first week had been hard. She had not dared leave the house alone. She hadn't even been across the street to the famous hotel, which she was curious to see, as she had read Philip Gourevitch's famous book about the genocide, *We Wish to Inform You That Tomorrow We Will Be Killed with Our Families,* and she had seen *Hotel Rwanda*—a fictionalized film account. She just hadn't felt comfortable going out yet on her own. She didn't yet speak enough French to get by—Rwandans speak mostly French to foreigners—so she felt very isolated. This is a fearless New York City woman, but there was something about the place that spooked her a little.

What's the reality? It is safe to walk around in Rwanda. Illegal drugs are not used much, which helps account for the low crime rate. House break-ins are rare, as there are bars on windows, steel doors, broken glass cemented in sharp points along the tops of property walls, and guards nearly everywhere through the day and night in areas where there is anything to steal. The main source of security, however, is that the people are obedient to authority. There are both positive and negative sides to that, as history knows.

Alcoholism is a problem in the rural areas, where a harsh wine is easily fermented from fruits and grains. An array of big banana leaves spread near the front door of a roadside house means the owner has some banana hooch for sale. But you don't see drunken people often in the city.

You will get many more smiles returned on a Rwandan sidewalk than in Manhattan or Boston.

For Alissa, it was the scars and the rough look of the place that intimidated. Only a few of the roads were paved at that time, which added to the frontier aspect. My not-yet-comfortable bride was just going to wait for me before venturing out.

Amidst the loads of booty Alissa unpacked from our luggage was what appeared to be an entire CVS pregnancy aisle— tests, thermometers, and vitamins. Alissa was planning to get pregnant but she wanted a couple of months to settle in, figure out what obstetrical care looked like, and then get moving. For someone who had always taken great care about healthy food and good water, Rwanda initially presented new challenges and strains.

My first day back, we walked around our hilly neighborhood. It was just a couple of blocks up to the center of the city, passing by the national bank and the president's compound. A few blocks over, we walked down the palm-lined street past UN headquarters and the World Bank, the US embassy, the Belgian embassy, and others.

On the back side of our hill—Kiyovu, it's called—we entered Cartier Mateus, where entrepreneurs set up their shops as African traders have done for centuries. You can barely squeeze through the crowds of people coming to exchange currency and purchase cloth, tools, meats, and, these days, pharmaceuticals and cell phones.

At evening we headed back to our more tranquil side of the hill and I took her to my favorite Indian restaurant. All of the seats are in a covered outdoor garden—the weather in Rwanda allows that.

The young manager, Amit, greeted me, "Mr. Josh!" He always knew everyone who walked in, and everyone got the very best table that evening, and was offered the very best specials, just for you, and the only truly special bottle of wine that had come in this week. He was Indian, but he was so New York that he made Alissa feel right at home. She had a place now. And someone who would always know her name.

"I love this place and I love you," Alissa said to me. There were little white lights around, as there had been on our first date on my rooftop garden. So this restaurant was a good move. She took a really deep breath. You don't do that somewhere new until you are settling in. She looked around and smiled serenely.

I asked Amit to turn down the waterfall so Alissa and I could talk without shouting.

Out came the amuse-bouche with three sauces—tamarind, a green curry, and a red-hot sauce—along with peeled and sliced carrots and cucumbers.

"These are safe to eat?" she asked me.

"I've eaten them a dozen times and haven't had a problem." It doesn't take long in any developing country before conversation goes to the fear of food.

"I've been in the kitchen here. For expats like us, with our delicate guts, Amit nukes everything in the microwave before it comes out, just to be extra safe. He would be mortified if you got ill, if anyone got ill. It would hurt their business and their pride."

She dug in to a *subzi taka tin:* deep-fried dough with fresh veggies inside. She loved it first with her eyes.

"Wait until you try the *dal maharani!*" I said, passing her the dark brown lentils in cream with ginger and spices. Their version of *palak paneer*—creamed spinach with homemade chunks of cheese—is worth the walk.

We had mango yogurt *lassi* for dessert.

"I think I'll be OK here," she said toward the end.

There are no Michelin stars in Kigali—the judges just haven't gotten here yet. One star means it's a good restaurant if you are in the area. Two means it's worth going out of your way for. Three, the top, means it justifies a whole journey. Maybe this was a three, or maybe we just needed a good meal. It was an evening that made a difference for Alissa, emotionally. Her tension fell away. She was Alissa again.

It helped that Kigali can be romantic at night. And then, by day, Alissa discovered that the "Hotel Rwanda" has a salon and gym. Now she really was fine.

Because the hotel was just across the street from our backyard, our team used the pool and the poolside bar as our after-hours and weekend hangout. It was sometimes easier to brainstorm a problem there, though the irony of dealing with poverty with a cocktail in our hands was not lost on us.

Alissa winced the first time she saw me send back a badly made margarita. She didn't want us to be Ugly Americans. But I had a whole rap about that:

"Sweetie, if you don't tell them when they are falling short, they will never get any better, and that means they will never really prosper." She shrugged unpleasantly. She whispered that I sounded like a colonial ass.

But, I was stating the truth. The hotels and restaurants and bars of thriving Nairobi, Kenya, are as good as they are—and they are very good—because of two centuries of complaints from safari-bound, leather-patched tourists in khaki. They were not the least bit shy about sending back a bad gin and tonic, if that drink can be made badly. Progress comes from competition, and you have to give the competitors the score.

Anyway, beer was always the surer bet to order. Mutzig and Primus were the main local beers available, and Heineken was just coming in. The wines were terrible.

I stopped ordering margaritas because they were just too disappointing. It was very hard to find a well-made margarita in Equatorial Africa at that time, at least outside of Nairobi— we were about five hundred miles west and a little south of all that. Besides, Mutzig is a terrific beer. The brewery, on the shores of Lake Kivu, buys up nearly all the nation's barley and is a top taxpayer, so you are doing some poor farmers and the nation a great favor every time you bend your elbow.

That was the main exercise, in fact, in the months before Alissa arrived with her yoga ways and got settled in. Then, once she had a favorite corner of the porch for her yoga mat and was ready to branch out, she was ready for more. She asked about the area's cultural activities.

Ahem.

CHAPTER 8

——〰——

Expats in the Mist

As Alissa eased into Rwanda, the climate appeared to agree with her (and me), and soon she was pregnant. Besides experiencing the usual cravings and fatigue of pregnancy, she felt—and I agreed—that we'd better have a lot of fun before the arrival of our first baby—a multi-month last hurrah of sorts. Unfortunately, since we'd both been so addicted to the long list in the *New York Times* of each day's countless cultural events, the "Things to Do" section of the newspaper in Kigali made for a really quick read.

It was awkward explaining to a woman who had grown up in San Francisco and Wellesley and Cambridge and New York City that the main cultural event here is the Saturday morning moto-polo game. A game like polo, but played on motorcycles.

"Really? That's it?"

"I think you'll love it."

"OK, then. It sounds fun...Really. I want to go."

She was my newlywed, newly pregnant, go-with-the-flow, Into Africa bride. She is a dancer, too, and a fine singer. She loves to see modern dance and take a turn. She needs those things. So what was I thinking, really, bringing her here? I was racked with insecurity on that subject.

Dr. Blaise was no help.

Blaise Karibushi, who had worked with the minister of health right after the genocide—when Blaise and the minister had to practically time-share the same desk—was now my country director for Health Builders. He was helping me to strategize on all fronts.

He grew up in eastern Congo and went to medical school there. Like so many others, his family had fled from Rwanda to Congo in the early 1960s. They flourished as cattlemen. By the time of the genocide they had well over two thousand head, a sizable herd. As streams of hungry refugees from Rwanda—first Tutsi fleeing the genocide and then genocidaires fleeing the rebel army—flooded into eastern Congo, Dr. Blaise's family wealth was literally eaten up. He decided to return and help rebuild Rwanda. Arriving in his Land Cruiser, he confidently told the new government that he wanted to reestablish the national tuberculosis control program. He was happy to be home and willing to do anything necessary.

Dr. Blaise was smitten with Alissa from the moment they met, and was concerned about her well-being in Rwanda. So when the subject of "things to do" came up over a drink, he was not in a mood to make light of it, nor to help me feel better.

"You're crazy to have brought her to Rwanda, so far away from the joys of her home," he said, standing over me. He is six feet seven, and he was not joking; he was upset by what seemed to him the madness of our move—borderline spousal abuse.

But a good dessert would usually satisfy him and calm him

down. We asked him to join us for a treat at our team's dining table.

The dessert was one that I had fixed with Joel, who was our cook even then. It was a strawberry-rhubarb crumble, with strawberries purchased from the well-worn plastic buckets of vendors on the street. The small wild berries reminded me of the farmers' markets during New England summers — strawberries that actually *taste* like strawberries, small, sweet, and with underlying tones of flavor lacking in their engineered supermarket counterparts. Alissa had packed a bag of Trader Joe's raw almonds, which Joel mashed with a mortar and pestle, then mixed into flour and butter for the crunchy topping. Dr. Blaise could no longer be angry.

"You both have such beautiful lives back in the US," he said more gently, while he registered his approval of the dessert by rolling his big eyes with the first tart taste. "It's great you both are here, really, but you are crazy. And Josh, do you think Alissa will be happy with the monotony? Think of what you have back home. The plays, the music, movies, the restaurants, television shows, the great stores, the everything, man. You have everything there, and nothing here. You are crazy. And your families! That's the biggest thing. I love you both, of course. But it's true."

"You just want to deal with me from across the ocean," I said facetiously.

"No," he said. "It's good you're here. It's the only way it will work. Thank you for coming. Alissa, thank you, too." He patted her hand with his, which was sticky with crumble. I know it wasn't also sticky with ice cream, as we hadn't brought over an ice cream maker from the States yet. We would figure all that out later.

Blaise had a point. We were crazy. One way or another, most people are. Most people are crazy in the other direction: turning their backs on beauty and adventure their whole lives. There must be a happy medium somewhere, but we weren't interested in it yet. Or was I the crazy one, and Alissa was just in love and coming along for the ride? No, I didn't think so. I kept reminding myself that she needed that sojourn in Tanzania when she was in college. She needs adventure as much as I do. Saying that to myself made me feel less guilty.

In those days—mid-2006—you might go to the poolside bar at the Mille Collines to find out if there was a moto-polo game on Saturday and if any of your friends were playing. These days, it's the bar in Heaven, a couple streets away. Expats from the United States, Canada, Europe, the UK, Israel, and other prosperous, generous lands congregate there to describe their week's adventures over a frosty mug of Mutzig beer or something more daring and expensive—maybe an *urwagwa* sour: an elixir of locally brewed banana beer, fresh lime juice, and homemade lemongrass syrup. Some social arrangements will be made for the weekend, including dinner parties, excursions to the national park, and of course dates. There were rarely concerts or games to attend, except local soccer. Moto-polo was always the most attractive option. But this was before Heaven, so we went to the Mille Collines and, yes, there would be moto-polo on Saturday. Alissa was game to check it out.

It's a gladiatorial event. Polo enthusiasts in their twenties and thirties, mostly from England and the former English colonies (including the United States), brandish bamboo polo mallets and ride breakneck on the backs of speeding, screaming, smoke-spitting little motorcycles. The players hold fast to the shirts and sometimes necks of their young African drivers, who maneuver brilliantly by dint of their regular jobs, which is to negotiate the only slightly calmer streets of Kigali as moto-taxi drivers.

After the game, they will drive you anywhere in Kigali for four or five hundred Rwandan francs (less than a dollar). It's the mode of transportation used by Rwandans and many expats to get around quickly. You hop on the back of their bright motorcycles, put on the mandatory—and often quite beat up—passenger helmet, and off you go to see if your number's up. It is considered uncool to hold on to the driver, so you hold a small rail behind you and hope that will do on the tight turns, the accelerations, and the speed bumps. That is when you think of how skinned up the helmet is.

There are thousands of moto-taxis and drivers in Kigali. They are everywhere, beeping at you if you dare walk instead of hop on. Saturday mornings, the best of them and their expat teammates will be playing polo on the grassy field. Watching and cheering from an overhanging bluff will be the members of the Cercle Sportif de Kigali, a country club of sorts where Rwandans and the Belgian descendants of colonial days sun and swim and play tennis on clay courts together. Expats can join or come for the day for a couple of bucks.

Umuzungu, or the plural, *abazungu,* is what Rwandans call the expats. It's the word for white people, or anyone who seems rich, and all foreigners seem so. "Muzungu in the Mist" is the slogan on a popular T-shirt sold to expats, who don't seem to mind the term.

Most expats accept the strangeness and the hardships of life here, though no one complains too bitterly, for they have a quality of life far higher than back home. The trappings of daily existence include drivers and housekeepers and cooks taking care of them, and they know they are deeply privileged to play the part of Westerners in a country where most homes still know hunger.

Many expats pay higher wages than the market demands for all this help, and many pay extra so that anyone working for them will have tuition money and good health care. They also teach English and household accounting and computer literacy and the importance of reading to children and a hundred other things to anyone they employ. It is, frankly, exhausting. In some ways, it is easier in the States, where people just take care of themselves and do not have to contend with constant management at home. If you chose to go it alone here, however, it would be considered possibly greedy, when you easily could have given someone a job.

For Americans, particularly, who are not used to having hired help, you don't want to become like some who nickel-and-dime their staff and insist on nearly constant work. *Please send me home before I become party to that,* is what you think when you see such things. It is another reason to go home after you have done what you came to do.

And you are far from home, and you get homesick sometimes. The soil and bricks and paint and rusty roofs and African print dresses that swirl around women on the streets cast reds and yellows that shift the tint of your vision in a way that confirms you are in an alternative dimension — and in an alternative moral universe. Any Rwandan you meet on the street, if twenty or older, knows terrible stories that will not be shared with you, or perhaps with anyone. We *abazungu* are and will remain outsiders, if only for that, even though the foods and flora of Rwanda, when they get deep enough into you, change the smell of your sweat a little (Alissa thinks it's changed mine a lot) and you think, well, you are becoming this place. But you are not. The Belgians who have been here for half a century are visitors, too.

The moto-polo game was loud and fun. But Alissa was not cheering. She was just smiling and holding her breath when the dust and exhaust swirled our way.

"I want to go home," she said as we walked back up the hill. "I'm showing already. I want to go home to have the baby when I get within a couple weeks."

"To New York?"

"No, all the way home. I want to go to San Francisco to be near my folks and my sister. I don't want to deliver here. I know you know all the best doctors. But, please, not even that good hospital in Nairobi, OK?"

"Yes. It's exactly what I think we should do. I thought we had talked about it."

"We did. I just want to be sure we do it that way."

———

Sometime later, my neighbor Pierantonio told me a story that made me share this moment with him. His Italian mother was pregnant, and they were going to stay in Congo for the delivery. As the date got very close, Pierantonio's father found out that her doctor was not in fact a doctor, just a man who had taken over his missing brother's identity. The delivery went fine, but from then on they made the difficult forty-five-day journey back to Italy for each child's birth. All we had to manage was twenty-four hours in the air.

Besides, we had to get out of Rwanda every ninety days anyway—the maximum length of a tourist visa, which is what we were using at the time. Work visas for longer stints were nearly impossible to snag. And ninety days is about long enough without some kind of a fix. Whether it's to America or France or the UK, South Africa, Nairobi, or some beach within reach, like Zanzibar, you have to go somewhere. It's too much, otherwise. That's why we had the ninety-day rule.

"Tell me about Zanzibar," Alissa said one night in bed. She wanted a story about beaches and nice stores and spas and chocolates on her nightstand.

"It is an island like no other, where everything is clean and perfect and very sexy," I began. She cuddled in.

CHAPTER 9

—∿—

The Gift Horse Makes His Pitch

When I left for my big meeting to present the Millennium Villages Project to the government, Alissa was on our porch, bathed in the morning sepia and reading one of the dozen childbirth and parenting books she had brought. The rest of her day would be spent sending out résumés. She knew the importance of the day's carefully planned encounter. Would we be staying in Rwanda or going home? This meeting would tell the tale. She wished me luck and assured me that they would love the project.

The meeting was not an option; you don't just waltz into someone's country and set up a major health and prosperity project—you have to get yourself invited. That's not quite the same as saying that a fireman needs to be invited to a fire, as there are good reasons why a country, even a very poor one, ought to have a say in who comes to help and how they do it. How would you feel if Norway set up a program in your neighborhood to help Americans lose some weight, and started ringing your doorbell at dessert time? Rwanda has its dignity, too.

I was granted a meeting with the prime minister and the cabinet. I knew some of the ministers personally, because my work had brought me to Rwanda before. But this was much more than the kind of drive-by consulting I had been doing before with Rwanda, helping them get access to the Global Fund money for tuberculosis, AIDS, and malaria. With this proposed Millennium Village, I was really asking to move in and co-lead a major initiative that crossed several sectors of government. It required high-level approval and assistance. One of the things I'd learned was that the various ministries of health in Africa tend to run their budgets at the whim of the ministries of finance, who hold the purse strings. So from the debut of this project, I made sure to position it not just as a poverty-reduction program, but also as a prosperity-creation one. That got the minister of finance's team engaged, and it would become our lead ministry.

As a practical matter, if your project doesn't have the blessing of the top levels of government, you will never get the kind of cooperation you need. Your days will be all red tape and endless delays and lost applications and needed signatures from people who are unfortunately out of the country for a few weeks. "Sorry, the minister is at a conference in Dar es Salaam."

The day of the meeting arrived. About a dozen men and women were sitting across from me at a long, polished wood table. It was such a young, new country that, for the first time, I didn't feel like some young punk briefing the government; I was in my thirties now, and I felt I was with peers.

Rwanda wasn't a government of leftover Cold War bureaucrats trained by the Soviets, which is what you would find in Ethiopia, and it wasn't kleptocratic Kenya.

Rwanda, from the very top all the way down to the lowliest bureaucrat, seemed to be about getting results for the people, and fast. The rush was on to create a prosperous middle class that could stop a poverty-driven conflict from ever starting again. If you were corrupt, it was almost as though you were on the side of the genocidaires. And you kind of were.

I thought I'd be presenting in English, but the prime minister asked that I speak in French. My French was good but not good enough for such an important meeting, but a colleague fluent in French happened to be with me.

To the assembled cabinet, we described what a Millennium Village was, or could be. They knew the general story, that the world—literally every country on the planet—had adopted aggressive goals for reducing poverty worldwide, and that the famous Jeffrey Sachs at Columbia had been responsible for setting up demonstration projects in Ethiopia and Kenya. They knew that tiny Rwanda had not been on the list, and that I had argued for it. They knew I was in a position to make it happen now.

I told them we would revive or build new health centers in the designated Millennium Village area, bring in agronomists to work with the farmers, and hire community mobilizers to help the people make economic enterprise decisions. I said we would do what we could for the local schools, and do whatever might be needed to turn a community around and create a model for other areas. I described our major donor, Stephen Lewis, whom they knew from his AIDS work. We would rely on the government to provide the teachers and nurses needed, and most importantly, to push forward with road, water, and electricity improvements, to bring the area into the twentieth century, if not the new one. We would make it sustainable so it wouldn't fall apart when we left—and, yes, we would indeed leave in five to ten years.

After our bilingual presentation, there was a silence. The prime minister squirmed a little in his chair. He leaned forward. It was of course natural for him to speak first.

"*Eh bien, Josh. Cela ressemble à un bon plan,*" the prime minister said. He liked the plan... but this was a courtesy that would undoubtedly be followed by one or more howevers. "*Nos préoccupations principales sont autour de la durabilité et dependence.*"

They were concerned about sustainability and the cultivation of a culture of dependency. They didn't want me to start something that they might not have the resources to maintain after we moved on. People from the West always came and then moved on, sometimes leaving empty, unfinished clinics and schools behind. They came with gifts—free medicines, shoes, fertilizer, books—but when those were gone, what then? You'd have a community accustomed to receiving and not to creating and purchasing. You'd have a community dependent on the outside. Dignity and motivation would be lost, and you'd leave behind something worse than you found. The Rwandan government had put its foot down in that regard: it would not allow initiatives that might create more disappointment and anger in a nation still so sensitive. The only thing preventing further deterioration—so far—was careful leadership and aggressive reconciliation programs. The country's new constitution, too, was an instrument of progress: thirty percent of parliament must be women. The cabinet has to be balanced. So they were trying very hard. There was no room for any showboating Westerners who might favor one group over the other or who might give glimpses of the good life and then yank it all away, causing anger and envy and dissention in a village. Until they processed all those considerations, the ministers could not give me an answer. The prime minister said they would get back to me as soon as possible.

There was silence for nearly eight weeks. I wondered if I

might have run afoul of some political problem within a ministry or some lingering anti-American sentiment. That sentiment is rare, despite the fact that the American government sat on its hands during the genocide—a fact that is well remembered and has caused President Bill Clinton to spend substantial amounts of his retirement providing support to Rwanda.

"It was our problem, not yours," is what most Rwandans will tell you, whether or not they believe that in their hearts. When they look at family photos of so many sweet people no longer in their lives, they must feel that the powerful actors in the world, who could have done something, abandoned them.

Finally, the phone call arrived: Yes, you can build your Millennium Village in Rwanda. "That is the good news, Josh," a minister said. "However, the bad news is you will have to do it in Mayange, in Bugesera District."

I didn't know many areas in Rwanda at that time, but I knew Mayange by reputation. Parliament, in fact, was presently putting together emergency funds for a rapidly worsening famine in that area, so it was in the news.

Mayange is pronounced with a soft g— "my-ANN-jay"— but everything else about the place was hard. Mayange includes about twenty-five thousand people in a cluster of five villages. It was the one community in Rwanda where a big project might not work, and they knew it. One minister told me: "We've already tried everything we know there, and they're still dying. Give it your best shot."

Poverty was only a symptom of deeper issues in Mayange. It had held a high concentration of Tutsi people before the genocide. In fact, beginning in 1959, many Tutsi had been forced into that area to starve—though their energetic farming brought them success, and the envy of other groups, for a time.

Mayange is just close enough to the soldiers in the capital, Kigali, so that the Tutsi could easily be killed when the time came. Indeed, it was where the genocidaires—a general name for the killers, whether regular Rwandan Army or members of the ragtag militia called the Interahamwe ("we who attack together")—tested their skills in a series of massacres leading up to the 1994 bloodbath. Those massacres, starting as early as the 1960s, had caused many Tutsi to escape the country. Many of those who could not go, because they were too poor or too infirm, who had good jobs or family reasons to stay, or who just thought they might be spared because they knew a powerful person, would, by the 1990s, find themselves in Mayange and its surrounding district, which was Rwanda's Warsaw Ghetto.

So, green light.

We knew we had some work to do, and we had to go in just right with the right people. We could not afford to land there in a way that made the discouraged people turn their backs and hearts away from us.

I got a good map and we began to look at aerial photos— the farms looked like hills of dust. Op-ed pointed here and there on the map.

"The ruts are very deep all the way," he said. "This bridge here is a bad place."

"In bad repair?" I asked.

"Yes, but bad in another way, too; I call it the Bridge of Death, you know—because of what happened there in the bad time."

The bridge was hardly discernible on the map, but no one will ever forget it.

CHAPTER 10

———•w•———

Rwanda Is Eight Thousand Miles Away from Where You Can Get a Good Job in Rwanda

I've sent my résumé to every organization in town and scarcely gotten a call for an interview," Alissa said in the quiet of our bedroom, a few nights after the government approved my project. She needed to hear some approval for her professional future in Rwanda, too. There are dozens of international health and development organizations operating in Rwanda. How could they not want her public health skills? I didn't get it. I would have hired her in a minute, if she were not family.

"They're not like you. They're not hiring locally the way you do," she said. "They only hire in the States and then ship people over here. I had a quick interview with one organization, but I need French, they said. And being pregnant doesn't help."

The big NGOs usually hire someone in the States, then pay a fortune to move them and all their worldly belongings over here. If they hire people already here, who don't need a cargo ship and all that, then they don't have big costs to pass on to the federal government or their donors. They like those big costs because it enables them to spend down their budgets—a key metric of success.

"Did you tell them what you did in Tanzania when you were in grad school? You did exactly the kind of thing they need here. I know because I see it every day. The health facilities are totally disorganized. That's what you're good at fixing."

"The one conversation I had wasn't that kind of conversation, and it was half in French."

By then I was on the board of a nonprofit called Generation Rwanda that was trying to get college money for the orphans of the genocide, so I suggested she volunteer for them until a paid job came along. It would give her an accomplishment in our new home, and a way to learn more French and maybe Kinyarwanda.

She was excited, since the alternative was Soprano house-mother, 24/7. "Give me the address," she said, ready to move on it the following day.

She started volunteering every day at the area's big orphanage. Every night she recounted her disgust to me: "There aren't even mosquito nets over the kids' beds, and it looks like it hasn't been painted since before the war. The toilets no longer resemble toilets, and I see donors coming in on tours and I suppose giving money, but nothing gets better. It's as if they want the place to look like crap so that they can collect more money."

I nodded in agreement with her diagnosis. Poor kids are often pawns in high-stakes games for donor dollars. During one of my first visits to Rwanda I visited an orphanage where kids dying of AIDS were on display to encourage donors to open their checkbooks. Once government got wind of it, they had it closed down and made sure that the kids received the treatment they needed.

At the orphanage where Alissa was working, she interviewed the older kids for their survival stories and their hopes for the future. Then, through Generation Rwanda, she put their stories online in search of US sponsors. It worked pretty well, and she was helping to get kids into college almost from the first month. But hearing their stories was tougher on her than either of us expected.

"Little Honoline probably ran through this area," she said after a gap in our conversation on our big porch one evening.

"Who is that?" I had never heard the name Honoline.

"Well, right now she is a gorgeous young woman—honestly, she could model for *Vogue*—she's the oldest girl in the orphanage. She's looking for a way into college. She was nine in 1994. She hid under the floor of a house near here. She was in a hiding hole—did you know a lot of the Tutsi and expat houses had hiding holes? I bet ours does, somewhere."

In fact, it had a well-built safe room with a steel door, but I hadn't come across a hiding hole. Of course, it wouldn't be much of a hiding hole if you could find it.

"She was near here, hiding in the hole—it was under a flagstone hatch in a garden area—hiding with a woman and a baby. They were friends of her family that she was visiting over the Easter holiday. They ran in there when they heard the killers on the street and the screaming of neighbors. They heard the killers crash into the house above them. They waited for dawn—for the killers to leave the house, but the killers kept coming back, looking for them, looking for the hiding hole. In the dark, they could hear them getting close, tapping everything with the tips of their machetes and the butts of rifles. The woman pushed Honoline back up against the flagstone so it might not seem so hollow if they tapped it. They did several times, but went on."

"Honoline had to keep the baby quiet in the total darkness. When the mother thought the killers might finally be drunk and sleeping outside, they lifted the flagstone and peeked out. It was just light enough to see that the house was empty, though there were snoring men sleeping here and there near the house. They climbed out and made a run for it."

I was hearing many such stories from Alissa. Each was remarkably different, the only common thread being the mention of machetes and terror. Many stories involved running, hiding in swamps, attics, anywhere. Some Tutsi were hidden away by their Hutu friends, just like Anne Frank. Many more were tortured and killed. The only real hope was to run all the way out of Rwanda, north to Uganda, perhaps, or west to Congo, east to Tanzania or south to Burundi, and to do it in the first hours of the genocide, before the roadblocks sealed everyone into killing zones. Rwanda is a small country, with the exits only forty to one hundred miles in any direction from Kigali. That is a long way for a nine-year-old to run, particularly with roadblocks and hunting dogs everywhere. Your heart tenses up when you look at the now-civilized roads and think of the terror of that time. Where would you hide if they were coming after you? Under a sewer grate? Where?

Honoline and the woman holding the baby, in fact, were quickly stopped at a roadblock down at the end of our street, Alissa explained. Honoline was separated from the woman and the baby at that point. She says she might have seen the woman and the baby killed — she will not talk about that, or perhaps the memory has been mercifully blocked. In any case,

Honoline somehow slipped through. She got past another roadblock with another stroke of luck. It must be said that not every killer could kill a child, and Honoline was so lovely. And there were so many people to kill that some slipped through in the mad rush of things as others were being chopped to the ground. The killers surely figured that the militia at the next roadblock would catch any who slipped by.

"She was finally caught on the edge of town, just before she reached the riverbanks running north to Uganda. She was roughly pulled into a line of people. She saw what the line was for." Alissa was moved to tell this story. She paused to gather her emotions, and then went on.

"At the head of the line, people were being yelled at and then killed. People who were too tall for the killers' liking were asked to stoop or kneel to be killed easier with the machetes. Women were screaming from the pain of deep slashes from dull machetes and screaming on top of that for their husbands or children to be spared. But there was no mercy at this checkpoint, and men and women and little children and teens were crying and screaming and being killed. There was no way for Honoline to run from the line, but only to say her prayers and move ahead as each person was killed. Bodies were being dragged away to piles that became part of the roadblock. The screaming and the spray of blood intensified as she approached the head of the line. There were then just three people ahead of her, and one was being killed."

Alissa paused again.

"Anyway, a big army truck suddenly pulled up to the roadblock and a commander yelled for all the militia men and soldiers to stop what they were doing and get aboard the truck; they had to go somewhere quickly. Probably it was the fact that the rebel army was making attacks from one of their strongholds, and some reinforcements were needed to deal with them. Honoline was left standing there, sprayed with the blood of other people, but spared and alive. She bolted as the truck pulled away, fearing rifle shots from the departing truck, but they were saving their bullets. She began her long journey through jungles, past more killers, sometimes running from gangs of killers with hunting dogs. She found other travelers to run with; some of them would make it and some not. Finally, she reached a camp in Uganda, where cholera would kill half of those waiting for food and medical help from the rest of the world. It came very late."

There was a long stillness as I just let the story find a place in my mind, though the mind does not easily offer up places for such stories.

"She can sing," Alissa said. "Can you believe it? She was with a big children's choir after the genocide and she toured all over the world, including the US. They went to Disneyland."

Disneyland after the genocide—what a world. The singing charity was supposed to help her with her tuition, but it didn't come through. She didn't seem upset about it; she had seen worse things.

Alissa was intent on finding Honoline a sponsor to get her into college—she was an exceptional student. Alissa would do that, as it turned out. But it was breaking her heart that so many others, who were just as worthy but whose photos and stories were perhaps not as sellable to donors, were languishing in the orphanage.

"There are no jobs for them, either," she said. "If they had jobs it wouldn't be so bad. They could at least get started and save up tuition."

She still hoped that her Harvard public health master's might get her a gig with an NGO, and she was simultaneously learning Kinyarwanda and French to get a leg up should an opportunity arise. It seemed to me, however, that she had found a calling. Every day, she seemed more interested in "her kids" and less interested in emailed rejections to her job applications.

"Screw them," I told her one evening as I closed the lid of her laptop almost on her fingers. "We're financially fine. Do what you think is important to do here."

A paycheck, though, is a statement of worth that doesn't mean much when you are getting one and that hurts your pride when you aren't. It was just that. She wanted that regularly arriving piece of paper with numbers on it that said "Here, you're worth something."

CHAPTER 11

⧜

Nothing Ever Changes

For a few weeks we clicked along: I was preparing the village program, and Alissa was spending her mornings in the orphanage. One evening I saw she was really drained. Her color was bad. She didn't want to talk much.

"So, what's going on with you?" I asked.

"A rough day at the orphanage," she replied despairingly.

"It's an orphanage, Liss. It's going to be crappy there every day."

"I know. But today was awful. Honoline told me that some of the older kids are slipping out at night and prostituting themselves. Some are doing drugs. I'm like Mary Poppins and they're in this really dark place. It's beyond me. How do you write those kids up to get sponsors? I'm not going to make it up."

We needed some air. We went to Republika, a restaurant and bar made of stones and filled with interesting people. I liked their *ngolo capitaine,* a rich stew of cassava leaves and fried fish wrapped in a banana leaf. She liked their veggie burgers. We arrived early as it tended to get busy there and pregnancy had turned her ravenous several times daily. If she didn't eat when the hunger started, it wouldn't be a pleasant evening for either of us.

The servers always took their time, but if you had things to talk about, that was fine. I had a beer and she watched me drink it. I watched her watch me. I saw something new: Maybe the pain of the continent was starting to find a home in her face—people's smiles change when they've seen too many hard things. It gets a little sardonic. And stress isn't good for a pregnancy. We hung around the restaurant after dinner so we could watch the expats and locals come and go. We were getting to know a few of them and would have little chats.

Back at the house, I offered her a way out, for now: "You could go back early. You could do some baby shopping in San Francisco. I could meet you when you're ready to deliver."

"I'm not interested in just running out on it, Josh, and I don't want Mom babysitting me for an extra month."

"Pick and choose, then. Save the kids you can. Find the ones like Honoline. It's a starfish situation."

"That's what it is. You're right."

That's an old story about a kid who is throwing starfish back in the sea because they've all washed up on shore. Some guy comes along and tells the kid there are a million stranded starfish, and they are just going to die. "Not this one," the kid says as he tosses it in the sea. "And not this one," he says as he keeps going. You think of that story a lot in Africa.

But the reality of our new life was draining. We had separated ourselves from most of the people and places and activities we held dear in exchange for a workload that scarcely left time or energy for joy, and joy is what keeps you going. Joy and debt, anyway—we still had a big mortgage back in New York.

Alissa was carrying the full management load at the Soprano house, explaining the same things over and over, every damned day. Big breakfasts and bigger dinners had to be planned constantly, with ingredients rarely arriving as ordered; gas tanks for the kitchen stove would come up empty and couldn't be refilled before the next day, perhaps having something to do with the house guard's fear that he had contracted malaria (it would turn out to be a common cold) and his spending ten hours in a waiting room; some vital piece of cooking or cleaning equipment would suddenly be blown out because someone had forgotten again to use the voltage converter; a visiting expert would make a peculiar request for a simple errand—something like shipping luggage that might seem easy to a Westerner but could take Alissa a half day here to arrange. And every moment of the day had to be managed in a patched-up concoction of English, French, and Kinyarwanda. She would lock herself in our bedroom with a book whenever her disaster management schedule allowed. She was wearing herself out, and I should have watched for that and worried about it.

Here is how tired she was: I was playing host to Bono of U2. He had come to take a look at what we were doing, and we all admired him for the ONE Campaign and all that he has done for Africa. After the day's tour of worthy programs around Rwanda, I took him to the poolside bar. I was telling him about my amazing and beautiful wife, and what she was doing for the orphans. Then I told him about Health Builders' aggressive plans for expansion. He seemed more interested in Alissa.

"You should call her and get her to come here. I'd like to meet her," he said.

So I called her. She was just across the street and could hop over in a minute.

"Oh, tell him thank you, really," she said to me on the phone. She said she was very tired from her day and just wanted to crash. That's when I understood how worn out she was: I love Bono, she loves Bono, and neither of us had ever met him, or a star remotely like him. But she was turning in.

It was exhaustion and I figured it was time to invoke the ninety-day rule a bit early. I took her to a lakeside retreat in Uganda. The Soprano house could fall apart for a few days while we Adam and Eve'd it in the luxury of a jungle that didn't know us and couldn't keep us to a schedule while we were in its greenery.

CHAPTER 12

Warsaw

Mayange, Bugesera District—before we go there, you need to picture the area in history: Before hundreds of thousands of Tutsi were packed into that region, starting in the 1960s, the community of Mayange and its larger district, Bugesera (hard *g*), was a jungle as you might still think of a jungle, with elephants and other noble animals ranging through.

Tsetse flies were a common and fatal hazard, as they transmit sleeping sickness. The ancestors of those very flies had killed Henry Morton Stanley's horse when the expedition came through here, looking for Dr. Livingstone. Stanley's miles-long supply safari was credited with spreading the disease widely throughout Africa. Stanley himself was said by some of his contemporaries to have shot black men by the hundreds, some for the smallest of infractions, and some—as he did with monkeys in the trees—just for target practice.

After he found Livingstone, by the way, Stanley was recruited by the perverse King Leopold II of Belgium to survey all of Congo—then known as the Kingdom of Kongo—and to annex territory eighty times larger than Belgium. Leopold ruled with remarkable cruelty: there were bonuses given for the number of native hands cut off as discipline for not working hard enough. It was not until after World War I that Rwanda fell under Belgian colonization, and its most poisonous legacy was the taxonomy of Hutu and Tutsi. So Stanley, who arrived first as a reporter for the *New York Herald,* left quite a shadow. Dr. Livingstone, who had come to find the source of the Nile and end slavery in the bargain, was of the opposite spirit.

As to the exact source of the Nile, the river still defies an easy answer to that question. It certainly does not begin at some spring in a meadow, where a historic sign might be pounded in, but instead in an impossible mosquito labyrinth of swamps that knit and turn for miles under a triple-canopy jungle. Debate remains today whether the farthest-flung source of the Nile is Rwanda's Nyabarongo River, which originates in the beautiful Nyungwe Rainforest, south of us, or if it is instead Burundi's Ruvyironza River. I have traced them both with the help of Google Earth, and I declare for the home team, the Nyabarongo River. Had Livingstone had an equivalent app, he might have saved a great deal of swamp time, but I have beat him to it, even with my late start.

You can't help think of Livingstone with some admiration for his pure grit, particularly when you see the cruel legacy of King Leopold in Bugesera. The area was considered, well into the 1960s, as a good place to die and not much else.

As more and more Tutsi were packed into what is now Bugesera District, their only way to survive was to cut wood and produce charcoal, which was then sold in markets for Kigali's cooking fires. By the late 1960s, the jungle was disappearing.

Pressure came to bear: not for the people, but for the animals. Baby elephants were moved to a national park and their giant parents slaughtered. Their bones are among the many bones just under the soil.

When the trees were gone, when the jungles were barren hills, the enterprising population turned to farming. After two decades of relatively productive farming (and dairy production — the district then was called Nyamata, meaning "land of milk"), the topsoil, abused by overcultivation and the elimination of any foliage that would hold the rains, rapidly began to fail; it had largely washed down the Nile. Any lack of rain now brought famine; any hard rain brought floods and more erosion.

When the genocide came, it came hardest to Bugesera district. Records are fuzzy, but survivors suggest that eight out of ten people were murdered. The survivors were those small enough not to be seen under the piles of bodies, or teens fast enough to get to the swamps before the teams of killers came chasing after them with hunting hounds.

In the years after the genocide, those who had escaped streamed back into the area. In addition, tens of thousands of returnees from the refugee camps of Burundi, Uganda, Tanzania, and Congo resettled in the area. The soil, however, was still depleted. The health centers were essentially abandoned. People were starving to death and too exhausted to do much about it. The land was essentially a red dust desert. The water supply was intermittent — it would drip for weeks and then shut off altogether for four or five months. Children were dying every day.

The government tried several approaches, including constructing *imidugudu* (resettlement villages) and sending countless aid organizations to Mayange, but every attempt was swallowed up by dust and despair. None of the interventions built a sense of community, which, though you might not think it at first, is essential to human survival anywhere. People don't stand a chance without community.

After our Uganda sojourn, Alissa seemed much better. She had the energy to do her volunteer work and the Soprano management with gusto left over for our evenings together.

By day, I was placing job ads in the local paper and networking with all my contacts in Rwanda and beyond. We needed organizers, agronomists, accountants, drivers, and public health experts. I knew there were many Rwandans who had these professional skills and were looking for work, thanks to what Pierantonio would later describe as the only good thing to come out of Rwanda's nightmare: of the hundreds of thousands who fled the country beginning in 1959, many were coming back—or their children were coming back—with great educations and higher standards for their country.

Many of the brightest of these returnees congregated in the front room and on the porches of the Soprano house to share ideas and help us plan. I hired as many as I thought our budget would allow. Unfortunately, other people had crafted the budget in New York, and it assumed we could get everyone inexpensively—didn't Africans come cheap? But returning Rwandans, coming from places that actually paid people well, had higher expectations.

We interviewed dozens, finding many who were looking for high-status positions in the city, when we were offering mud and hard work.

But every few days there was someone like Chantal, a tall, elegant young woman who was very clearly intent on helping people at the village level. Dressed in flowing African colors, she told us of her dream to create women's cooperatives that would produce beautiful products for sale so that the women's families might prosper. She didn't ask about the pay; I had to raise the subject. She was a yes.

The returnees were very interesting to me, not only because of their stories of resilience, but also as a historical oddity. I was always interested in useful ways to understand poverty in the world, because understanding a problem is always the first step toward finding solutions. Along that line, something that fascinated me was the observation that landlocked countries are usually the slowest to develop. I'd first seen that while living in desperately poor, landlocked Bolivia in the early 1990s. The exchange of ideas and products, access to foreign markets, and the arrival of competition are necessary to move a country forward. The United States has ports along its twelve thousand miles of coastline. Italy is nearly an island, ringed with ports to send off its adventurers like Marco Polo and Columbus—and Caesar before them. Britain, Japan, and most other highly developed countries have easy access to the rest of the world. Interior countries generally have a harder time. There are spectacular exceptions, such as Switzerland, which adapts by assimilating with the countries surrounding it, which have the ports, but the rule generally applies in devastating form.

So it was amazing to see all these Marco Polos in Kigali, ready to share their treasures from the developed world. Banks and telecom companies were snapping up returnees with degrees from very good schools in the United States and around the Western world. We found a few with gritty development skills honed in the genocide's aftermath: Rwandan agronomists, community organizers, and health experts.

Dr. Blaise, as head of our Health Builders operation, helped me sort through the stacks of applications. He could tell who was sincere and who would probably be able to work well with the different personalities in the still-new government agencies. His time leading the government's tuberculosis program and later in charge of the funds coming from the Global Fund to Fight AIDS, Tuberculosis, and Malaria had honed his people-judging sense.

The world knew what to do about those killer diseases (not to mention many others) but had been doing very little. USAID—the development branch of the American government—was hopelessly slow in implementation, and had even lobbied against providing AIDS medication in Africa. In one notorious incident, USAID's head argued that Africans didn't know Western time and therefore could not take their medicines regularly enough for them to be effective. But the new Global Fund money smacked down such ignorance and was followed by a major new injection of AIDS-fighting American money from the miraculously enlightened Bush administration. That program, awkwardly called PEPFAR (the President's Emergency Plan for AIDS Relief) quickly made something of a hero of George W. Bush in Africa, even as his stock was falling in America. His huge contribution of AIDS money, combined with the Global Fund money from developed nations (including yet another shot of US money), was to provide the biggest public health investment Rwanda, and many countries, had ever seen. For the first time, very poor countries could design and direct their own health programs. Jeff Sachs, instrumental in lobbying for the Global Fund, said it was the first time public health programs could think about billions of dollars instead of millions. In Rwanda, Dr. Blaise was the guy to bring the money home, so his savoir faire was priceless.

I first met Blaise when Health Builders was active in several countries, helping governments quickly prepare proposals to the Global Fund. Sachs warned me that if the Global Fund didn't receive requests that were at a different scale than anything previously imagined in public health, the fund wouldn't be able to justify raising billions of dollars from member nations and would quickly flop. You can't tap the industrial nations for billions if the requests coming in from the needy nations are for antiquated projects, a few aspirin, and bandages.

Blaise was one of the dreamers on the ground in Rwanda who understood the necessity of ambition. We quickly became good friends. He wanted the Rwandan programs to run like a well-managed business. He asked me to start bringing him business management books from the States, which started to fill my carry-on.

Rwanda's president, Paul Kagame, was setting a marathon pace and serious tone for the nation, according to Blaise. Everyone seemed to be trying to build up the ranks of government with capable technocrats. Anyone who took bribes or ran a bad program would run afoul of Kagame. The national goal was to raise Rwanda to good health and prosperity within a few decades. There was no room for corruption in their plans, and that set them apart from nearly every other developing nation.

Annette Karenzi was one of the first people to respond to our ad for a country director for the Millennium Village project. Dr. Blaise and I liked her application and felt that she exuded the confidence that would be mandatory for the challenges ahead.

Annette, like many Rwandans, grew up across the border in Uganda, where her parents had fled from the earlier stages of the genocide. Her mastery of English set her apart from the other young women of her village.

In the summer of 1994, with the Rwandan Patriotic Army in control of smoldering Kigali, Annette left her parents to make her life back in Rwanda. Her family placed her in the home of an uncle, who kept a very close eye on her. She quickly got a job reading the news in English at the major radio station. Her uncle's driver took her to the station, waited for her to read the evening news in English, and then delivered her safely back to his home. Her social opportunities were thereby limited. It was, after all, still a very dangerous and difficult environment. Bodies were still unburied in many places of the city. Dogs were still being shot. Many scores were being settled, and defiant Interahamwe killers yet roamed the countryside.

Not far off her daily drive to the radio station was the compound of a young doctor, Major Ben Karenzi. He, too, was raised in Uganda. He had done well in school, gone on to medical school, and was practicing in South Africa successfully when he decided to go back to his home community in Uganda to find a bride. While he was there the war began. He was recruited to be one of the first field surgeons in the army as it charged into Rwanda to overturn the government and end the slaughter.

Under the direction of Paul Kagame, the remarkably effective commander of the Rwandan Patriotic Army, the army gained a reputation for good medical care. That gave courage to troops, as the opposite—when troops fear that the smallest wound will kill them—quickly damages morale. When the war was over, Karenzi was given one leadership position after another.

Colonel Karenzi would later tell me that after the war, he was amazed to see in the mirror that he was still alive. He did not expect to be. He had seen too much death. He often thought he was living his last day, his last minute. When he had come with the army toward Kigali from the south, he passed through the carnage in Mayange. Though he was by then a seasoned warrior and had seen many things, the situation in Mayange was such that he has never been able to go back there. He is a hard and serious man, but he cannot speak of the place without stopping in midsentence, grasping for the words to describe what he saw.

After the war Karenzi thanked God that he had survived, and asked in a second prayer if he perhaps might now get on with the business of finding a bride. He put the word out to his family and his many comrades-in-arms that if they knew of a very bright and available woman from a fine family, they should let him know. The message went to those who had lived in his home village in Uganda. When a transmission like this goes out in Africa, it goes quickly and to everyone in the most amazing ways. In ancient times, the king of Rwanda could get a message to every household within the same day. It is even faster now, of course, but not by much.

It happened that the driver and security man who worked for Annette's uncle—the young man who took her to the radio station each evening—was from Karenzi's home village. He described her to people who then described her to Karenzi, and a plot was hatched. However, Africa being Africa, by this time Annette had heard that someone senior in the army was interested in her.

"It will not be easy for him to get me," is what she told the women in her family. "He is a big man who thinks he can get me, but I will not let him. He cannot get me." But the joyful game was on.

One day, on the way to the radio station, her car took a sudden turn.

"This is not the way," Annette said to the driver.

"I just have to make a quick stop," the driver explained.

"I cannot be even a minute late. There is no being late for a radio news show."

"You will not be late," he assured her, as they pulled up to the gate of a compound, where two soldiers let them pass.

"Why are we going in here?" she asked the driver.

"Someone wants to meet you," he replied. "It will just take a moment."

Annette immediately understood that "a great conniving" was afoot. Her willful suitor had somehow corrupted her uncle's driver. She could do nothing but smile at his cleverness and her own entrapment. She walked into his house with her smile and her laugh, and then-Major Karenzi, dressed in the green shirt of a soldier, thought her laugh was just from a joyful heart, not from a game. She was thinking she had better be smart now, so she was actually laughing at herself.

He fell in love with her right then and insisted she have a cup of tea, which they had as the sun went down in an unusually beautiful orange ball that Annette remembers very well today. Then he drove her to the radio station himself so she would not be late.

Annette liked him. In his favor was his good English. Another plus was the fact that he was a doctor—her own father is a medical man—and he was of her same Christian faith. She wanted to refuse him, to win the great game, but she could not. She liked him too much.

Annette's father quickly gave in. He knew the reputation of Major Karenzi and told her, "What can I possibly deny this young man, who has given us back our country, and who has made it safe for us to come home? What can I possibly deny him?" So he gave his brilliant, beautiful daughter to him, as the young major had requested through the formality of family representatives.

After six head of cattle changed hands temporarily (they were symbolic, and were given back), the marriage was sealed in October 1994, even as the war was barely over and the dead bodies were still being taken to the many vaults being built all over Rwanda.

Annette had three children by the time I met her. She had recently completed her master's in sustainable international development at Brandeis University. She was a strong believer in pursuing health through building up the spirit and institutions of a community, so she was a perfect fit for what I thought we needed to do in Mayange. When we met, she had been up all night in the hospital with her little son, Tunga, but he was all right, and she, despite her lack of sleep, was obviously brilliant. I wanted to hire her straight away, but Colonel Ben was now the permanent secretary of the Ministry of Health, someone I dealt with regularly. I didn't want to hire someone we couldn't fire, and I didn't want to hire her if it looked like an attempt to curry favor, especially in a country so keen on avoiding corruption. I would have to ask him if hiring her posed a conflict of interest.

"Josh, what you and I have to do together will not be affected if you hire her or if you don't, or if you hire her and it doesn't work out. It will not affect anything between us," he said. He has the slightly bloodshot eyes of a man who has looked into many eyes of friend and foe for the last time, and he has a strong handshake. I did not doubt his word, so I decided to hire Annette to lead the effort in Mayange. When I reached her by phone, she had already heard from Ben. They were both excited about doing something for Mayange.

Donald Ndahiro, our chief agricultural expert, was my next perfect find. He is a quiet man, calm and methodical, as you might expect of someone who is patient enough to watch plants grow. He had good contacts in Rwanda's agricultural college, from which we hired several more agronomists to help us work with the farmers. He was born in Kampala, Uganda, in 1967 to parents who ran from the Rwanda killings in 1961. His father was a tailor who died from diabetes. His mother managed the family cattle and fields and her ten children. Only one of the children died, and that was in the war.

You might expect that Donald and his nine siblings, growing up in the dust of poverty, would be destined for much of the same dust, but Africa is a surprising place. One of Donald's sisters is the director of a nonprofit in Kigali. Another is a law school professor. One brother is the director of a religious organization. Two brothers are in the UK getting master's degrees; another is an engineer creating broadband coverage in Rwanda. One brother married an American and is studying in Virginia. One brother is still on the family farm, helping his mother. This is the picture of Africa now. This is how it is transforming itself.

As for Donald, he has four children and a wife. As a kid, Donald liked to herd cattle, which he did by himself at the age of eleven. Because the number of cattle a family owned determined village status, he was embarrassed that they did not have as many as most families. His father kept selling them in order to give each of his children a good education. In time, Donald saw how this was more important than village status. It was the future.

With Donald in place, our initial team was finally assembled and ready to go to Mayange. The only way there was over the bridge that Op-ed dreaded. It was just a bridge, and care must always be taken when crossing bridges in poor countries. I had passed across it before, pausing to make sure the steel plates would support our wheels. But I did not know the bridge as Op-ed knew it. You can walk down a street in any city — even your own — and not know that a remarkable thing happened on this corner or down that alley. If you are very sensitive to such things, perhaps you feel a blush of dread or a hint of joy as you move through such human landscapes. My sensitivity to this bridge, to Rwanda's dark and bright corners, was an education just started.

CHAPTER 13

—∞—

Bridge of Death

On a good, sunny day, navigating the road to Mayange involved over three hours of climbing in and out of ruts deep enough to find the axels and bumpers of the most Africanized vehicles. There is such a thing, by the way, as an Africanized vehicle. Land Rovers and Land Cruisers and a few other makes come to Africa with big running boards, safari-style cargo racks atop, tougher and higher suspensions, supplemental fuel tanks, and, most visibly, snorkel pipes that come from the engine, up alongside the passenger side of the window. That pipe allows the engine to keep going in waist-deep water, and it allows the engine to stay cleaner, gulping its air a few feet higher up from the surface of the roads, which are often traveled in fast, close, dusty caravans. I think the main reason you see such vehicles, however, is that they look very cool, and many of the charities operating them want badass vehicles pictured in their brochures and websites. Our vehicles were picked up on the cheap, however—no sexy snorkels.

The only smooth section was the narrow steel bridge over the Nyabarongo River, which is the upper reach of the four-thousand-mile Nile, just as it begins its last long, open-air curve toward the deep green tunnels of the Nyungwe Rainforest.

Abed drove slowly over the bridge leading to Mayange, not only because it was narrow and old, with loose steel plates for a roadbed, but also because he knew very well that it was a solemn, if unmarked, memorial. He stopped midbridge.

"You see, this is where they were killed." He said it in French and spread his hand out the window to indicate the full expanse of the swiftly moving Nyabarongo below us. Thousands of men, women, and children were marched down the road from the villages and then forced to jump off the bridge to their deaths in the raging river. Jump or be shot. Jump or be hacked to death. Many miles away, their bodies were pushed to the surface as they shot over a waterfall, their arms and legs swinging in flailing cartwheels that gave onlookers the impression of people playing in the water—but they were all dead. Their bodies would float north all the way to Lake Victoria, where the shorelines were solid with corpses from this and uncounted other mass murders along the rivers of the Nile.

We continued across the bridge and soon passed the infamous Nyamata Catholic Church, where thousands of people were massacred in 1994.

Mayange, a cluster of five villages, is just a few kilometers beyond the church. As we arrived, the only thriving business we saw was that of a woman, Jacqueline, who prepared people for burial. She was doing well.

The children did not rush our vehicles with shouts and smiles, as is the custom throughout the developing world, especially Africa. They were too weak. The adults stared at us with sunken eyes. They had seen other trucks come and go, bringing only dust.

Donald the agronomist had a clear articulation of the causes of Mayange's hunger.

"You see how the hills are all eroded," he said, pointing at the red earth flowing down the hillside. "They cannot hold the rain and they cannot hold the soil itself. That must be fixed." We were looking at a huge expanse of brown-stubbled hills. It seemed impossible.

To orient you: Kigali, the capital, is fairly in the middle of the roundish nation. We were about halfway down toward the Burundi border. Fifty miles to the west of us, and a little south, was the Nyungwe Rainforest, known not only as the mystic source of the Nile but also as the home of an astounding thirteen primate species. Congo, just to the west, has lots of gold in the ground; Rwanda has golden monkeys. Today, Rwanda has the better deal, as the monkeys bring tourists, while the gold and minerals bring only exploitation, corruption, and misery to its neighbor.

North and west of the rainforest—fifty miles due west of where we were in Mayange—is Lake Kivu, one of the Great Lakes of Equatorial Africa. It is sixty miles long, north to south, and about twenty-five miles wide. In more peaceful times to come, when memories fade a bit and there is security between Rwanda and Congo (skirmishes that are echoes of the genocide still play out), this land will be one of the prime honeymoon spots of the world. It is Jurassic Park without the dinosaurs. In 1994, the rainforest was a refuge and the lake was a deadly barrier to escape.

The Nyamata Catholic Church, which is right across a field from where we had decided to rent our little office—is to me the moral center of the five villages of Mayange, and the whole district. Though services aren't still held inside, it is very much a church. The shirts and trousers and dresses and shawls and baby clothes of the victims are stacked high on the pews. Underground vaults below and behind the church are filled with the neatly stacked skulls and bones of forty-five thousand men, women, and children. The dark and narrow vaults can be entered, though it is heartbreaking to do so. I used to be able to do it.

There is a memorial plaque at the side of the church for an Italian missionary, Tonia Locatelli. In 1992, Locatelli sheltered people in the Nyamata Catholic Church, while killers gathered at its gates. Having seen massacres in the area during the prior week and fearing a massive slaughter in Nyamata, she got through to the BBC. The BBC called the communications office of the Rwandan government and is said to have asked, "We have a missionary on the line, and we understand you are about to kill several thousand people at a church in Nyamata. Can you confirm that?" That attention stopped the present massacre, but a week later the nun was shot dead in front of her little house.

The fact that the church saved the people once, even at the price of the nun's life, gave the villagers confidence that the church was a safe place to go. When it started again, in April 1994, thousands fled there. Nearly seven thousand people crammed into the church—standing room only, children in back. It is not a large church, so that is hard to imagine. It must have been like a Tokyo subway car. Four thousand more were just outside in the front courtyard of the church.

When the Rwandan Army arrived they surrounded the church and erected a chain-link fence to enclose the church and its overflow crowd. They pounded drums and taunted the crowd with, "We shall kill the cockroaches! We shall kill them all!" The term "cockroaches" was a horrid label for dehumanizing the Tutsi. The soldiers jabbed at people through the fence with their bayonets. More people from the village were rounded up and brought into the enclosure. Finally, an order was given to the militia by the army officers: "Hutus, do your work. Clean out the cockroaches from your church."

They pushed into the courtyard and began killing people there, to terrible screams and shouted prayers. Just inside, a priest was quickly baptizing newborn infants as they were passed overhead to him so they could enter heaven. The killing was not mercifully quick: it went on for a long time even before the killers entered the church, which was locked tightly from the inside. A grenade finally opened the door. The killers cut off the arms and heads of six people in the anteroom, and used the arms to push through the bars to the inner church to taunt the next to be killed: "See how we will kill you cockroaches?" they yelled. They then entered the area where people were packed so densely. Soldiers sprayed machine gun bullets, then sent in the militia with their machetes. The babies were killed by wives of militia members, who swung their little heads into the brick walls.

The priest, the head teacher of the Catholic school, a doctor, and three others were tied to the pillars and killed with hammers to their skulls. When they fell, the killers taunted their bodies, laughing that they should use their elite brains to help them stand up now.

A pregnant Hutu woman who had married a Tutsi man was singled out for singular torture so horrific that I cannot describe it here. Four pregnant Tutsi women were similarly tortured.

If you did not want to be killed with a rusty machete or

beaten to death with clubs with big nails sticking through them, or see your wife and daughters impaled as these other women had been impaled, and if you had money, you could buy your death by a bullet, or buy bullets for your wife and children.

When the pile of dead made it hard to get to the living people in the back, the killers began to throw grenades. The holes in the tin roof are kept there to remember. The spray of blood from the machetes and the nail clubs and the hammers and the guns and finally the grenades soaked the interior in blood. The altar cloth is still there, brown and stiff with a bloodstain that must surely endure as long as this earth.

When you hear such stories from area survivors, there is a moment when you ask yourself, what am I doing here? Why should anyone care about people who could do such things? But you remind yourself that the cultivation of an empathy strong enough to overcome what we hominids are capable of doing is the cultural artifact of civilization, and civilization is the artifact of security, and security is the artifact of at least some modicum of prosperity. Prosperity is sometimes not enough, as we saw in Germany and China and Armenia and Bosnia and the Americas and so many other heartbroken places, but it is a precondition of civilization, without which you can do nothing civilized.

A young man who works as a guide at the church was a small child at the time of the killing. He described to me how he escaped with one brother and one sister from one of the villages farther south—they escaped the roundup and so were not taken to the church. Six other siblings and his parents were killed. He and his brother and sister survived in the swamps to the west, along the Nyabarongo, coming into the dry forests at night to hunt for small animals. They ran back to the swamp each dawn to escape the roaming bands of killers and their hunting dogs.

Many brave people who had escaped to the neighboring countries in the years before 1994 ventured into Rwanda during the worst of it to check on family members and to help the survivors find a way out. The young man finally met such a fellow, a friend of his family. In this way the children survived. He is now a student majoring in political science and he works at the church to earn his way. He told me that, before they met the family friend, they crossed the hills toward Lake Kivu, where they were able to pass as Hutu children for a time. Lake Kivu, as I mentioned, serves as a long barrier between Rwanda and Congo. In the hundred days of genocide there was another Tutsi child pretending to be Hutu. That was Solange, one of the cooks at Heaven Restaurant, whom you will meet.

When we arrived in Mayange, we knew the hard history of the region, and one other thing for sure: To rebuild a sense of community from those pieces would be difficult at best. But there was something to do first before we could do anything else: People here were starving to death. They needed to eat.

CHAPTER 14

—◦◦◦—

Rule One

If you're involved on the ground long enough, you'll come up with a handful of commonsense rules of thumb to guide your work. I keep coming back to five—one for each digit of my hand. The first rule, represented by my best-fed digit, my thumb, is pretty obvious: People who are starving cannot be asked to do more than eat. Many of the twenty-five thousand survivors and returnees in Mayange needed food, and they needed it immediately. You can't ask starving people to save themselves. You feed them. They get their strength and their wits back. Hungry people, dying people, can't do the creative things they need to do in order to move forward. They can't act as a community.

If, after you feed them, you do not get them to solve their own food problems, but instead you just keep handing out food, then you are not doing them any real favors, and you are also wasting aid money that could be used more effectively.

It happens all the time.

—◦—

After our big team breakfasts, Alissa would head to the orphanage to work with the kids and the rest of us would head to

Mayange to begin the hard work of reopening the health clinic and establishing our community mobilizers throughout the villages. The most important work for now, however, was done over the phone: Coming and going slowly on the nearly impassable road, I called for support from other groups and experts. Mostly I was trying to get donated food and medical supplies from the UN, from donors, and from the Rwandan government.

Now that our team was visible on the ground, we were also dealing with individual problems: a farmer with a fungus-infested foot that was three times its normal size—it had to come off; a young boy with a spine virtually destroyed by tuberculosis; a thirteen-year old girl who had been brutally raped and had a resulting fistula that made her incontinent. We had to respond to the distinct illnesses and traumas, but we also had to deal with the larger issue of mass starvation.

This was basically international lobbying work, and we were blessed to have good cell phone coverage, even in remote Mayange. It is a fact that you can get better signal strength in some very odd places in the world than you can in some parts of Manhattan. Indeed, I could call my parents in Ridgefield, Connecticut, on my cell phone from the dusty and seemingly infertile fields of Mayange.

I didn't have to sugarcoat those calls. My dad is a doctor and I could tell him what I was seeing. My mom has been with me to the deepest jungles of Papua New Guinea and the Amazon, so she doesn't flinch when I describe hard places.

"I'm sure it's rough, Josh. How's Alissa doing?" she would say. "How's the baby bump? Tell us when you know which color baby clothes to send." That sort of thing. Dad was clinical. He is good at long-distance medical diagnosis, which comes in very handy.

Why the good cell phone systems? Well, it says a lot about how America operates in the developing world, and how the rest of the world operates. Rwanda and a thousand other remote places have good cell signal because international investors from South Africa, Libya, Luxembourg, and especially India have jumped into markets like these. India and China are all over Africa. While the Americans typically send free food and medicine, those other countries send business-people and investment capital. Both approaches are needed, but the business-oriented operations make a profit and so can move faster and farther and actually help build up a modern economy rapidly. Cell phones themselves are small and cheap. They arrive by the barrel from developed countries and are sold for a few dollars. You might see a woman who sweeps the street for a dollar a day stop to take a cell phone call from her sister. She will be smiling as she does so. The cell phone has been a great addition to happier living worldwide, but especially in developing countries, where it is always urgent to know that someone is all right, and where to find the best price for your farm's produce.

There were never many telephone poles in hilly Rwanda. A better use for copper wire is getting electricity to more homes, and though copper phone wire had connected a few thousand people in Kigali, wireless technology was cheaper and much faster to install over entire regions. Modern communications in many parts of Africa and other developing areas leap-frogged, moving almost directly from jungle drums to cell phones.

The simple cell phones are good for more than just conversation: They have opened the door to remote banking, health care tracking, ambulance dispatch, small business creation, and education. The people of Africa will probably be voting on their smart phones before we are in the States.

But on the muddy road of 2006, it was just voice calls. Many voice calls. I was trying hard to get food shipments sent from the UN World Food Programme. If you want trucks loaded with food from the UN to stream into your neighborhood, it will take a lot of calls and some serious documentation of need. The world is a hungry place, and you must compete for those prized pallets of food.

Ranu Dhillon, the one young expert I had brought with me from the States, worked with the nurses of the health center to measure the thinness of children's arms. You have seen bone-thin children in charity posters. Believe it or not, the UN has mandated armbands to determine how skinny is too skinny, and how skinny is not yet skinny enough to warrant food support. It's logical and maybe necessary, but shocking nonetheless. It's shocking to tell a very hungry kid that he is not hungry enough yet, not wasted away enough yet. But everyone was hungry, so we made the measurements.

We found that a third of the population—almost nine thousand people—met the criteria for severe malnutrition, while most of the rest were moderately malnourished. Unfortunately, a third is not a high enough percentage for the area to qualify for World Food Programme assistance.

Part of the "problem" was that since people were eating mostly weeds and cassava root on a good day, they were dying slowly of malnutrition instead of quickly starving from an abrupt famine. Cassava is a green plant that gets about six feet high; in Latin America it's known as manioc. The roots— growing as big as ten pounds—can be milled into flour or cut into pieces and boiled like potatoes. They don't have much nutritional value, but they are filling.

Mayange's malnutrition had been a long time coming, with years of deteriorating soil and drought after drought. But long-term malnutrition was now rapidly becoming outright famine. The coup de grâce, or non-grâce, was the arrival of a destructive cassava disease called mosaic virus (for the way it dapples the leaves before it kills the plant). When you try to pull up a healthy cassava plant, you're a bit like a human trying to pick up Thor's battle hammer. The locals dig out the roots and cut them. The plants grow back. But with mosaic virus, you can tug a bit on the plant and it gives way, showing atrophied roots. Donald found that all Mayange's cassava leaves bore the crisscross mark of doom.

Policies or no policies, people were dying. Donald, Annette, Ranu, and I agreed that the first corollary of our Rule One should be that when people are dying of hunger, we won't take no for an answer from anyone who has warehouses full of food. If the UN said no, which it did, we would just consider that an unacceptable and therefore inoperative answer — as if we never had received it.

We had a robust back channel: Jeff Sachs was close to the leaders of many UN agencies, and they, in turn, were close to the people at the very top. The people telling us "no" were only following rules, though this was clearly a case where the rules needed to be ignored. A wink from the top office would do it, and, thanks to Jeff, the wink was forthcoming. Supplies were soon on their way to the Indian Ocean port of Mombasa, Kenya. From there, trucks rumbled fifteen hundred muddy kilometers westward across Kenya, then through the north of

Tanzania, skirting the south shore of Lake Victoria, and finally into Rwanda. Before they arrived in Mayange, the little clinic needed to be fully revived, not only as a good health clinic, but also as a well-organized food distribution center.

Abed was always silent when he drove us, though I could tell from his body language when he knew something I should know.

"You didn't like what I said on the phone a minute ago to the UN," I said, as he negotiated deep ruts through the mud by the river bridge again.

He shrugged, meaning it was nothing.

"I think I was talking about how we were planning to use the medical clinic as a food distribution center. The UN wants to know if we have the capacity to manage all that, so that's what I was talking about," I said.

"So you were thinking something about that?" I prodded.

"It's fine, boss," he said, though it was *c'est bien, chef,* as we usually speak in French. "If they send enough food, everything will be fine," he said. "But if they are only sending a little, they should send some soldiers in blue helmets, too. We have a saying, boss: the stomach never lets go." It means hunger is a dangerous animal with teeth, or something like that.

He was right. Enough food was on the way, but we should be careful not to let it arrive a little at a time. When it arrived, it should look like more than enough for everyone, so there would be no panic for it, no corruption in giving it to family members first—that sort of thing. There had been enough damage already to the area's sense of community. The first convoy must be a big one. The lines must be organized. No mob scenes.

We knew that the expat team members should not be the

people handing out the food. If your town ran out of food, would you want someone from another nation handing you the food, or would you want your longtime neighbor to hand it to you? You would want a neighborhood committee to have figured out how to organize the distribution. That way, your dignity would be intact. Your children would see neighbors doing something together to feed their families—they would not see their parents looking like helpless victims. We prepared the medical clinic to serve as a food distribution center, but we insisted that the food operation be organized and staffed by nurses and local volunteers. This would be a first big step in restoring a sense of community. Though most of the people were weak, they agreed to help and began planning for how it would be done fairly, with the first food going to the hungriest families.

We wanted to jump-start the dead economy, too. A good way to do that would be to pay the farmers a little for the terracing work that Donald said had to be done, even if they were improving their own fields. It would also be a way to make sure the work got done, even if the farmers didn't yet know the value of proper terracing and row planting. Through international partners, we would pay a dollar a day to revamp all the fields of the area. That would add up to a lot of money, but Stephen Lewis and our other donors demanded results, and this, we thought, would get them.

There were plans for three lines at the health center: one for health care, one for food, and one for training the farmers on the new terracing and planting methods at a model farm next door. The district government, which was functioning and caring, helped identify the families who should be first in line for food when it arrived. Our clinic staff measured and weighed children who obviously should have been put on the priority list but had been overlooked.

Still, even before the food arrived, the health clinic needed to get back in business. For this, I had an ace up my sleeve: Ranu.

Ranu, as I mentioned, came over from the States to help. Though he is a full-fledged doctor now, he was at the time a medical student. Whenever I was lecturing at Columbia, he would be in the audience taking down everything I said and following me afterward with a list of questions. He was a kid, dressed with baggy everything and his shirt buttoned just at the top.

Ranu's parents emigrated from Punjab, India, to Trenton, New Jersey, where he grew up surrounded by poverty and gangs. He had an epiphany one day: he realized that if he didn't immediately find a high purpose for his life, it would be a short life, ending badly. He had been challenging teachers and any authority, but he soon began to challenge poverty itself; he decided to become a public health doctor, to the amazement of his street friends. By the time he latched on to me he was already a medical student. He was easy to spot in an audience: a maroon turban shadowing his bold Indian face, bushy black eyebrows constantly bouncing to register his amazement at a new fact, and then another. He smiled beautifully when he wasn't concentrating and scribbling.

He offered himself as a volunteer to help with any work I saw fit to delegate to him. I had no system for interns so I always said no, though I was impressed with him. He had already traveled to his father's homeland in India to establish support services for children displaced by political violence in the Punjab, in the far north of India. The Punjab is adjacent to

Pakistan and to Kashmir, so it was brave work. Then, while in college in Philadelphia, he created a group to help inner-city kids develop leadership skills, and he helped get medical services for poor immigrants.

Ranu was often on my mind: I wanted to be a mentor to him and I thought that he could be a great role model to me in terms of energy and confidence and optimism. When that rooftop party resulted in funding for a Millennium Village in Rwanda, I finally had something for him.

"Ranu, Alissa and I are going to Rwanda to do something fairly big. If you really want to work with me, you can come."

He stuck out his hand for a handshake.

"Not so fast. Little to no pay, abominable challenges, no time off," I said.

"Sounds perfect, Josh. I'm in," he replied. It would mean a delay of his school plans, but he wanted to do it.

It was Ranu who first spotted the "really fantastic and beautiful" vacant "Soprano" house that would become our headquarters and group house. He immediately started interviewing for household help and scavenging for the essentials, such as a stove, a fridge, and a microwave. Laundry would be done out back by hand and line dried. He learned Kinyarwanda fluently while I was still struggling with basic greetings. Now and then I'd try to say something in Kinyarwanda to a farmer in Mayange and he would softly correct me later.

He quickly endeared himself to the vitally important permanent secretaries, and to their secretaries, in the seven ministries of government we had to deal with. When the résumés began to arrive in response to our ad for local experts, his wise comments were often the decisive opinion. The credit for the fact that we were ready to roll when we got the green light must go to him, and to Dr. Blaise, of course, and to Annette and Donald.

With the food trucks presumably on the way, Ranu was the guy to get the health clinic up to speed. A clinic building was in place, but it was essentially abandoned and off the water and power grids. A huge sign declared "Mayange Health Center, Project of UNHCR with support from the Government of Japan."

"Ranu, do you think this sign should come down?" I was half joking. I didn't know if it should or not.

"Let me ask," he said, shouting something in Kinyarwanda that I did not understand. Two men ran over and ripped the sign down.

The process of resurrecting the clinic began. The first few times we showed up, we found the front door locked and sick patients languishing on the steps, some of whom had been carried several kilometers in makeshift bamboo ambulances. We easily found nurses to work in the health center. They were already living in the area, and within walking distance of the abandoned clinic. But they had given up, as it had no management or payroll and no supplies or drugs or lighting. There were fluorescent lightbulbs in the ceiling, but no power connection. By this point, the health center's nurses were coming in just a few times per week. They were splitting doses of the dwindling supply of donated drugs, and then splitting those doses further. They knew that the dilutions probably wouldn't help, but at least everyone would have the same chance, and they, the nurses, would not have to decide who lived and who died — God would. As the famine overtook malaria as the top killer, the nurses just stopped coming because the only thing to see was death. When we assured them that medical supplies were on the way, they returned in their white uniforms.

Ranu organized them. His command of Kinyarwanda was nearly perfect, so he ordered them about and was ordered about by them, just as if he were native to these hills. Although the infrastructure was awkward and seedy with small rooms and paint peeling off the ceilings, Ranu knew that the most important first step was to restore dignity to the facility itself. He sported cleaning gloves and a mop and, with the whole team, got to work sanitizing and painting the entire facility for the first time in years.

Ranu wanted to reestablish respect for the nurses, too, so he called for a meeting with our team and the nurses and elders. First we went around the circle introducing ourselves and getting to know the people of the area. I told everyone that I was a new arrival without any kids yet (everyone found that quite funny); Donald talked about his roots in the area; others said they were married to this or that person, or they had lost their families in the genocide, and they have this many children— or used to. When it was Ranu's turn to introduce himself, he stood and said, "My name is Ranu Dhillon, and I have many girlfriends." And he sat down.

It felt like the first good laugh heard in Mayange since our work had begun. The men exploded and the women snickered behind their hands. The nurses blushed, as some people assumed he meant them. He suddenly had their hearts, and they would listen to him and believe that he was there for them. That he spoke fluently in Kinyarwanda was the icing on the cake. That, and his part in making happen what did one Friday afternoon: the rumble of distant trucks on the dusty, rutted road, the deep-drumming answer to the prayers of twenty-five thousand people.

CHAPTER 15

⟶⟋⟍⟵

From the People of the United States of America

The red dust of the roaring truck convoy drifted above the road where it topped the desolate hills between the Nyabarongo River's Bridge of Death and Mayange. Whole families, notified by Africa's mysteriously instantaneous communisphere of cell phones and neighbors, moved as quickly as they could from their mud houses to the clinic, where, by the hundreds, they formed in the orderly lines that had been planned by the elders. Some mothers and fathers, so thin and weak, could barely make the trip. In the worst cases, neighbors made the trip for them.

Arriving by the ton now was a corn-soy flour blend, grown in America's Midwest and then shipped a world away in canvas bags. Included in the shipments were big tins of cooking oil and thousands of small sacks of sugar on plastic-wrapped pallets.

I had a little flashback to Ethiopia, where I had first seen packaging marked, "A gift from the people of the United States." It was very moving when I saw it.

I watched the nurses give the first careful spoonfuls of prepared food to the most severely malnourished children—they didn't want those families to have to make their long treks home before a first good meal. In the coming weeks we watched as new recipes were concocted from the few new ingredients and then joyfully served by happy parents to their still sunken-eyed children.

Medical supplies came, too. Ranu had the health center running beautifully. The nurses were all in love with him. Perhaps in part for him, they wanted the health center to be one of the best in the country, which is exactly what it became.

Rule One was now a thumbs-up in Mayange. Day by day, we could see the children looking healthier, the adults energetically tending their fields, and we could see some joy. When our vehicles arrived on a village road now, you would see what you always like to see in such places: the children cheering and running alongside the vehicle with wide smiles. Ranu and the nurses were making big dents in the malnutrition-driven illnesses that had swept through Mayange and were now being swept out.

Nonetheless, this wasn't success yet. With each Mayange acre supporting a family of six to ten, it was clear that long-term family planning was needed, and that farming had to be improved to support the very dense population—the densest in rural Africa. Donald had to get the farmers themselves into successful production of crops that could support all those families.

In many ways, Mayange was more refugee camp than community, but unlike a formal refugee camp, we couldn't tap the UN for food much longer.

Dr. Blaise, who had been watching Ranu's success, had a moment very much like my moment in Greenwich Village:

"Josh, I think Health Builders should operate in places like Mayange—in other words, at the district level, not at the national level. Health Builders is too high up the food chain. For example, I think we should help make sure the clinics are well managed, as Ranu has done. This will help us in many ways. The management of the clinics is critical. Ranu is brilliant, but he will not stay forever, and there is only one of him. We need to fix a dozen health centers in Mayange's health district, and that is just the beginning. All the districts need this kind of help. If you fix only Mayange, it will be like the one flower in a land of bees, and it will be overrun with demand."

"We don't have room in your budget to do that," I replied. "It would take more staff."

"We have the staff! We have me and my crew!" he laughed. He was willing to do what many people in his position would never be willing to do: leave the comforts of the city to spend his days making muddy rounds in the villages.

It would mean changing the mission of Health Builders from national-level consulting to fieldwork, and that meant talking to the donors and working it out. But I didn't want to argue with Dr. Blaise. He is a really big guy.

And he was right. Plus, I knew that his way, we would learn things that could help us improve health delivery far beyond Mayange. He was a maniac for good management. He had nearly memorized the business books I had brought from the States.

When Blaise first showed up to look closer at Ranu's operation, he had suggestions for better records and goals. It was rather like a merger, and he was the visiting new CEO. Ranu was fine, but the nurses didn't like having an extra boss. There was some culture shock. Ranu smoothed as many feathers as he could, but the nurses pushed back, informing Ranu and me that they knew what they were doing and didn't need to be told what to do by a six-foot-seven giant from the city.

With some coaxing, they all sat down and listened intently to his description of the systems he wanted to set up.

"Pretend this isn't some neglected health center! Make this place a successful business — you've got customers, you've got products; you're the employees — *tugende! Tugende!*" That means "Let's go!"

Every employee needed a job description. QuickBooks needed to be installed and used. A drug procurement and tracking system was needed to stop drug shortages; and most importantly, the new national health insurance program needed to be used by everybody.

Blaise wanted careful tracking of the number of births, family planning consultations, malaria and other diagnoses, and the nurses' hours. He pulled out slides to show the staff how the visual tracking of all these would work and would be interesting and would even be a little fun. He showed how good accounting could increase their budget for the things they needed by cutting back on things that were wasted.

There were soon charts on the waiting room walls to track vaccinations, checkups, prenatal visits, birth weights, well-baby visits, and many other measurable activities. These new efficiencies enabled the clinic to serve patients faster, and that attracted more patients. The clinic went from treating 10 patients per day to over 120 a day — and treating them very well.

The nurses got it by seeing it work. All they ever wanted, anyway, was to be the best clinic in Rwanda and maybe the world. For that, they could stand an accountant or two and some charts to keep up. But it was a new world. They knew that whenever they saw Dr. Blaise's hulking shadow in the waiting room, everything had better be shipshape.

Of course, one thing needed to happen before the computer arrived: Although an electricity tower was visible from the steps of the health clinic, the lightbulbs had still never turned on, and indeed, the community of more than twenty-thousand had not one single electrical connection. For over a decade the people of Mayange had lived in the dark in spite of the looming electrical cables high overhead. Working with the mayor and the electrical company, we lobbied for electricity.

In two weeks, a crew arrived without notice and poured a concrete footing for a transformer. The next day they installed a switch, flipped it on, and departed.

Miraculously, at Mayange Health Center, where the UN had installed Japanese-funded fluorescent tubes a decade earlier but had never managed to turn them on, every single light turned on. The nurses celebrated—no more treacherous births by candlelight, and no more hikes to Nyamata to charge their cell phones, which were critically needed to arrange hospital transfers.

Just a week later medical information and data would be entered electronically. But before that, on that very first night of light, long after the day's patients had departed, a flood of children came to do their schoolwork. They set themselves up in the waiting room, in the clinic halls, and on the steps. Student eyes that had strained for so long by candlelight or by the flicker of "three stone" cooking fires—built of a few rocks the size of melons in their homes or just outside—relaxed now to do their studies under the bright light of something very new and wonderful.

CHAPTER 16

Rule Two

If you want the staff in the clinics to do a certain thing," Dr. Blaise explained to me, "for example, to take a baby's vital signs, to ensure the mother has a mosquito net over the bed, and to give standard immunizations, then you only need to make check boxes for those things on a form, and tell them the form must be followed and completed. Otherwise, those things will not be done reliably, no matter how many times you ask for them to be done." I was learning from a master—from someone who believed that health was the key to prosperity and that public health could deliver services effectively. "And if you want them to check those boxes, then you must have effective management, and make certain the staff are paid well and on time and have the medications they need."

Why, after all the fundraising and new charities and billions in foreign aid from successful countries and full-hearted volunteers heading off to all corners of the world and donated goats and sponsored children, is there still so damn much poverty in the world? Yes, the apostle Mark wrote that the poor would always be with us, but he did so long before the rise of the tremendous powers we now have to raise people up. The stubbornness of poverty seems to derive from the willingness of the haves to let their programs for the have nots simply fail. The War on Poverty in the States was marvelously successful, until it was let go. That is a common story, worldwide. It suggests that poverty programs are created for our own satisfaction and rationalization, not for true and permanent results. While most development assistance has evaporated without a trace—eaten up by business-class plane tickets, hotel stays, conferences, and never-to-be-read reports and pamphlets—there are also too many abandoned schools and clinics and other things of great human value littering the landscapes of the poor—facilities funded by well-meaning people with short attention spans and no true belief that poverty can actually be eliminated. The despair in Mark's words has, for two millennia now, undermined our faith in ourselves to actually end poverty.

Rwanda was a crucible for our efforts because we worked alongside a government that insisted it would end poverty, and not necessarily with much outside assistance. We quickly realized that the big trick in our work was not only to improve performance in the short term, but to build management systems that would work long after we had left. That goal requires having faith in the people you are helping, and a strong belief in the idea that problems can be fixed, not just made a little less horrible while you are there to watch and be pleased—a brief entertainment for your moral sensibilities. My daily challenge, then, was to convince donors that building out management systems would save mothers' and children's lives now, and for years to come. Unfortunately, most were more interested in sexier stopgap Band-Aids—drugs, high-protein emergency foods, and other tangibles, rather than durable management solutions.

To create that kind of permanence in Rwanda's health care system and elsewhere, we sometimes had to take advantage of the culture's negative habits in order to establish long-lasting benefits. Developing countries, for example, are often very bureaucratic. Stacks of forms, which give the impression that something is being done, are often sad substitutes for real progress though they may enable higher employment. Jobs are essential, of course, but silly, useless jobs do not actually contribute real wealth and progress to a people, nor do they raise jobholders to their truest potential.

Rwanda, too, is very much about forms and reports, but such processes are not a cover for a lack of progress here, as tremendous advances are being made. Still, Rwanda, as Dr. Blaise was making me understand in a new way, is a very authority-centered society. Kids in rural schools are routinely punished for the silliest things. I know kids who have been beaten at school for raising a hand to go the bathroom. Others are punished for speaking out of turn, so that soon enough they only want to hide behind the other students. They quickly learn not to raise their hands or ask a question that might be thought stupid. They get so beaten down, both in school and at home, that they will do only what they are very specifically told to do. They will not risk a creative idea.

Forms and charts are a refuge for those who want to hide from notice and judgment, and Dr. Blaise understood this well. Forms are safe. If the form is followed, who can blame someone for anything? See? The form is right here, and it is filled out properly.

If the form indicates that a woman's family planning visit is due, then something must be done. The form must be correctly completed, so the directions on the form must be followed and each item checked off. The clinic's chart showing the total weekly family planning visits must then be updated, and the curve must go up, not down. Regular reports must be sent to the Ministry of Health in Kigali, and the district mayor's status will rise or fall with the health statistics of his area. By slipping the right new forms and charts into this bureaucratic mind-set, improvements can become almost automatic, though good leadership is always necessary, too.

Dr. Blaise was not afraid of leadership. He could stand in a doorway like a British colonel, hands on hips, expecting that something be done forthwith. He personified the second of our five rules for development, which is that high standards must be imposed without cultural shyness. For me, the pointing index finger represents this rule: It is not cultural imperialism to demand high standards in a developing country, where those standards improve performance and upgrade the institutions that serve people and help them have better lives. The imposition of high standards is almost always a great gift to that society. To see poor sanitation in a newborn nursery and to say, "Well, we're not in the US, after all, and this is their way," is soft bigotry of the worst sort. To save lives in this world, it is sometimes necessary to stand and say, "This won't do; this won't do at all," and then see to it that things are improved. Ranu did this with a little laugh that preserved everyone's dignity, and correction soon followed, and Dr. Blaise's business measurements set things on ever-upward paths. We were imposing Western standards, indeed, but only those that might generate better health, better education, and enough prosperity so that people might enjoy the brighter aspects of their own cultures.

When people are starving or ill, they don't mind your leadership. When they are not starving or ill, it is time for you to insist they put their own fists on their own hips and hew to standards—even unfamiliar ones—that will improve life. It is cultural imperialism when new standards exploit people, but it is *not* cultural imperialism when they are instituted to raise others to good health, to higher personal potentials, and to a decent level of prosperity.

Our own Western high standards are not mere cultural affectations. They are valuable, hard-learned recipes for better living, and we should not be shy about them. We should not demand that developing nations find their own Louis Pasteurs and Jonas Salks. Our first charitable instinct should be to share what we know from our own history, and we should share it with confident determination, pushing aside unhealthy and cruel traditions where we find them. For example, the idea that any development emissary would accept as the local norm something like female genital mutilation or even female isolation from education is not cultural sensitivity, but cultural cowardice. To equate it with, say, our own culture's male circumcision—for the purpose of saying we all have our customs, and we should therefore not point a finger and demand change—is a failure of critical thinking and true helpfulness. In a nutshell, one should not go traipsing around the developing world if one cannot stand up for civilization itself and assert some leadership in doing so.

It can be done nicely, as Ranu showed us every day.

Here's the even larger takeaway: Whether we want to acknowledge it or not, there is indeed an American empire in the world—a Western empire, really, as Britain, Canada, Europe, Australia, Israel, and other advanced economies are all represented here with their energetic young expats and their development money. For the most part, this Western empire operates culturally instead of militarily, but it is real, and it is ours to administer as brilliantly as we can for the good of absolutely everyone. If we can bring more people out of misery, then we can tell our CIA and our military to take the day off, because the misery of poverty drives much of the world's anger and danger.

The most important reason to demand high performance standards in development work is that you should be able to leave someday. If you have not left behind a culture of high, ever-improving performance standards, everything you have labored for will fall apart very quickly, leaving behind disappointment and new danger. In Rwanda, it was ingrained in us from the start that encouraging a culture of dependency would be the ultimate destroyer. If you give out too many things for free, it is hard to make people feel industrious and entrepreneurial. That even applies to the advice we give out. We knew that the people of Mayange should teach themselves if our work was not to fall into the red dust like all the efforts before us. Donald, Annette, and others were deep in the mud of these efforts for the farmers, just as Ranu and Dr. Blaise were reinventing the African health clinic.

CHAPTER 17

⚬⚬⚬

The Biggest Fear

We were all working very hard, in days that began before dawn and ended long after dark. What we were doing in Mayange was exhilarating but stressful. The emergency food and medicine were helping tremendously, but we knew that was just a temporary fix; it would not last long, and we needed to get the local food supply growing and put a long-term health program in place.

We also had to ensure that Mayange didn't become a magnet for all the poor and sick in the region. Thousands of families in our area were counting on us, and tens of thousands more outside, and that is very heavy on your shoulders. Blaise and the team worked fast to upgrade all the health facilities lest Ranu and colleagues be overrun. Alissa forgave me my long hours and my exhaustion, but I could see that her work was dragging her down, too.

I knew we both needed a break of some kind, but I waited one day too long. We both woke up one morning with what felt like a terrible hangover, though we had not been drinking. A doctor diagnosed us with malaria and gave us medicine for it. I could be treated with the new first-line drugs—artemisinin combination therapy—which was already having a real impact on reducing malaria deaths around the world. Unfortunately, it hadn't been approved for pregnant women, so Alissa had to take doses of the old first-line treatment, which is just quinine. You've tasted its bitter disposition in really good tonic water. The colonial Brits considered it a "tonic" against malaria, which is one reason the gin and tonic became popular. But the quinine dose Alissa had to take was terribly high, and on the second day of treatment she went deaf in one ear. I freaked. I had a pretty good address book of doctors, so I called the minister of health to come over and check her out. After a quick look at Alissa, he reassured us that it was a common side effect and that she'd be fine.

A few weeks later it was time to go back to the States, not only because of the ninety-day rule, but because Alissa was now in her eighteenth week and we wanted our doctors back home to check her out. Rwanda's two main hospitals were getting better, but not if you had complications. Any real trouble meant you had to hire a plane to get you to Nairobi, and that would take too much time. Just before Alissa's bout of malaria, we had a twelfth-week ultrasound that looked good, and we were excited to get the next one (and find out the gender of the baby) in New York. We were giddy all the way back and scarcely noticed our six-hour layover in Nairobi and five hours in London.

In a New York medical office, the baby seemed awfully quiet. The sight of the ultrasound made the doctor's face fall, just as it had frozen the nurse's face moments before. I squeezed Alissa's hand, which was cold and trembling. The doctor passed the jellied wand again and again over her round stomach. Alissa had the pained smile of Africa.

The pregnancy was over. A surgeon was not available immediately, so Alissa had to go through a long weekend with the dead baby inside her. The weeks following the surgery were difficult, too. But we were in New York, and then in San Francisco, and the distractions of those great cities, and the love of family, moved us, little by little, away from the horror and the sadness.

I would not have blamed Alissa if she had decided right then that our life should be in America, and that we should leave Africa to the Africans and to the younger, or at least hardier, expats. You can imagine the feelings of her parents, of my parents, who were hoping for a grandchild and did not fully trust this African adventure.

"We can do it like we did before," I said to her over dinner near Central Park. "I can fly back and forth like I did before, and we can make it work. We have a place here. We can be here. You can stay here." I said as convincingly and supportively as I could.

She gave a long answer, noting that when she told her friends of the miscarriage, they all reported their own mishaps. Ours was no unique misery and no reason to change course, as there was much work and challenge left for us in Rwanda.

When we arrived back in Kigali, Dr. Blaise was at the airport, tears streaming down his big face. His wife was crying too. They presented Alissa with the best flowers Africa had to offer that day. She cried when she saw them, overwhelmed by the emotion that she was coming home in some new sense. His gesture made all the difference, and it helped erase some of the doubts she was feeling—I could see that as she sat beside me in the darkened backseat, holding the flowers like Miss America while Apollo sped through the night streets. She didn't see me staring at her; she was watching out her window for our familiar landmarks. The moto-polo field meant we were nearly home.

The Soprano house was lit up bright and skull-white in its jungle nest. Its lighted bedroom windows testified to the fact that many of the original team members had dispersed to more private quarters. Most of the team, and the birds, would greet us the next day.

As we entered, we tried to be quiet, but the big front room, which had been good for so much camaraderie and optimism, was now useful only for holding our small pile of bags and amplifying every echo. We looked at each other and smiled, but wearily. We would just have to start again, was the prevailing feeling. It wasn't a joyful sentiment, really, but a matured one—we had a life here, and we had each other.

"Let's see if the troops haven't depleted our wine reserves in the kitchen," Alissa said. There was a decent bottle, and some bananas and papaya from the yard. In silence, in the fluorescent-lit kitchen, we arrived again.

I decided to take a day off with Alissa before heading down to Mayange. I knew every move going on down there, thanks to frequent text messages, and I knew they could do without me more easily than Alissa and I could do without each other. We slept in. We slept long past the birds' rude riot, and long past any chance to say hello to anyone in the house. Jet lag is a good excuse for privacy and some leisure together, and it should be used whenever it presents itself. Life is otherwise too busy without the little time-outs we can fudge.

The Rwandan sun embraced us that afternoon, and we saluted it during our yoga practice on the terrace. We stretched out the kinks from our journey and started to plan out the week. Alissa had already spotted a number of household areas that would need her supportive guidance, and she was excited to get back to the orphans. We walked that evening to the Indian restaurant, which also felt like a kind of starting over.

CHAPTER 18

Accept No Substitutes for
Muddy Shoes

Dr. Blaise, like everyone who has learned to keep moving after horrible times, knew to show up at the house the next day to have coffee with us. When I suggested that Alissa and I might take it easy again, he smiled and shook his head.

"No, Josh, we are going on a field trip! Alissa should go to the spa today at the Serena Hotel. I would like us to leave in a few minutes, as we are going very far."

He had planned a trip to the farthest-flung health center in Bugesera district: Nzangwa. Dr. Blaise and I bumped passed Mayange—waving to the children who spotted us and ran along for a ways—and continued until the land changed and we could see the military training area for miles on the right side of the road. The lush jungle remained there, as it hadn't been farmed, nor had the trees been taken out for charcoal. It was easy to imagine the elephants that had roamed just a few decades before. On we continued until we could just glimpse the Burundian border, and then we went off-road, jarringly so, until we arrived at what was allegedly a health center. At first I didn't believe it from the outside—it looked more like a couple of very poor homes, linked together by mud brick corridors. On closer inspection, I could see where perhaps there had once been solar panels on the roof—we were very far off the grid.

"What do you make of it?" I asked as we walked around. It wasn't deserted, but nearly so. We came across an old man who told us he was living at the facility because he needed insulin shots and the refrigerator was powered by propane; his family visited him weekly. He pointed us to the nurses' area, where we found a straggler. "So, what's going on here?" Dr. Blaise asked, waving his arms at the peeling paint, dirty floors, lack of everything. Reluctantly, the nurse told us that the director had taken down the solar panels for his own home. Under a desk, we found an unopened carton containing a computer and printer, ostensibly for tracking and data collection; they wouldn't get anyone very far without electricity. As we toured the facility we saw that it was as bad as Mayange had been when we first found it: no organization whatsoever. "Blaise," I asked gently, "what can we really do here, so far away? We can't be here even once a week." Blaise responded confidently: "You'll see."

See what? I wondered. I knew Dr. Blaise would be interested only in real results, but this one seemed well outside our halo of operation. Just the same, I trusted that he knew what he was doing, even if he was going to let it be a mystery for now. I trusted him, just as our main donors trusted him.

Donors, I should say, can be a pain in the ass. We had avoided the kind of donors who just want their names on schools or clinics so they can feel good, even if the same dollars, if spent in better service to the community's deepest needs, could have helped thousands more. Sometimes a shabby school building is OK to have for a few more years if new money can inoculate the whole community against childhood diseases and assure that there will actually be some kids to fill the school.

Health Builders' biggest donor would have been high maintenance to most organizations: he wanted measurable results. Rob Glaser and his team had made a big bet on me in 2002, and with his backing and his business approaches, we— Health Builders—had helped governments obtain over a billion and a half dollars to fight AIDS, tuberculosis, and malaria. That was a stunning return on investment even by Silicon Valley (or in his case, Seattle) standards. Still, Rob wanted better measurements of our effectiveness. How could we say that this grant resulted in this many lives saved, when there was such a mulligan stew of grants, NGOs, and UN agencies in the field, not to mention social and demographic changes? By working in the offices of presidents and health ministers, we were so far up the food chain that direct results were hard to accurately and honestly measure.

When Dr. Blaise pushed to close down the Health Builders headquarters in other nations and go into the field in three districts throughout Rwanda, part of his sales pitch to me was that Rob would appreciate the fact that the progress would be very, very measurable. "Rob will like that," he said, raising his eyebrows. "You give me a desk in Mayange and wherever else you go, and we will organize the improvement of health care. We will come down off our high horse."

He was right, as usual. I had, without realizing it, drifted too high again. In Nigeria, Kenya, Ethiopia, and Rwanda, we had real offices and programs, and conditions were changing, but not as fast as they should have, given the dollars that were now flowing.

Rob agreed. We quickly wrapped up operations in the other countries and concentrated on making our districts in Rwanda the healthiest places in rural Africa.

In the weeks that followed, Dr. Blaise and I toured dozens of health centers throughout Rwanda. The staff often greeted us like high-level diplomats visiting far-flung consulates and inquired whether we would return. They had seen their share of one-time visits over the years.

We saw that rural health centers did not have the foggiest idea how to account for income and expenses or for the inventory of drugs and other supplies. They could not budget for their own staff. Our starting point was to set them up with QuickBooks and training. They loved it—in a land that loves order, forms, and reports, this was the panacea they'd long craved. For the first time, heads of health centers had a handle on money coming in and money going out.

Newborn visits, the distribution of mosquito bed nets, and a hundred other things were now a part of their computer tracking, and the simple act of having to update a chart meant that mosquito nets would be forced out of health center closets and into the homes of villages.

Unlike so many African nations, Rwanda's government truly gave a damn about the public's health. Aligning ourselves closely with the Ministry of Health, we figured out ways to reinforce their policies with good business practices.

One of the ministry's biggest innovations is Mutuelle de Santé. Essentially, it is a community-guided health insurance program. We pushed the implementation of Mutuelle in Mayange with great success, but it wasn't catching on as quickly everywhere else, because the health clinics weren't giving clients much for their money. We quickly realized that in order to make

Mutuelle effective, pushing out good clinic management would be essential. Under Dr. Blaise's guidance, the team started tackling the invisible parts of public health: finance, human resources, strategic planning, pharmaceutical stocking, and procurement.

We also recognized that the problem wasn't just at the health center level; we had to reorganize the insurance program's local offices, too, where people had been delayed for needless hours because the clerks were not filing forms by the person's name, but by the date of their last visit! If you needed help at the Mutuelle office then, you had to remember when you were there last, and then they had to go through all that week's records. If you forgot, they'd spend hours going through the prior year's archive.

Everywhere Dr. Blaise and I went, we saw situations where people were dying because of bad health center management, and usually for lack of very simple fixes.

I thought I saw an oasis of good management the first time I drove into the driveway of the Nyamata Hospital, which was just north of Mayange. The hospital is the next level up in district health care, offering care for more complicated medical cases than what is expected in health centers. Despite the fact that Nyamata served a region of three hundred thousand people, there were only about thirty people in line for health services when I first arrived. I knew that a hospital would usually have hundreds of people in line or waiting patiently on benches for hours on end. I figured that only thirty meant that something was working well here.

I made inquiries. Was there some unusually resourceful medical director here? Had the medical staff been trained elsewhere and were therefore moving patients through very quickly? Did they have twice the normal staff of nurses? Was there some donor who had provided them with a bottomless purse to deliver world-class medicine?

None of the above, was the answer that came back. The hospital was so bad that people had stopped going there for regular care. They went there only as a last resort, or to die. I toured the facility. It had a lot of potential. The staff of sixty nurses and six doctors was about right for the area's needs. It just needed management vigor throughout. The mattresses were stained and stank horribly, yet a full supply of new mattresses was stacked and forgotten in a storage area. I came across a post-caesarean patient in the maternity ward who seemed ready to go home. She was indeed, she said, and had been ready for four days but they wouldn't release her because she had no way to pay for the ambulance trip home. As a result, she was taking up a bed, and her baby was taking up a crib, for a few-dollars ride that would be nothing to the hospital but was an impossible amount to the woman, who had nothing, it seemed, but a baby.

Soon after, we offered our services to the district mayor, whose job rating by the national government depends on good health outcomes, among other things. Yes, please, I'll support you, was his response. We found a new hospital director, who got the hospital and its finances cleaned up within two months. The new director fired some corrupt and incompetent staffers, held meetings to identify the biggest challenges, got the X-ray machines running for the first time in two years, and provided the caring inspiration needed for a rapid rise in employee morale and community reputation. The lines got very long, which, in this instance, was a good thing. Now we could work on getting the lines down for the right reasons.

It wasn't a white American coming in to fire one director

and hire another and generally shake things up; it was big, tall, NBA-sized Dr. Blaise. This was the kind of on-the-ground work he had been doing with such great effect to fight tuberculosis right after the genocide. He was his old self again, busting up furniture, kicking ass, and getting things done.

At the health center and hospital levels, we could make rapid changes in people's lives. It was a rush. What we were doing was very different from other NGOs. They had their staffs in Kigali, or whichever other developing nation's most livable city was available. They would visit the field irregularly or never. We were there every day, every minute, with most of our staff living in the districts.

I have always liked *New York Times* columnist Nicholas Kristof for naming his blog "On the Ground," because it captures the fact that there is no substitute for being there. I had learned that lesson as a kid, visiting Ethiopia. I had forgotten it and then remembered it that night in Greenwich Village when I decided to jump off the international consulting money-go-round. The wisdom of the mud left me again for a time, until Dr. Blaise's insight and Rob Glaser's prodding taught me the lesson yet again.

A few months after that first "field trip" to the distant, nearly abandoned health center, I went to visit a refugee camp on the Burundian border and figured that I'd stop by Nzangwa Health Center just to check in. The ride was just as long and bumpy, but this time the health center was freshly painted, solar panels were on the roof, and the mud had been scrubbed off the concrete floors. There was a line of patients and a full staff. I walked through the clean halls and saw nurses tending to patients and medicines being dispensed. It was a miracle. I called Dr. Blaise.

"Blaise, I'm standing here at Nzangwa and have to say that

the team has done a miraculous job turning it around! It's clean, there's electricity, and there are patients! I didn't even know you had started down here."

He laughed so hard I had to hold the phone away. "Josh, we haven't started working there—we just made two field visits to assess what was going on. When they figured out that someone was watching them, they made the changes themselves!"

What a lesson: measurement, even observation, even the *rumor* of it, is transformational. If you remember your high school physics, it resembles the Heisenberg principle: you can't measure something without changing it. This was a certainty. It was another reason why programs must be administered on the ground and why the experts and heads of organizations have to be in the field not just on annual VIP visits but often, and in the mud.

CHAPTER 19

—⁓—

Soil and Optimism

There's no better phone call to receive than one from a motivated donor. After reading an article about our work in *Forbes*, a wealthy businessman called me to express interest in building new health centers for the communities that had none. Dr. Blaise's whole team celebrated—it was hard just doing management work, and they believed that great health systems *and* a state-of-the-art health center would inspire the others even more. The dream for seeing a healthy district in Bugesera, home to Mayange, was swiftly becoming a reality. That would help take the pressure off Mayange Health Center and the others that Dr. Blaise and the team were improving. Alissa was excited to see my progress and was about to see a transition in her work as well: Generation Rwanda, the organization with which she had been working, was hiring its first executive director and Alissa's time would soon be freed up.

"I have some news," she said when I returned one evening from Mayange, covered in the area's signature red dust coating and happy to be home. I expected a problem with one of our guards, who of late had been spending more time drinking than guarding.

"I'm pregnant again."

We hugged and talked about the timetable, the necessity of delivering in the US, all that. Knowing of our impending time back in the States, I felt that the pressure to perform had been ratcheted up.

Seeing the team's achievements in the health facilities gave me hope that we could succeed in other areas too, but Abed was more pessimistic. "Boss," he told me, "a farmer who has not hoed, his family will not eat." The land in Mayange was rough and cracked like cement under your feet, yet Annette and Donald had to determine how the farm terraces should be reconstructed, and how the new seed should be planted. Now that the members of the community were not hungry, now that they could see their children eating and gaining weight, they softened and came to hear Annette and Donald under the few surviving trees. I wanted to be there, but I knew it would be best if I drifted away so that all eyes would be on them. It had begun.

In the weeks that followed, the insights that the team collected astounded me. Annette came into the office one day with what sounded like a riddle:

"Josh, I had a meeting with all the community leaders to find out how to make progress and see what they thought was the single biggest problem in the community."

I was fairly sure what those concerns might be: food security, a water system, electrification, and a better school. Wrong.

"They said alcoholism. The men are using what productive fields they have for bananas for banana beer and it is holding the community back!"

"Did you ask them how to fix that?"

"They think that it is all about despair. If we convince

everyone that prosperity is possible, they will change. They will not drink or use their fields for that."

How could you know something like that from Washington, or even from Kigali? You have to be on the ground to really get somewhere.

The cheerleading for a better world in Mayange had begun, and people were listening. The first thing the team had to get across was that every hectare of their hilly fields had to be progressively terraced in wide stair steps. Long trenches at the outer edge of each terrace had to be dug to catch the runoff water long enough for it to percolate through the flinty soil. The second thing to learn was how to plant the seeds in plowed rows, not the old way of scattering seeds into the wind.

Except for a few innovative farmers, most were deeply suspicious of our lessons. Some chose a small portion of their fields for our techniques and continued with their old ways in the rest. We soon learned that the only way to combat the farmers' skepticism was to grab a shovel and start doing it right beside them. We hoped the farmers would see that if we deemed it worth our sweat, it was worth theirs, too.

Donald and I had been in close contact with international agricultural experts for advice, and trucks were now arriving with the recommended maize seed and with soil additives tailored to the area. Working with local government, we cut a deal with the individual farmers: we would provide fertilizer and seed, but they had to contribute a small portion of their harvest to silos that would protect the community from future famines. There was another catch: they had to enroll their families in Mutuelle, the health insurance program, since we wanted them productive and healthy, but not dependent. One of our interns from the States—a sophomore at Columbia—

discovered that a major disincentive for health insurance was the need for a photo, which required a trip into town. He calculated that the cost of transport and photography would cost the average person more than the health insurance itself! For the cost of a twenty-dollar webcam, he set up his own photo shop at Mayange Health Center; soon everyone was posing for pictures and those bags of seed and fertilizer were moving by handcart along the dirt roads to the distant farms.

As I moved around Mayange—from farm field to clinic to community meeting—I would now see Annette and Donald and our other staff people out in the fields, up on the hillside terraces, working shoulder to shoulder with farmers young and old, male and female. Annette, remember, was a city woman from Kigali—something of a radio star. She was there out of love, as were Donald and the others. So were we all.

The person who I'm sure made the biggest dent in Mayange's hardened soil was Jeannette Mukabalisa, our lead community mobilizer. She was another great find, though initially I wondered if she would be right for the job. She is from the mountains in the north of Rwanda, and her father was in prison, suspected of taking part in the genocide. There are no secrets about your family in Rwanda—everyone finds out who you are pretty quickly. Could the daughter of a man suspected of genocide stand in front of a devastated community of farmers and instruct them on anything? At such moments you have to make a leap of faith and trust that people mean what they say about reconciliation. She was brave to take the job.

The farmers were resistant to Jeannette's help at first. She was a bit different from Annette, who dressed elegantly in flowing African colors even when she was in the fields with a hoe or shovel, showing how progressive terraces must be engineered.

141

No, Jeannette did not look like that. To fit in, she dressed more the part of a farm woman, and she got her sandaled feet in the dust. She wore dirty trousers, not pretty prints. She had a motorcycle license and rode one of our project motos at breakneck speed to get to the faraway farms and back in time for a meeting or a training session. She was sometimes just a cloud of dust on the road, seen through the bushes. You heard the roar and saw the dust and you knew, and the farmers knew immediately, that it must be Jeannette. Aware of how her own family history might affect the memories of these farmers, she was courteous to an extreme, careful to not make anyone feel stupid for not knowing what she knew about farming; she was all business, though warm and often smiling.

In time, the farmers accepted that she was one of them. They took her advice and worked beside her.

I thought of Jeannette's leadership as part of the brave reconciliation underway in Rwanda. People were really trying. Women whose families opposed each other during the genocide were sitting down and weaving "peace baskets" together as a sign of the new times.

Besides, we were in a big hurry to get the terraces carved, the soil in good shape, and the seeds in the ground before the rainy season arrived—if it would come at all.

From Kigali I'd bring Joel's cookies to the team in the field—literally—and try to get them to look beyond our current challenges. I was pushing for more fruit trees, raising money for the next project that needed doing, encouraging the start-up of some small enterprises that could be connected to the tourist trade. But it was really the project's own internal energy that was driving progress. The community itself was a living thing again. It had Ranu's sense of humor because he

142

donated some each day, and it had Jeannette's roaring stamina, Donald's expertise, Annette's happy organizing, and Dr. Blaise's charts and QuickBooks.

And it had the lack of rain, still with us. The shadow of the genocide was still with us, too.

I was driving through a brushy area one morning and saw an older farmer planting seeds very carefully and correctly — burying them in a deeply scored line. I had not noticed him at any of the meetings or seen him in the fields before. I stopped to visit.

"You are doing a good job," I said in Kinyarwanda. Yes, he knew he was doing things the new way, and was proud to be a part of the effort. I asked him if he was new to the area, as I had not seen him before. He grew serious. He had been smiling, but he stopped.

"I was just released from prison," he said. I knew what that probably meant. He leaned forward on his planting stick as he considered whether to say more. But the essence of Rwanda's recovery is confession, and he knew that his confession, just like farming in this better way, was the difficult but right way to move forward. He gestured up the dirt road toward the next little farm.

"In the bad time," he said, "I killed my neighbors." He looked at me. He sighed and repeated, "I killed them." He looked at the stick, his hands holding it.

There was nothing I could say in return, except to thank him for telling me, and to say again that with today's work, with the planting, he was doing a good job.

CHAPTER 20

———

Like Starbucks

Within a few weeks, with thousands of farmers now at work on the hills, it was possible to see the difference from afar. The broken chaos of the hills was becoming organized by the terraces and tree saplings. It was beginning to look like purposeful agriculture, not like the results of drought.

I came home each evening, all caked in Mayange's red mud, to Alissa's growing belly. One night I also returned with a headache from the combination of the dust that I'd inhaled, the jarring road, and a management struggle underway between our agronomists and our community mobilizers. Alissa knew I was drained, so she made me drink a big bottle of water, waited for cognitive functions to return, and then pulled it out of me.

"The agronomists think that they kick ass, because they're helping everyone get on their feet and food in their bellies. They just don't have respect for the mobilizers, not even for Jeannette, who rules. She and her mobilizers are the ones who really get the farmers to listen to the agronomists. She knows that. The agronomists would be talking to themselves in the shade without the organizing. It isn't even a chicken and egg question; she's clearly the chicken. Organizing is key. So she and the other mobilizers are feeling unloved. The divisiveness is hurting us as a team."

"How are you going to make peace? Do you just tell the agronomists to open their eyes to that?"

"The agronomists are busting their butts right now, and they think the mobilizers are slacking off. There is some truth to that. That may be the underlying reason for the dispute. Plus, what may look like chatting and hanging out to an agronomist may be valuable networking and organizing to the mobilizers. They don't understand each other's way of doing work."

"You'll figure it out."

"I'm sure I will."

I wanted to figure it out with her, but she had enough on her mind and still hadn't hit her stride since coming back to Africa.

She was attacking her volunteer work with a fiercer dedication to making a mark here, to making it worth the sacrifice we had already made to be here. But I knew that the lack of progress at the orphanage and the paltry opportunities for the orphans to advance were dragging her down.

There was a pause as she chewed on some words. "I have an idea," she said. I could tell she had been saving it up. "Can I talk about it, or are you too wrapped up in figuring out the situation with the agronomists?"

I wanted to hear it.

"Why don't we start a coffee shop or something, like we talked about?" she said. We had once considered the idea when we were on a much-needed ninety-day-rule break in Uganda. "There's no place to get good coffee here," she continued, "and we could give a lot of the kids jobs."

It was a beautiful notion. Rwanda grows some of the best coffee in the world, but all for export—you couldn't get a decent cup here. It was frustrating, because on my treks, especially around Musanze District, up north by the gorillas, I saw billions of the shiny red, ripe beans growing within an arm's reach of the road.

Like Pavlov's dog, the sight of an establishment that sold coffee always made me desperate for a good cup. I tried the coffee at every hotel and restaurant in Rwanda. It was usually terrible, almost as if cigarette butts were in each cup. You'd think that a big hotel, with its grand old colonial espresso machines, could make a great cappuccino. Once in a while, yes, but usually it fell short. Rwanda just wasn't getting the good beans to stay within its borders yet.

Alissa isn't a big coffee lover, having soured on drinking it while a barista at Starbucks. It made her jittery. Not me—I hauled pounds of gourmet, fair-trade Dean's Beans from the States and ground them up every morning, just as I'd done in New York. A truly fine cup, coming out of my French press decanter, was the thing each morning that told me I was somehow in charge of my day. It was my security blanket that stretched back to childhood. As a kid, I loved the smell when I accompanied my mom and dad to New York City, where they would mix and match beans right from the barrels at Zabar's. But for Alissa, this was about more than coffee.

"Well," I said to her, "why don't you look into it?"

"You won't help?"

"Of course I'll help. What do you want me to do?"

"I think it should be outdoorsy, don't you? Can you think of a place? Have you seen anything for rent that might work?"

I said I would keep my eyes open, but I suggested that she

find a rental agent. Ranu, of course, knew everyone in Rwanda by this time, so why not start there?

. "OK. Good. I'll ask him if he knows a good agent," she said. She gave a smile of wonderment, like the one she gave when she first saw my rooftop garden.

Coffee wasn't a foreign subject for us. I had worked with coffee producers in several countries over the years. Coffee was still a hot commodity but, with more areas coming on line as producers, the competition on price was pushing field-worker wages lower. For that reason, I wasn't interested in selling Rwanda on more coffee plantations. They already had such good beans and so much potential for what they could do with them, including making a splash in the local hotels and restaurants.

During my work in Latin America with coffee growers, we always presented the instructive case of Brazil. For years, Brazilian suppliers mixed their good beans with their bad beans as they were more concerned about meeting quotas than about quality. When quotas were lifted and Brazil's growers started selling their best beans into the local markets, all of a sudden Brazilians became consumers of high-end coffee, and a great new market was created for the growers—a market with nearly zero transportation costs or environmental impact. Plenty of countries in Africa could walk that same road, I thought. In fact, my consulting firm had a few years earlier suggested to the government of Uganda that they should develop the gourmet end of the coffee trade, showcase it locally and develop local demand in Uganda, and then go for the high-quality end of big markets like the United States. Our recommendations, presented to President Museveni by the coffee association, didn't make much of a dent in his thinking: he shortly after announced that the whole association should pursue the then-dwindling instant coffee segment.

But we still thought the idea was sound, and Alissa, thanks to her time at Starbucks, knew the drinks and the equipment and what it was like to end the day smelling like a sack of beans. She had enjoyed that experience, and the job had bolstered her otherwise frugal spending habits. She felt that a job as a barista was a perfect transition into employment for the older unemployed kids she was working with every morning at the orphanage.

When you are an expat in a frontier such as Rwanda, it may feel much like the American Wild West did in the late 1800s: Every idea you can imagine seems possible. You will grow with the territory. You will learn by doing. Besides, how could the capital city of Rwanda not have a great place for a cuppa? There were probably seven thousand American and European expats in Rwanda, ready to line up alongside the hundreds of thousands of Rwandan returnees for their morning lattes. They would come for the coffee and the snacks and the views. They would also come to meet their friends and new people. Socializing in Kigali was still hard. Dating was harder. A place to go, to be, would make it easier.

But most importantly, every café job would be someone's ticket to food, to college, to a good future. As important as the paycheck would be to Alissa, it would be multiplied in the hands of the people who worked for her.

Alissa had finally found her mission in Africa.

CHAPTER 21

—ᴥ—

The Elites Strike

It started the next day. Alissa and Apollo went on an expedition south to the town of Butare, where a coffee tasting center had been established by growers to improve quality and boost export sales. On her return, she began scrambling around Kigali with a rental agent, then another, then another. They are not all top-notch, she learned. Some just knew the guards at properties and had no idea how to contact the owners. She was given the runaround a few times—spending whole days with self-described agents who didn't even have valid listings. But she was earnest in her quest: open air, good view, a location close to government and international organizations.

As Alissa continued her search, I didn't feel so guilty heading with Dr. Blaise to new districts where we were expanding our work. Alissa would welcome me home with stories about all the wild goose chases, and she was happy. Her latest agent seemed honest, though he was showing her properties that clearly would not work.

"Put your foot down," I told her. "Tell him he is wasting your time and his own."

I could tell she wanted to be gentle, because he was a genuinely nice guy.

"You're not being nice to him if you're not letting him get a commission. He wants you to tell him exactly what to do. Tell him what your standards are for this property. Tell him not to bother you with properties that do not meet the standards. They are used to people being strong. Do you think his wife doesn't put her foot down if he brings home mutton instead of the beef she asked for?"

She took a deep breath. Yes, she saw that it would be the right thing to do.

In spite of Alissa's entreaties, he simply couldn't manage to find any good properties. So she brushed him off and began peering over walls and knocking on doors by herself. Besides, it was a good way to learn the town and the language.

She texted me throughout the day so I would know where she was and what she was finding. Mostly she was finding places that were perfect and not for lease, or for lease and all wrong. Then, one afternoon about two weeks in:

"Found it," she texted. "You won't believe it. How much money do we have for this?"

I guessed she had found that a wealthy politician's massive new house was for rent, or something along similarly expensive lines. I texted her that we could talk about it that evening. I didn't mention that I had just gotten some bad news about her coffee dream.

The news was that an American who had grown up in Rwanda and his wife, who had also worked at Starbucks, were opening a high-end coffee shop called Bourbon Coffee in downtown Kigali, blocks from Alissa's great property find. Backed by local and international investors, they had big plans

Twenty-six bags and counting

Observing the ninety-day rule: Alissa and Josh on Chapman's Peak, Cape Town, South Africa

A death duri[ng]
the early day[s of]
Mayange: th[e]
funeral of Ke[vin]
Kwizera *(Ra[vinder]*
Dhillon)

Adam (at cutting
board) training
in the kitchen
(Sarah Ruxin)

Alissa picking
maize with
Apollo

Alissa teaching Heaven's first front-of-house staff

Alissa, pregnant with Maya, at the Heaven construction site, 2006
(© Yoray Liberman)

Alissa with the gorillas
(Amy Ziff)

From left: Alissa, pregnant
with Elias; Maya; and Elodie

Collecting the bones of Epafrodite Rugengamanzi in our yard

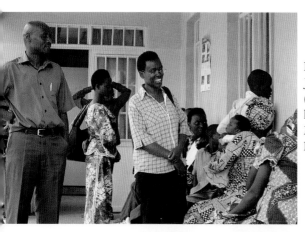

Donald and Jeannette (third from left) outside Mayange Health Center

Melsa with Elias

Harvesting disease-resistant cassava for propagation

Heaven, just before service

Solange and Joel in Heaven's kitchen

Josh and
Blaise at a
health center

Elodie and
Maya celebrate
Hanukkah
Kigali-style

Eggplant
pancakes
with mango
chutney

Ngeruka Health Center *(© Mackenzie Knowles-Coursin 2012)*

Passover family portrait *(Asna Nkundumukiza)*

for expansion in Kigali including two other locations (today they have a branch just steps from the World Bank in DC, and others in Manhattan and Cambridge).

I thought the news of Bourbon Coffee's rise would devastate Alissa, but instead she took it in stride. It was nothing compared to some other things, I guess, and she seemed to see a way forward. I also think that it confirmed her own business instincts since it was just what she thought should happen—it was just bad timing given her plan.

"Listen, let's start a real restaurant instead," she said. "Not just coffee. If we can get that property I found today—it has *such* a great view—it will be the nicest place in Kigali, and we can still create jobs—lots more than with a little coffeehouse. A big, beautiful, gourmet restaurant, the best in Rwanda, maybe the best restaurant in Africa someday, a real destination restaurant, Michelin stars and all. The place is actually big enough for all that, if we can get it."

It was like she was on a foodie high and could really see this thing materializing just as she had seen neighborhood gourmet eateries pop up along the streets of San Francisco.

She walked me to the property, where the agent, waiting, let us in. It was evening. Two massive trees framed a view of the hazy city below. Mud houses and low, modern buildings, sprawling marketplaces, the US Embassy, streets glowing with the evening's motorbikes and buses stretched to the distant hills and then to the foot of blue Mount Kigali. "It's romantic, isn't it?" Alissa said. I didn't have to answer.

Over the next few evenings we sketched it out. She understood that it would cost more money than our home equity line from New York could support. We thought perhaps our parents and friends would help, if we had a good plan. I am a fundraiser, of course, though never for something like this. As it all started coming together and they felt the excitement of the dream, our families said they would be pleased to help. Alissa went straight to work on the details. For management, she was eyeing Amit, the manager of the Indian restaurant where lately we seemed to be having our conversations.

"Wouldn't he be right for us?" she whispered to me. He was young and very skilled in chatting up the customers, as we had seen. That is a very rare skill in the hidebound countries of central Africa, where fearful upbringings in families and schools, as I mentioned, have cowed many people into a passivity that cannot easily be unlearned.

Amit was different. He was like us.

"And he's Indian!" she said, raising her eyebrows as if I should understand that he might help us with the Indian owner of the property she was looking at. Many years ago, the old Indian owner had created the first corporation in Rwanda and was now very wealthy. The property had been rented as a home since the genocide, but he liked it and was apprehensive about the big changes that would be necessary to convert the property into a restaurant. He certainly didn't need the money. It might just take another Indian, a hopeful young man with whom the owner might identify, to make him think differently.

"Amit," Alissa said sweetly when we had paid the check and were standing atop the steps of the entrance. "Would you like to come visit our house sometime soon for tea? It is only four streets away."

He looked confused. It was not a normal customer's request.

"Why, of course, Ms. Alissa. Perhaps I could come tomorrow?"

The next day at the house, Alissa offered young Amit the

job of manager. He accepted. Together they made a rendez-vous with the old Indian owner of that perfect location the following week. Setting eyes on Alissa and young Amit weak-ened his resolve, and he agreed to allow the lease and the res-taurant construction. Now, full of happy energy, Alissa needed an architect.

CHAPTER 22

—⁓—

Rule Three

Almost anywhere else in Africa, Alissa would have spent all her time and money in the next few months dealing with hundreds of outstretched palms, each one waiting for a bribe to make the next thing happen. Here in Rwanda, it took an official fee of twenty-five dollars and all of twenty-four hours to establish a new business, obtain the necessary paperwork, and move forward.

In the same way, we were getting good support from the Rwandan government for our work in Mayange. District leaders stepped forward to encourage community cooperation and to reassure everyone that all actions were being taken in concert with the community, the government, and the project.

Our smooth, corruption-free experiences in Rwanda led to the foundation of our third rule, which is simply that you can't do successful, sustainable development in hopelessly corrupt countries. Development work in a corrupt nation just enables the government to spend its own money—which should be helping its people—on guns and mansions and money stashed in other nations.

What would happen if we told the most corrupt governments

to take a hike? What would happen if we concentrated our aid dollars on the least corrupt nations needing help? The rise in prosperity in the honest nations would create tremendous pressure on the others to clean up. The pressure could come in the form of revolution or it could come from diplomatic and economic pressure. Whatever the case, Rwanda provides a road map that many other nations should consider replicating.

Rule three is the middle finger. It sounds like a harsh rule, and you must certainly make exceptions in times of short-term humanitarian disasters, but in most other cases it is the right rule.

Every time corrupt leaders travel to the West, students and human rights organizations should greet them with great protests. This is simply not a practice today; they mostly get a free pass. Why aren't there protests outside of the consulates of nations that have the wealth needed for public health but choose instead to let their mothers and children die? There are good websites that rank these "kleptocracies" by degrees of thievery (Transparency.org is my favorite), so organizing against them should be easy. The most corrupt fifteen percent of nations—twenty-five countries, more or less—should be on the foreign aid black list, except, as I said, for dire emergencies. Otherwise, let's encourage the corrupt rulers to build their own roads and health clinics and schools and water systems. It's crazy that we have enabled so much corruption for so long.

All these thieves have to do is look the least bit like a fan of democracy or claim they are bulwarks against terrorism, and developed nations pull out their checkbooks. Never mind that these regimes steal everything from their own people, never mind that no real progress is made. The resulting despair, in fact, seems a likelier root of terrorism.

Businesses can and should go into such countries, as wealth raises the middle class and, over time, usually increases government openness. But pure aid to kleptocracies should be ramped down as reform pressure ramps up.

Rule three was the reason very few African countries seemed as right as Rwanda for our program. Rwanda may have its share of bureaucracy, but it is not a kleptocracy. It's a place where a good program doesn't die the death of a thousand bribes, a thousand misallocations, a thousand brothers-in-law who must have a piece of every pie.

Dr. Blaise felt strongly that the private sector was the key to Rwanda's future success. From the first moment he heard about Alissa's restaurant idea, he would invariably ask how it was coming along. He wanted to be the first and best customer, and he encouraged her to locate it near the government center. One good business, in Blaise's view, would be worth dozens of not-for-profit, ultimately unsustainable projects that might just bring more dependency.

Alissa, in fact, was doing well. She found Straton Uwizeyimana, one of Rwanda's best architects, to help make use of the beautiful lawn overlooking the city and the property's giant trees. He was nearly donating his services because he liked the idea. I expect he liked Alissa, too, and her insistence that the two trees on the property be protected and built around, not torn down. She was passionate on the subject of those trees, and she is hard to say no to when she is passionate, and pregnant.

Knowing how much longer everything seems to take in Rwanda than you might intend, I told Alissa that she might have to put the construction work on hold so that we could get back to the States for her delivery.

"This is moving forward" she confidently replied. "This will be my first child, to be followed closely by my second, and it's happening ahead of schedule," she said. "I'm sure I can do it. Straton thinks it will go fast. I've talked it over with him."

The architect was planning with her before I was. You work in the bush, you miss out. I told Op-ed of it the next morning on our journey and he smirked and said, "There is a saying, boss: the two fingers can't help but live together."

"What does that mean?"

"It's natural that they are close because they are working so much together."

"You're not helping," I replied uneasily, stewing over how little time Alissa and I had been spending together.

"It's just a saying, boss."

Alissa and I trusted each other. In expat communities in the tropics, relationships can get complicated quickly, but that's something for unmarried people and married people whose spouses are living in another country (expat married men in the company of modelesque Rwandan women are common-place). Without all the extracurricular and cultural activities that keep everyone engaged back home, the tawdry details of all the twenty- and thirty-somethings' latest relationships offer compelling entertainment. We've long thought that the young expat escapades in Rwanda provide fertile ground for a reality TV show. The show wouldn't feature just the sexual encoun-ters that at times dominate the lives of that crowd. Many of them spend their days imagining and carrying out elaborate gags, surprises, and trips. We've been to surprise birthday par-ties in the middle of the fruit section of Kimironko Market, admired home-crafted marathons through the hills of the gorillas in Musanze, and jealously watched the stream of images from adventurers who have driven a renovated delivery truck from Kigali to Cape Town with days spent on an old steamship crossing Lake Tanganyika. Indeed, the expats knew how to have fun here; we just had a different conception of what fun could be.

Just the same, I knew I was away from Alissa too often and for too long. It would be tough for each of us to maintain our pace without burning out. Nonetheless, we knew that we were each building tremendous things and that one day, we'd be in for the big surprise: building is the easy part. For Alissa, who had never built anything in her life, construction would be her greatest challenge and joy.

CHAPTER 23

—◈—

Roots

Straton, Alissa's architect, was famous in Rwanda and beyond for his beautiful Bank of Kigali, Hotel Chez Lando, and other signature structures. He had charmed Alissa and me during his personal tour of Kigali. While showing us one of his impressive housing developments, which looked like it could have been plucked from suburban San Francisco, he noted, "I wanted all the yards to be wide open, with none of the African-style high walls and fences. The financier wouldn't stand for it. How I wished to have interconnecting backyards for the kids to run across! Maybe someday!"

He would not be the sort of architect we could afford, except that he wanted to do this for Alissa, perhaps because she wanted to build the restaurant from the native materials of Rwanda. Most Rwandan construction relies on materials trucked in from Kenya or beyond.

Straton stood with Alissa on the property of the Indian man's modest home. The big lawn sloped steeply downhill from the house toward a high wall along the road, and the wall hid a beautiful view of the city from the lower part of the lawn. But in Africa, the wall is important. This one did not have broken glass cemented in sharp points along its top edge, as most do, but it was high enough to secure the property at night, and it needed to stay.

"Your restaurant will need to float over the ground like a tree house, so everyone can see over the wall to the city below," Straton said. He was suggesting a grand porch that would let the yard's slope fall away beneath it. He proposed a great roof over that deck, creating, very economically, an outdoor restaurant that would take full advantage of Rwanda's year-round perfect weather. The old house on the property could serve as wash-up area and office.

Alissa turned the subject to the pair of giant, ancient ficus trees.

"They are so important to the site," she said. "You'll have to design around the trees somehow," she told him. He agreed. The trees would help cool the whole property on hot afternoons, and would be an aviary to provide what is certainly the main music of Africa.

"Can the construction workers not hurt the roots?" she asked. The roots danced over the ground, sometimes far from the trunks. Straton was sure they could avoid them.

For the restaurant, she wanted a name like "haven," or "retreat," but they are not commonly understood English words. We talked about it each evening. Nothing seemed right.

The name "Heaven" just came down on us one day when we met a woman whose daughter was named Heaven. It was a good name for a place that appeared to float above the earth, high up in the air.

Alissa filed the necessary business papers to secure the name, and then took her registration to the post office to get a post office box for the business. Delivery does not come to your door in Rwanda.

She told the clerk that she wanted a box for a new restaurant that would be built at No. 5, Rue du Mont Juru.

"Ah, yes, heaven," the clerk said in nice English. Alissa was confused, as she had not yet told the clerk the name of the business.

"How did you know that?" she asked. We had thought of the name only the previous evening.

"How did I know what?" the clerk said.

"That it is called Heaven."

"Madame, Mont Juru—*Juru* means heaven."

We did not know that *Juru* (or, to be precise, *Ijuru*) in Kinyarwanda meant heaven. Alissa was stunned and just stood there with her jaw dropped. It seemed like a great sign, that the Fates were paying attention to this thing.

Rue du Mont Juru goes uphill from a main street in Kigali and ends at another road, where the compound of the president happens to be. Because it was only two streets from the team house, we knew the area well and had often walked it. On several occasions Alissa, walking alone, had been shocked to see human bones being exhumed alongside those roads where there was construction. Another reason, perhaps, for a gentle word like Heaven to come to rest there.

CHAPTER 24

─◦⌁◦─

The Cook's Expertise

Joel, our cook at the team house, heard the story of the post office and told us that the road might be named for heaven, but it had not always seemed like heaven to him.

When the genocide began, he was in his own house, quite close to that street. He had just moved there to be closer to his brother's family and to the big house of Mimi, the Belgian woman who had recently hired him as her cook. Mimi lived atop Rue du Mont Juru in a house that was later taken down with many others to make a park area for the president's compound.

Fortunately Joel was a newcomer, so his neighbors did not know if he and his wife and three children were Tutsi or Hutu. That uncertainty gave him some precious moments to prepare a plan. He is a cool and thoughtful man, so he knew what to do.

"Bring me your identity card," he said to his wife. His children were too young to have them.

Across one line of the identity card was a line of words: "Hutu, Tutsi, Twa, Naturalisé." (The Twa are an ancient minority people — Pygmies — who then lived in thatch huts in the remaining jungles, much as they always had.) Each identity card had all of the ethnic possibilities, except one, crossed out in ink. The cards of Joel and his wife had all the words crossed out except Tutsi, which is what they were—or rather what the Belgian colonists had decided their grandparents were.

In the kitchens of Belgian families, Joel had earned his living with a knife. He now found the sharpest one in his own kitchen for this most important moment.

Over the next few hours, as the genocide raged on the streets outside, Joel kept his hand from shaking. He worked like a brain surgeon to scrape the ink from the word "Hutu" without making the paper look disturbed. There might be a pounding at the door at any minute, but he must do it carefully. Then, with an ink pen that matched the ink of the other, he crossed out "Tutsi" as best he could. They thus became Hutus.

Hundreds of other Tutsi from the neighborhood did not have Joel's option: they were well known to their Hutu neighbors, or they were on lists of Tutsi, and they were pulled from their homes and killed. Those who could escape ran with their children to the big church at the bottom of Rue du Mont Juru and prayed and sang together. It was one of the most heartbreaking acts of the genocide that many Catholic priests gave up these people and even helped the killers kill. Nuns did not, but priests did.

On one of those days, a bus pulled up outside a Catholic office within sight of Joel's window. The Tutsi families who had gone there instead of to the church were told that they would be protected, but that they must go back to the neighborhood under guard to save their neighbors who were still in hiding. They boarded the bus and were taken to the street.

One by one, they were pulled from the bus and killed, some by being set afire. Joel and his wife could see and hear this horror, and the sounds of screaming were constant through the night.

When a great pounding finally came at his door, Joel opened it to see a half-dozen blood-spattered soldiers and militiamen. The head soldier was a man Joel recognized. They had gone to grade school together in another town. The one soldier in Kigali who knew that Joel was Tutsi was the one to come to his door.

Joel's family was being dragged out to be killed when Joel told the soldier that there was a mistake. "We are not Tutsi," he said with as honest a face as he could manage.

"But, Joel, of course you are." The man grabbed the identity cards from Joel's shaking hand.

The soldier looked carefully at the cards. If his eyesight was too good, or if he was too certain of his childhood memory, this would buy the family only a few more seconds of life before their painful deaths under machetes already dulled from so much killing. Their screams would join the hellish choir that was now a constant over the city.

"How strange, Joel," the man said, sitting down on a bench just inside the door. "My memory is that you were Tutsi."

"How can that be? How can you have thought that? You used to make fun of me and call me that, but of course I was not Tutsi. It was your joke."

"Well, be careful." The soldiers left. Others would be back to check the papers again. It happened again and again, for what seemed forever.

It was just the beginning of Joel's hundred days. Somehow, he knew he would have to get up Mont Juru, past two or three roadblocks to the embassies, with his family if they were to survive. But how?

Mimi, the Belgian in whose kitchen he worked, fled the country, but not before getting a small fortune in cash to Joel so that he could get some food for his family while he worked on his plan. He knew that the militia members were coming back through the houses, rechecking identity cards much more carefully. That would be it, unless Joel could be brave enough to walk his family past the checkpoints and get to the Tanzanian embassy atop the hill, where he hoped they would be let inside.

The battle raged through Kigali and around the people packed in that embassy as the Tutsi army finally overtook the national government's army and the nightmare ended. It was July 4, a date Joel knows is special to us, too.

After the genocide, Joel became one of the administrators of the system of outdoor neighborhood courts that heard stories of the genocide and sent many people to prison (but refused to do so when they found the evidence weak). The outdoor neighborhood genocide courts were generally famous for their fairness, considering that they were run by people who had no legal training and who had suffered their own great losses. Any regular legal system would not have been able to process the quarter-million accused killers.

Called the Gacaca (pronounced *ga-cha-cha*) courts, they were useful in a psychological way, too: Everyone was legally compelled to tell what happened to them, or what they did to others, providing a kind a group therapy on a national scale. By telling your story to a large gathering of others, you let some of that weight slide off your shoulders and onto the shoulders of the whole community. Yes, you carried that community burden, too, but it was shared. People could begin to move on. The great heaviness of that load, a sadness that seemed like a fog over every street, was still present when we arrived. In 2006 it had begun to rise, when the cumulative effect of the government's reconciliation work and the sign of a good future for all Rwandans, not just ethnic group members, began to make a difference. But it is always there. How could it not be?

With so many cases before those open-air courtrooms, there were international allegations of injustice. But it is hard to know what better thing could have been done. Knowing Joel so well, I know that at least the courts under his authority were fair and serious. He is a round-faced Atticus Finch in his demeanor and in his patient kindness.

Joel and his wife, like so many couples who survived, adopted some of the orphans of the genocide, and they care for them yet today. So to say that Joel is a cook does not quite cover it. It is unusual for him to share his story, and he shares only the parts that can be said aloud in company. We do know that his brother was killed within his earshot and that his brother's wife, a Hutu, helped them eventually escape across the barricades and find shelter in the Tanzanian embassy.

CHAPTER 25

Breaking Ground

Before a new project in the States would have been out of the blueprint stage, Alissa was breaking ground. Indeed, she had arranged with Straton that there wouldn't be a true blueprint since that would be costly. Instead, they would work with a rough document and build and design as they went along. The contractor promised her she would have a finished restaurant before we needed to leave for the States.

She was busier than I had ever seen her, and happier. She was overseeing construction, planning menus, and thinking about all the hiring for the different positions. Honoline, the young woman who had escaped the killing line so narrowly, was by then studying management. Maybe she could help in the restaurant's office, or be maître d'. Alissa was mentally plugging the young people she knew into perhaps two dozen jobs that would be available.

When I got back to Mayange each morning, Ranu would already have the health center open for the day and the lines moving well. The food distribution, still required for some, would also be underway. Annette, Donald, and Jeannette would be running a class under a scrawny tree with a new batch of farmers, or they would be out in the fields with them.

Often there would be a woman standing beside the parking area of our little office. She was tall and high-cheeked and always impeccably dressed in long African prints. Her name was Jacqueline. She was what we came to call an "early adopter" of our techniques in Mayange. They had benefited her, and she had emerged as a major community leader. In addition, she was the person you would go to if your child had died the previous night of malaria or malnutrition. The weight of this misery gave her face a distant but peaceful look, as though she had long ago died herself and was just staying around to do what she knew how to do. She was only in her early forties but you might have thought she was ten years older.

One day about four months in, she approached me as I was putting a wrench to a community tap that was still bone dry.

I was in a fairly good mood already that day because things had been going well, but she seemed as though she might not be the bright spot in my morning. She walked toward me with the dignity of death itself.

"Mr. Josh," she said. *"Mfite ikibazo!"* It meant she had a bone to pick with me.

In her mix of French and Kinyarwanda, she said that she had spent much of her time organizing funerals and that she had made something of a living doing so. But now, she said, there were no more funerals. "So I want to thank you very much for ruining my business." With that, she smiled a lovely, shy smile, and her eyes welled up. She put out her arms for me to hold. When someone's hands are dirty from farming, he or she does not extend a hand to shake, but rather a clean arm for you to grasp. Jacqueline did that—I held her arm—and she then went about her many other businesses for the day.

Much of our recent success was her doing, too, and I told

her so before she left. For her own family, she had quickly adopted our farming practices and was now planting seeds in lines, and also putting in high-profit fruit trees, pineapple plants too.

I tried to remember how many days it had been since we had pushed a shovel into the dirt to make a new grave. I couldn't remember—a few weeks, perhaps? Things had changed. The mood of the people, and their energies, had risen. We were approaching that wonderful point when they have more ideas for improvements than we can keep up with, and we have to step back and let them take over some of the areas, and then more.

All we needed now was rain. It was in the prayers of every family, including my own.

Rwandans have a funny relationship with God, which they convey through a story that anyone can tell you: "God worked very hard for six days creating the heavens and the earth. But on the seventh day, he needed a break, so he picked Rwanda as the place to take a much-needed sleep. God sleeps in Rwanda, then keeps busy at work everywhere else."

This story has two meanings: The negative take is that God is not in Rwanda to protect you or answer your prayers, that He comes here only to shut His eyes. The other interpretation of "God sleeps in Rwanda" is that the country is a mile up, cooler and more beautiful than any other place, and so, naturally, this would be where God comes when He is not punching the clock—His favorite place. It was the second interpretation that we needed to believe.

Prayer ceremonies were organized to ask God for some rain. Recent droughts had been cruel to Mayange, and we had bet our operation that Mayange's weather luck would change with our arrival. That kind of gall can be one of the worst sins of well-meaning development types, but we didn't have a choice; we had to just trust our hubris and our connections. If we could get food trucks out of the UN, after all, we could certainly get a little rain out of God, who requires far less paperwork. If He was absent during the genocide, perhaps He would be all the more willing to help now. So the people of Mayange forgave God as much as they could, and they met and prayed for rain. We joined them in their prayers. God did not seem in any hurry to send us rain, but He sent us a guardian angel named Angelique, a joyful young doctor who would become the chief doctor of our clinic and overall health advisor.

—⫶—

Angelique arrived at the perfect time. We couldn't rely forever on Ranu's volunteerism to keep Mayange Health Center moving forward, and the sooner the whole project was completely Rwandan, the better, so I quietly put out the word that we were looking. Dr. Angelique was soon at our door, pregnant with her first child, but promising that she would take her baby wherever the community needed her.

I was skeptical at first. I was sure her résumé and lively energy could get her a plum NGO job based in Kigali, so why was she willing to work for our dusty project? I asked her.

"It is just such a surprise to see an NGO actually doing something," she said. Like so many Rwandans, she had seen hundreds of millions of American and other aid dollars wasted on reports that usually just recommended more reports, more studies, conferences, adoption of principles, better communication, more meetings, government protocols, and more reports from the follow-up meetings. Most of the dollars ended up back in Washington in the form of consulting fees. We, on the other hand, were actually building health centers and bringing seed and fertilizer and putting people on the ground; it was, and unfortunately remains, highly unusual.

"If we had one percent of all that money that comes and goes to do things like what you are doing in Mayange," she said, "then we would be doing amazing things everywhere in Rwanda."

Her encouragement was important to us. But she brought far more than that: she brought a pragmatic Rwandan attitude that showed the team, time and again, that we'd do everything possible for the people of Mayange.

While we were heading back along the bumpy road from the field one day with her, a young child flagged us down. The little girl told us that her mother was ill and needed help. It would have been so easy, with the sun setting and the health center just a few kilometers down the road, to shrug this off, especially since we were constantly bombarded by one need or another.

But Angelique grabbed her stethoscope and we made haste. The mother needed to get to the hospital. We eased her into the cab of our pickup truck. Seven-month pregnant Angelique rode in back. That image is all you have to remember to know everything about her.

We knew that everything we did well in Mayange would have the chance to be reproduced all over Rwanda, and Angelique was part of that. She would go on to become one of the top three officials in the Ministry of Health and earn a PhD, and with her help the Millennium Village of Mayange would indeed become a development model for the rest of the nation.

CHAPTER 26

—◁◈▷—

Rule Four

Two days into the construction of Heaven, Alissa stopped by the site to take some pictures of the first stages. She stood in horror at the foot of a trench where men were kneeling to hack and saw away at the interwoven roots of the two great trees. She screamed for them to stop. They assumed the pregnant woman was crazy, but they stopped. She called me, sobbing, to tell me that the workers had cut many of the main roots. She exploded at the contractor and broke down in front of the seventy workers.

None of them could understand her concern. It was the normal thing to remove trees from construction areas. It would be a big problem to leave these roots intact, they thought, as trenches for plumbing and electric had to be installed, and an old septic tank needed to be removed. It was not as if they had accidentally severed them with a backhoe—they had attacked the roots with saws and machetes.

For Alissa, the two trees had become more than trees. I think they somehow symbolized Africa and our work here. When she first saw the property, if she had been told that she could have the land for free but the trees must come down, I'm sure she would have walked away.

There are a few Rwandan trees more beautiful than the ficus; the giant African Tulip Tree, for example, sends a canopy of reddish-orange flowers high up over the landscape. But this old couple, with their thick green leaves and massive trunks and interwoven branches, looked just like something from the Garden of Eden. You could probably climb up into them and live there. Hurting them seemed the perfect symbol of insensitive Westerners coming in with their bulldozers and doing more harm than good. Expats like us always have that worry, and we should, because unintended consequences have a horrible history, here. Dr. Livingstone had the kindest intentions, but his long absence brought the scourge of Stanley, followed shortly by the colonists. You can't blame it all on Livingstone, but would he have come if he could have foreseen his role in the opening of Equatorial Africa to such exploitation? I will answer for him: No.

Alissa wondered if the trees should be propped up somehow, or even put out of their misery. Donald, who as an agronomist knows a great deal about trees, drove up from Mayange to look at the damage and give a prognosis. He looked at the trenches and the holes and the size of the exposed cross sections of the cut roots. He sat there on his haunches for a considerable few minutes.

"You should wait, Alissa," he said. "Wait and see what the trees decide. If they want to live, they probably can do it. Maybe they will talk each other into it."

He called them Umuvumu trees.

"The Umuvumus are wise old trees," he added. He explained that the grand trees are often the gathering points of villages. Their wide leaves give protection from the rain and shade from the sun. That they might be old survivors was at least hopeful.

Still, Alissa decided she did not trust what might happen if she was not there to watch every move of every worker.

Her response to the problem was something we expats do. We don't understand why the local people act the way they do sometimes, and we are sure we have to do it all ourselves. I was doing the same thing in Mayange until I turned things over to Donald and Angelique and Dr. Blaise. It's hard to do that when you have exact ideas about how things should be done. Of course, when you are first setting things up, it is understandable and often necessary. I was sure that if she really wanted the Umuvumu trees to be part of Heaven, she was doing the right thing to stand her ground. Once Heaven was up and running sustainably, then it would be time to enable local entrepreneurs to learn the business and eventually take it over. We would be leaving someday, and the permanent things we left behind would be the things we stood aside from and allowed to be sustained and grown organically.

We have seen dozens of projects and businesses over the years that have been entirely reliant on outside funding and expertise go kaput the moment those funds and expertise depart. It's a cliché in the development world, but a true one for sure. Learning over and over again the need for sustainability became our fourth rule, represented by the wedding ring finger: We are not here as a lifelong commitment. We should not be married to our programs. We should ultimately never be the essential party, even though we do have leadership responsibilities at the beginning.

The better NGOs—and there were not many of them—would nurture Rwandans to lead their efforts, and they would find ways to make the improvements sustainable, then they would leave. Think of how a homebuilder starts the homeowners' association, but then bows out. That is the right model, even when you know the association will have troubles.

Don't start anything that won't be sustainable after you leave—and do leave: that is the rule. That was why we treasured our relationship with Angelique and others in government. In 2010 we opened our first gleaming new health center in Bugesera, and every year since we have opened others there and in the hills of Musanze. Before commencing each center's construction, we first forged agreements with the government to staff them permanently and we obtained cofinancing from the local districts, so they would feel ownership. There were no signs announcing "Brought to you by foreign donors." We wanted our donors to know that they could give, have impact, walk away, and know that they'd done something lasting.

We knew that we had to encourage farmers to create co-ops so that they could begin to hire their own planners and instructors and marketing people. The people are always their own best organizers and workers and celebrants of success. When foreigners stay too long, they become a reason for people to doubt their own abilities. When foreigners come with unsustainable projects, they are often doing it for their own pleasure or as an excuse for fundraising and salaries, not for love.

—◦—

Watching the work closely over the next days, Alissa was horrified to see the men working without hard hats or other safety equipment. When the steel came for the undercarriage of the great deck and for the roof over it, men dangled from precarious perches while welding and hammering, and all without harnesses or goggles or helmets—and it's not as if people don't get hurt: they do.

Rwanda is a litigious culture: if you are considered a rich Westerner, you will be sued for the most amazing reasons. This is easy to understand, as desperate people are desperate people, and you must expect it and you must always have a good lawyer on standby to respond to their actions. When workers were injured we paid for their care. Fortunately for them and for us, the injuries were all very minor. But it raised Alissa's anxiety level to be watching this, so she started buying hard hats and goggles, and trying to get the men to wear them.

She was also watching her belly grow with the baby and feeling that every moment counted. She needed the construction to be finished and locked up by the time we left. She talked with the lead builder in the morning and asked what would be accomplished this new day. If a wall needed to be built next, she would say, OK, have it finished by the end of the day. The lead mason would say, no, this will take four or five days. Alissa would say, no, you get as many men as you need to get it done today, but get it done today. "And stay away from the trees."

In this way, Heaven started to take shape in half the time the architect had expected. He was amazed each time he dropped by.

When the steel work was finished, the time came to fetch the wood for the deck. Wood is a very expensive commodity in Rwanda, as the big trees good for lumber were long ago cut for firewood. As fast as they can grow back, they are cut for quick profits. In times of drought, farmers in Mayange, for example, will sell the wood from their own homes, even if it means removing the roof beams in places. So wood is a precious thing, and Alissa needed a great deal of hardwood for the grand deck of Heaven. To make sure that the right wood was purchased, she asked her most trusted worker to go on the journey to the forest in the south of Rwanda to obtain the wood. At a cost of $10,000, it would be one of the largest expenses.

He agreed to go. He got the right wood. Then, before coming back to Kigali, he stopped at the wood mill to have the logs cut into the right lengths for the deck.

When he returned to the city, Alissa saw immediately that the wood was cut into very narrow strips instead of the necessary planks. The carpenter hemmed and hawed, lamely explaining that he thought this way, the wood would go twice as far. Of course we knew that women's heels would catch in the deck if the narrow wood was used, and it would look bad. It would be hard to nail down without it splitting and making people trip. A disaster.

When the truck full of ruined wood arrived at the site, Alissa called me in Mayange not exactly crying but not exactly not crying. She said she wanted to fire the general contractor and finish the project herself. That would be a lot of stress on mother and child, but she was sure I had to agree. She sent the contractor away and looked around at seventy men who did not know what to expect next from her and who barely understood her halting French.

Op-ed was philosophical when I explained what had happened. We were on a dirt road when Alissa called.

"There is a saying," he said. Well, of course there is.

"If you are building something and a nail breaks, should you stop building altogether, or should you change the nail?" he offered.

The wood would indeed be salvaged and used to create tables and chairs and some ceilings. For the deck, another truck was sent to the forest and to the wood mill, and Alissa was on the truck this time. She changed the nail, and she was the new hammer.

She came back with the wood cut correctly. She should have slept for two days after that journey, but a farmer's young son in Mayange had been gored in his head by one of Africa's big-horned Ankole bulls, and Ranu would not give up on him. He administered first aid and somehow got him alive to the hospital in Kigali in the health center ambulance. Then, suddenly, another boy needed heart surgery. We got him to South Africa and Israel for two surgeries, which, by the way, were funded anonymously by a prominent rock star.

In all these emergencies, Alissa would be one of the people to drop everything else and spend time at the Kigali hospital while someone was waiting for transport or recovering. She took art supplies and movies on her laptop or whatever would make their time pass more easily. At the same time, she was managing the construction project and overseeing the Soprano house, and she was very pregnant.

Was it again too much? Is it impossible to relax in Africa? We were both so eager to dive into meaningful things, but maybe they were eating us up. Maybe the source of the Nile is quicksand. We were grateful to the director of immigration for the ninety-day rule, but that wasn't really enough right now. How would we find the time? We would have to wait for our trip to the States when the baby was due, but that seemed very far away.

───『✦』───

CHAPTER 27

Good Projects Bring the Rain with Them

Dry weather beat down on Mayange. Winds blew little curls of dust along the roads. The people began to look at me and our agricultural staff in the way that people look when they realize they perhaps should not have trusted you so much. What part of *long-term drought* had we not understood?

"Help from abroad always comes when the rain has stopped," was a saying Op-ed told me. Over the years the people of Mayange had noticed that when disaster struck, the *abazungu* and government often swooped in to save the day. Then the rains would begin again and the help would depart—a classic vicious cycle of dependency. The farmers had some hope because of our arrival, but their hope was getting strained. There was an uneasy gap as we waited—a community holding its collective breath.

A void of leadership in a time of uncertainty is a great danger. We all tried to look confident, but Jeannette did more; she did the great thing: she started weekly community meetings under a tree in each village. She'd have an agenda, teaching this week about cash crops, the next about infrastructure, and another about co-op management. She was teaching them what was possible, far into the future, if they worked together with a positive spirit. This got them out of the old ways of thinking that had been narrowed by poverty and isolation— starving people think only of today, and that is a hard habit to break, even when you are no longer starving. She gave them the big picture of economic development. Once they could imagine all those markets and potential earnings, she asked them to make their own decisions. Should they repair more farmland terraces to improve future earnings, or use the next few days to put in watermelons, which will sell well in Kigali markets in six months?

"The rain?" she said, "Of course it will rain!"

"Who are you that you know it will rain?" an old woman, who lived and farmed alone, asked her.

"Because new projects like ours bring the rain with them," Jeannette answered. There was a general nodding of heads, as this was believed to be true of new projects and it was even a well-regarded saying.

"But why did you take the signs down from everything?" a farmer asked. "Are you truly a project if you don't have signs?"

"We took the signs down because this is your place, not ours. This is a new project, but it is your project. Your poverty or prosperity will be your own, not ours. We have just come through to give you some education, and then we will leave. You should put up your own signs," she told them. After a time, they would do that—signs that declared that this cassava processing plant, or this farm cooperative, or this craft workshop, was a project of the Mayange Community. Then later came a stream of small businesses with their own signs:

"Cinema Mayange," "Downtown Saloon" (which actually referred to a hair *salon*), and "24/7 Supermarché" (which was only open from nine to six).

It deeply matters whether you cultivate dependency by handing things out or instead nurture self-sufficiency, and a shared vision of an agenda for improvement within the community. You offer yourself as a resource, but you insist that the people must decide how best to use you. We were doing all that, but maybe we had failed them anyway by presuming too much of nature.

Donald was calm. "It will rain. It doesn't need to rain much, the way we planted and enriched the soil. We're fine." But with each passing day he seemed a bit tenser.

We started privately sharing half-baked weather theories. Perhaps the deforestation of Mayange was so severe that the rain clouds couldn't form over us. We'd sit up on the hillside and wait for clouds we could see in the distance. We watched as they drenched neighboring districts, then parted to keep Mayange dry. Alissa, on the phone, would say Kigali was getting soaked, were we? No.

"Well, anyway, it looks like dark clouds heading down your way," she would say as an encouragement.

"Yes, we see them, too," I would respond, knowing they would pass us by.

Ranu, for once, had no jokes about it; he just drilled down into the health center's issues. He and Dr. Blaise and the nurses and Dr. Angelique were making it a better operation each day—charts on the wall showed the activity and the improving health of the people. The whole Mayange health team celebrated when a woman came in one day not with a life-threatening illness, but with a sore back, wondering whether we had anything to help. The road improvements underway would soon make it even easier for more patient visits, though Ranu worried that the heavy road equipment was kicking up too much dust for the fragile respiratory systems of children still recovering from malnutrition. The rain, if it would come, would settle the construction dust. He demanded rain from Donald, who said he was working on it.

With government support, we were now delivering cows to families so they would have milk. That would keep us busy until the rains—hopefully—came.

High-producing European dairy cows, mostly of Irish stock, were given out, one per farm family. The cows looked around for some green hills and I could sense them wince. Nevertheless, with the feed we provided to them they began producing as much as twenty liters per day each—four times the production of the frail local cows of the region. Good nutrition for the family, plus as much as six dollars per day profit, was a remarkable and immediate improvement to family wealth in the villages.

Cattle have always held an important role in Rwandan society. They are a key source of protein and an important status symbol. Over the last couple of years, the government, working with Heifer International and other groups, had promoted a policy of "one cow per poor family" in an attempt to improve nutrition and family prosperity. That's where the cows were coming from—the government's program, along with American donors such as Heifer and Send a Cow. Lots of people were impressed by Rwanda's audacity—Bono said to me once, "One cow per household and one laptop per child— these guys have ambition!"

All that was asked of participants—as per Heifer's program—

was that they pass their first-born female calves on to another family, and then again from that family onward.

Cows don't produce milk from thin air, of course. They need protein, grain, lots of water, and a slew of vitamins and minerals. What they had been chewing instead was low-protein, nutrient-deficient elephant grass. That's why we started pushing for more communal stabling—to get the cows more of what they needed and have a convenient spot for vet care.

The cows did very well on all that, but ideally we wanted the maize crop to come in. Maize is corn, as you probably know, and we used a variety called Katumani, developed in Kenya. It is a hardier, less sweet variety than is grown in the States, but it cooks up well. If we were going to see any of it, though, the rain had to come, and it had to come gently—not in floods that would wash out the new, unhardened terraces and their seeds.

Annette, our project lead, helped organize more staff prayers for a change in weather. People gathered in the main room of the office and asked God to please help with some precipitation, "for these are Your people, Lord, and they have worked hard to respect Your land and Your seeds and the manure that is not Yours in an unseemly sense but is provided roundabout by You, and now it is time for Your rain, Lord." People from the community, who had been doing their own praying, were looking in through the doors and windows, and they joined in each "amen."

We had done everything we could do, and the five thousand households had done all they could do. I tried to be patient. Alissa could see that I was very stressed and that I was doubting everything about our mission and our adventure as a couple.

But Alissa believed my rains would come. For herself, she had her business plan and she saw the restaurant taking shape every day. She knew it would have a huge impact on many lives. It's what she came to Africa to do.

So, yes, the whole thing had been a leap of faith, but she had found hers. She was fine, out there in midair. That gave me courage.

CHAPTER 28

—⟨∾⟩—

What Jacqueline Saw

Jacqueline, the burial lady, was standing out beyond the road one afternoon when the dust blew around her. I saw her through the office window and thought she would make a good *National Geographic* cover photo for the story of our failure here. She was looking up at the sky in a forlorn Scarlett O'Hara way. Every time I looked up from my work—Blaise and I were planning our expansion into thirty-nine health centers across three districts—she would still be looking my way, but up and over our little building. I looked at her again, and there was a sudden darkness around her and a great boom of thunder from above and behind us, as if she had conjured it. We had not seen the rain coming but Jacqueline had. She was happy to stand in it for a while, and occasionally wave to me like a little girl. Ranu, out on the road, called my cell phone to say that the village school kids had left their classrooms to frolic in the rain. Even the banana wine–soaked drunks in their ramshackle bars were out in the streets celebrating, and Ranu was dodging them as he drove back.

For the next several weeks the rains came every day. The rains could have washed everything into the Nile, but they did not. They came gently, as if understanding that the community was still new to line planting and progressive terrace farming.

Six weeks later, Dr. Angelique stood laughing with us in fields of green and golden maize that were thicker and higher than any seen before in Mayange—double the yield of any previous good harvest. It would have been a bumper crop even for Iowa, I said.

"Yes, even for Iowa," she agreed. She knew Iowa. She knew much about the States, having traveled around the country after earning her master's at Brandeis. (Our American universities and their scholarships to foreign students are our most important and most appreciated foreign aid investment.)

"But this is not right, Josh," she said. "Nothing much grows in Mayange except some diseased cassava, bananas, and pigeon peas. Everyone knows that nothing much grows in Bugesera. You are ruining the motto of this place," and she laughed.

It was the community's victory, and so the community celebrated. A great festival and dance were held. Traditionally, communities have a harvest festival where all are invited to eat and drink and dance, but this community, in all the years anyone knew, had never had enough food for a harvest festival. So this was very big. Traditional dancers and musicians came from afar. The national government of Rwanda, represented by many high officials and ministers, took the occasion to announce its "Vision 2020 Umurenge" plan. In essence, it was a plan to reproduce core elements of our program in every rural village of Rwanda and combine them with lots of other government initiatives to wipe out extreme poverty by the year 2020. This is the kind of replication you long to see: you want to see the government officials take your programs and scale them up on their own—this is what can make programs sustainable for generations. It was the kind of moment I had dreamed of since Ethiopia.

Donald and Jeannette and Annette were deeply relieved. If everything had failed, I could go home, but they could not. They knew this harvest would have a great effect on many communities and on this government and perhaps others—it would be historic.

Later in the evening, I wanted a smooch on the unfinished deck of Heaven with Alissa. Maybe I would have a glass of wine and she could have some passion fruit juice. With her ever-expanding belly, she hadn't been up for the long ride to the festival in Mayange, and I wanted to share this milestone more personally.

She led me out onto the great deck. I hadn't seen it in days, and it was more finished than I expected. A papyrus-reed ceiling soared above us, pink in the evening cast; the twinkling lights of Kigali were spectacular on the hills beyond our hill.

There were still systems to install in the restaurant, but it was getting close to the time we should go. Our young Indian manager, Amit, now living in the Soprano house with us, had been busy preparing the overall plan of attack, even as construction workers were still pulling wires and fitting pipes.

Then, just when we were about to leave for the States, he disappeared.

He left a note to explain that the Indian businessmen who had brought him to Africa to manage their restaurant had informed him that they would pull their sponsorship from his work visa if he did not do as they said. They forced him to go to work managing an Indian restaurant in Kampala, Uganda, and he simply did not have the heart to tell us in person, so he slipped away by night. Uganda is immediately north of Rwanda; its southeastern border is the west and north shore of Lake Victoria. He was not far, but he was a world away from us now.

We knew he must have been crying as he wrote it. He was a joyful young man, but now he was back in the clutches of an upper caste that would keep him as their work animal.

A waiter at the Indian restaurant whispered news of him when we next dined there—in Kampala he had quickly become very depressed. Then news came to us by a note from the waiter: Amit had allegedly accrued gambling debts and failed to pay his sister's dowry. Unable to face his sister, he jumped from a building to his death.

We were devastated, but Alissa had no choice but to keep moving. She quickly found another manager. He was quite good, but, soon after we left for the States, he was hired away by the people who were setting up the Bourbon Coffee franchise. They seemed to have unlimited funds, and they offered him double what we could afford. We encouraged him to follow that opportunity. Still, he said he would keep an eye on Heaven while we were gone, and, in fact, he helped install a few key features, including the big, hand-built gas range and ventilation hood.

We would be away for a couple months. We would come back to Africa with a beautiful daughter, Maya, but to an empty restaurant and, in more ways than one, no clue how to proceed.

CHAPTER 29

～∞～

Adam in Eden

For the annals of travel, note that we arrived back in Kigali with twenty-six pieces of luggage, each at the airline limit of fifty pounds. Baby supplies accounted for some of it, but most of the duffels and boxes and cases contained pots and pans, chef's knives, color-coordinated cutting boards, pastry tubes, even a cash register. Our American Airlines check-in agent at JFK was horrified and started looking through the rule book to see if we could really do this. If we paid, we could. Alissa had read the rules very carefully.

You can buy kitchen supplies in Rwanda, but they are not the quality a good chef would want, and they are remarkably expensive, even for the poor grade, so it's much cheaper to pay for the extra baggage. Better manufacturing companies will soon come to Africa, and the markets are already waiting. Even now, you could keep a couple of motorcycle and cell phone factories running around the clock.

Apollo met us inside the terminal. You already know something about Op-ed, but Apollo is worth knowing, too.

Taller and narrower than Op-ed and almost always smiling sweetly, Apollo was born in Uganda, to the north beyond the gorilla volcanoes. His parents were farmers who fled Rwanda in the 1960s. After the genocide, when Apollo was in his early twenties, the family returned.

He was then taken under the wing of an old family acquaintance, John Rucyahana, an Anglican bishop. Bishop John started the Sonrise School, Rwanda's most impressive primary and secondary school, which primarily serves the poor. With the help of dollars from Arkansas donors (there is an inexplicably large number of Arkansas expats in Kigali), the school's students quickly became the nation's best. When Little Rock donors Dabbs and Mary Cavin decided to come to Rwanda for a few years to help the school and establish a microfinance bank, Bishop John recruited family friend Apollo to be their driver. Dabbs had worked at Hillary Clinton's Rose Law Firm and does a remarkably good imitation of President Clinton. Apollo, always the quiet presence in the driver's seat, learned a great deal during those two years about America and, really, everything.

The Cavins swore by Apollo's honesty and his expert driving. When they headed home to Arkansas, they asked us if we needed a good driver. We did.

In his thirties now, Apollo is tall and bright-eyed, always amused to see you or some new situation. He was the calm spot among the horde of anxious taxi drivers and baggage handlers as we arrived with our thousand pounds of bags and a tired baby.

Apollo is smart about his country and its history, though you will not know it unless you ask him serious questions to pierce his smile and his reticence—he is the quietest man I know outside of holy orders. But if I ever needed to get my family out of Rwanda in a hurry, I would go to Apollo and ask him to figure it out. I have traveled so many miles with him and know him so well that I can predict with great confidence how he would react to that conversation. If I said, "Apollo, I want to get my family out of Rwanda tonight, but I don't want to fly out," he would not ask why. He would just nod and ask which direction we might go—to which of the four nations surrounding Rwanda. If I said I wanted to go west to Congo, he would smile and ask if I was sure that would be the best place to go, as there is fighting there. If I said yes, then he would ask where I wanted to cross the border. If I said I wanted to cross Lake Kivu on a bamboo raft, and did not want to go there on main roads, he would say that, yes, he knows some other ways to get there, and we can stop at his friend's place and get some rope and saws to make the raft. He would ask when we wanted to leave and what we wanted to bring, and whether he should ask Joel to make some sandwiches. I am sure the conversation would go that way. If it were a real situation, I'm sure he would get us to the lake and across it safely.

His duties this night were less serious: he organized a few men to grab our dozens of bags and load them into and on top of our old Toyota Land Cruiser, with a spare pickup truck following for the overflow.

The streets still had a few tired but colorfully dressed women carrying loads of fabrics and foods to morning markets. Other big loads blossomed from handcarts and overloaded bicycles. There was music coming from late-night shops. Hearing the music, you might think you were in the Caribbean, as Equatorial Africa is where such music is born— rap and gospel and ancient tribal rhythms, all mixed together. It is music to move to, which is useful in a land where survival is about motion. Men and women will return your smile and wave back, if you wave. But you should just wave from your wrist, not your elbow. A bigger wave might mean something else, like stop or come here or run away from here. So you keep it to just the hand.

But the people on the streets were not looking at our smiles or our waves, they were looking at our bulging load of luggage. Many expats, first moving to Rwanda, ship their household belongings from home in forty-foot containers, which arrive by ship in Mombasa, Kenya, and are then trucked to Kigali via Kampala, Uganda. We had always traveled light. But this time we were like the old-time safaris, when English and German gentlemen brought their beverage bars and favorite mattresses by land.

Apollo didn't make the turn up the hill to the Soprano house as usual. With a baby now, we needed our own place. For now, it would be the old house on the Heaven property—a few months later we would move to the house where the bones were buried.

The next day, I had to go check on Mayange, so Alissa was left to wander through her finished restaurant with baby Maya in a sling. It seemed Maya could take naps only in a sling, and that habit was taking a toll on both our backs.

That evening, Alissa told me she was at a loss about how to proceed. There was still lots of finishing that had to be done with Alissa's eye for detail. Organic-looking paint colors had to be chosen, stone and brick work needed further attention, and the plumbing was yet in shambles. Chairs and tables and napkins had to be fabricated; plates and glassware had to be run down. Then there was the lingering question of how to move from physical completion to an operational restaurant.

We both thought in silence for a few minutes. Maya fidgeted.

"Remember how you said how much you liked meeting Adam, Sarah's husband?"

She brightened. She was seeing the idea.

My cousin Sarah had just married Adam Cohn, a New York City restaurateur who had been chef at a Cajun restaurant in South Africa and now had a place in the East Village. He absolutely loved Africa. He had gone to South Africa in 1994—quite a year for Africa—for a friend's wedding. He happened to end up alongside three million other people at Nelson Mandela's inauguration. Mandela, in his remarks, addressed the Westerners present by saying, if you want to give us a hand, come do business with us. So Adam stayed and helped develop restaurants. Sarah had heard all his stories and wanted to see Africa for herself.

Maybe Adam and Sarah would like a three-week African honeymoon of sorts? We tallied our frequent flier miles to see if we could cover their tickets. We could.

They agreed immediately. His restaurant was doing well, had a good manager, and could spare Adam for a few weeks. It might be a last opportunity for the couple to have a great adventure before starting a family. Adam told Alissa to go ahead and hire some bright people so that he and Sarah would have a crowd to train when they arrived. Alissa put out the word to the orphans. Applicants were soon lined up at a table in the Heaven courtyard, under the Umuvumu trees with the severed roots. Every strong wind worried Alissa— that the trees might come down and pound her restaurant into smithereens.

When Adam and Sarah arrived, they rented a motorcycle (without a driver) and bravely took off each morning to explore Kigali's sprawling, open-air food markets. Adam's test kitchen soon featured the best foods of Africa, blended into recipes that expats, tourists, and Rwandans might all recognize and love. Sarah trained the front-of-the-house servers.

One of the great difficulties of training people from another culture to cook and serve food is that if they don't like the tastes of those foods, they will never get the tastes right for those who do. Adam, therefore, worked to create menu items that the cooks and servers would also love. That sort of thing takes great skill and thoughtfulness.

The best guacamole in Africa, featuring Rwandan avocados that taste a bit tarter and richer than their brethren in the States, was on our tasting table each evening at the cocktail hour—and thankfully Alissa could have a glass of wine now.

The anxiety of taking the first steps toward opening had passed, and Alissa could start to relax. The pros were in the house, and they would stay long enough to perfect the opening menu and train the staff.

It didn't help that most of our fledgling staff had never dined in a restaurant. The hardest part about training the serving staff was just getting them to smile. Other skills could be learned later. Adam understood that they functioned best as a group and responded well to group sports training exercises, as all were serious soccer fanatics. He started the training sessions with a huddle where they put their fists together and then exploded them outward to the cry, "Guacamole!"

Adam latched on to a young man, Seba, one of the orphans, as his sous-chef. Seba had been the Millennium Village team cook out in the field, stirring up delicious African stews and multicourse meals to give even the crabbiest community mobilizer something to look forward to at day's end. Seba helped

Adam find the best foods at the best prices. Rwanda is a green-house, but many foods still have their season. Mangoes, straw-berries, mushrooms, and rhubarb come into season just like the fall fruits of New England or Washington State.

Honoline, who was now a Generation Rwanda scholarship recipient taking business courses at the university, was hired as office manager. Others we had known from Alissa's volunteer work filled other positions.

Then there was Fabrice.

Fabrice Uwimana, a young man with a happy face and whimsical dreadlocks that twist up at all angles, was from a working-class neighborhood of Kigali. Before the genocide, his father worked at a transport office and his mother sold fruits and vegetables at the big Nyarugenge Market. Fabrice had two brothers and two sisters. When the genocide began, he—just eight years old—fled east to the Tanzanian border with his father and a younger brother and sister. Just as they were about to reach the border, his father was pulled from the car, thrown into the bushes, and killed. During the commotion of his father's murder, Fabrice pulled his little brother and sister into the bushes, where a cow herder found them and took them carefully through the backcountry to the river that marks the border with Tanzania. With the old cow herder's help, they tied banana stalks and sticks into a raft and crossed the river, paddling with their hands. In Tanzania, Fabrice learned that Hutu militiamen had burned his family's house back home and killed his mother, his grandfather, his older sister, and a cousin. They had been held inside their house as it burned.

After the hundred days, Fabrice found his way into school while his sister took a job cleaning for UN troops, who had returned a little late to be useful. Fabrice finished high school, all the while washing dishes at a little Chinese restaurant that paid him $1.50 a day. He and his sister often went hungry in order to pay the rent. They once peeled potatoes all night at a little restaurant where they had ordered and eaten a good meal and then fessed up that they had no money and would do whatever was needed.

Fabrice's hard life is not visible on his face or in the spring of his step. He likes to sing. When he started at Heaven his dream was just to go to university in Kigali, but there was no financial means. With the job, of course, everything was possible. He would start the first day after the interview. He stood under the Umuvumu trees near Alissa's interview table as he tried to grasp the big fact of how his life had just changed.

At that moment, interviewing people in the shade, Alissa noticed that something was happening to her two giant trees. It turns out that the Umuvumu tree is a kind of banyan, sometimes called a stilt tree. On the side of the tree opposite the cut root, the tree had suspended some thin tendrils from the lowest branches. These thin ropes had rooted into the soil. They would surely now grow into thick and strong crutches. The tree had adapted, as life in Africa does.

What better symbol can there be for Rwanda than this tree? At first, we had no idea what it was and no knowledge of its special powers to heal and move on. In fact, in many of the prisons still holding those who participated in the genocide, there is an Umuvumu Tree Project to bring peace and reconciliation through confession and apology. Umuvumu trees often gave shade to the neighborhood courts where people gave testimony after the genocide. Today, many people still gather under the Umuvumu trees, though now it is for neighborhood projects. The last Saturday of each month is called

Umuganda, when everyone takes the morning off — by law! —
to work together on community improvement projects and to
get to know each other.

It is hard to imagine how they do it, but Rwandans try to
meet face to face with the people who killed their loved ones,
or with the survivors of people they themselves killed.

One of our friends, Jean-Baptiste Ntakirutimana, went
through a similar reconciliation with his mother's killer. In a
note, he described it to us:

> I inquired first about his life in prison, his family and his
> state of mind. He said he was expecting that I could kill
> him, which he thinks was the way of doing justice for
> having killed my mum. He added that no one else
> dared kill my mum, because they knew her and liked
> her. She was brought by two militia to our village and
> they called for people to come and kill her. No one
> was allowed to loot from Tutsis before killing all their
> family members, so he felt he had to kill her. Since they
> thought I was already killed in Kigali, where I was
> residing, the only hindrance to take all the family
> property was my mum. So she had to be killed. By the
> time he started explaining how he killed her I partly lost
> consciousness. I prayed to God to give me His spirit to
> revive me and give me more strength to continue, as I
> felt it was His mission that I was on. Miraculously, I felt
> warmth from my head to my feet, I felt like a big rock
> melting from my chest and my head. I felt very
> refreshed, cleaned up my tears and carried on the
> conversation, tremendously relieved from my whole
> being. I then told him that I have personally been

forgiven all my wrong from God and that it is in the
same spirit that I was coming to him offering him
pardon myself. Then it was like a huge veil off his face;
he started smiling with a lot of words of gratitude. He
started holding my hands and telling me many other
things I couldn't expect about himself and the reality
around the genocide. He agreed to go and see other
people whose family members he killed.

There are few therapists in Rwanda—at least not like we
have in the States. Rwandans have to work through their ter-
rors in simple, straightforward ways. You sometimes have to
marvel at each person's determination to have a life, to find
happiness, and to get past the impossible, no matter whom
they must forgive or what they must forgive, in others or in
themselves.

CHAPTER 30

Rule Five and a Thousand
Heavens

With Adam and Sarah still in Kigali, we had a soft opening for Heaven—a party for more than a hundred of the people we had met since coming here. Adam's dishes were a great success, particularly the filet mignon smothered in cassava chimichurri.

For Alissa, standing on the deck, welcoming her new Rwandan friends and first customers was very satisfying, even though she is an introvert by nature.

She was a little proud, and rightfully. After all, she had trucked the deck she was standing on out of the jungle, forced the great roof into the sky by sheer determination, learned the necessary parts of two foreign languages, and hired a great crew of young people who now could see their futures, and she had somehow found the strength for all of it as a pregnant woman and now as a new mother.

I kept my day job, but Adam and Alissa pressed me into evening duty in the kitchen as we headed toward the formal opening. It was fun, but I was fast learning the difference between being a cook, which I consider myself, and being a chef. Chefs have to organize and efficiently make use of perishables going bad while ensuring that each person in the kitchen knows his or her station. I could cook for a couple dozen once in a while, but was in over my head when it came to the finer points of getting the sous-chef to create a perfectly balanced mango salsa day after day and getting the grill master to cook an herb-basted whole tilapia to perfection. The kitchen was only one area of challenge, as we wanted to have the best food and the best bar. The latter was initially Alissa's domain. The water for drinks and for ice had to be purified. The swizzle sticks were split from sugar cane. Morello—not maraschino—cherries had to be tracked down for the Manhattans. Alissa's Mojito instantly became—not just in my opinion—the best in Equatorial Africa.

That emboldened her to create a Japanese Plum Cosmopolitan—made, by the way, with organic tamarillo juice. Then she created her version of a Dawa, an East African vodka cocktail with fragrant honey and citrus juices, whose name translates to "medicine." On nights when the kitchen struggled to get meals out in less than an hour, we'd start taking our medicine early to help us deal with unruly customers.

Our starters featured guacamole with green banana plantain chips, banana flower salad, and a stellar gazpacho. For a country with so many avocado trees, it was amazing that we introduced guacamole. Later on, we'd introduce the country's first avocado fries with a spicy chili mayonnaise. For entrees, the sweet potato gnocchi with sage–brown butter sauce was a standout, as was our burger on a homemade bun with our own ground beef (with some bacon ground in) and tangy barbecue sauce. We had rotating specials of curried Indian eggplant pancakes with mango chutney and brined pork chops with creamed matoke and papaya sauce. For dessert, the molten chocolate brownie with homemade ice cream was, and remains, the biggest hit.

The menu was a political statement: quality is possible here, and with local ingredients and local staff—not a staff imported from Kenya, as the hotel restaurants typically have.

For better or worse, the menu established us as "the American restaurant"—maybe the burgers, guacamole, and Cosmos did that. But our presence meant that the other restaurants would have to get more creative and more quality conscious, which would help promote the tourist and business trade in Rwanda. Jobs, from busboy to bank president, would be created as a result.

On the night it formally opened to the public, Heaven was the best new thing in Africa. To the assembled guests, Alissa introduced the whole team that had put Heaven together, from the stewards to our two amigos from NYC.

In her remarks, which were extemporaneous but eloquent and confident, I saw her as she had always wanted to see herself.

Dr. Blaise, who looked like the special Rwandan Ambassador to Heaven that evening—tall, strong, dressed to the nines as always—hugged Alissa and told her she had done a great thing.

"In the long run, Alissa, this place will do more good than a dozen charities coming to Rwanda. If every poor place had a thousand Heavens like this and a little more justice, there would be no poverty."

I was listening. The pinky finger of our handful of rules is to trust the market as the biggest player, even if the power of the market looks small now. Rule Five is a reminder to never be afraid of the profit model, as it can carry the heaviest load of long-term development. Profit brings sustainability, not to mention dignity.

Most international development schemes rely on two legs: a hint of government action and NGO charity. But a third leg, the market, is the strongest of the three and is often overlooked. No nation, not even the United States, has enough public and foundation money to send all the kids to college who qualify, or cure all the illnesses that plague us. But small jobs and private incomes do the trick. The little finger, often overlooked but actually the strongest finger of the hand, represents this rule.

The restaurant opening was a big moment for the people's future, and Alissa made it happen.

Dr. Blaise's words seemed like a truth so important that I knew I should look more closely at everything I was doing, too. I began to look at the profit model as it might apply to dairy production. If we were ever going to boost childhood nutrition to modern standards, we were going to have to get quality dairy products distributed as an affordable staple of family meals. The only way we could really do this well, and expand it quickly, would be by using dairy farming cooperatives and large-scale, sanitary production facilities to produce products that would not need refrigeration. Could we do this as a charitable enterprise? It was too big and would be unsustainable. It needed to be done as a business, so I began romancing the idea among the kinds of people—inside Rwanda and internationally—who might be interested. This project continues to mature, and I don't think I would have been inspired to begin it if not for Alissa's Heaven and Dr. Blaise's comments that evening.

CHAPTER 31

—◈—

Yes, There Is a (Cash) Bar in Heaven

Bourbon Coffee, the operation that beat us to the punch, is a good place to go in the mornings or midday to see business deals getting done. You will see business types from India, China, Belgium, and many other places across the table from well-dressed Rwandans. All of this commerce is bringing Rwanda rapidly into the modern age, and Rwanda has climbed up through the ratings of best places to do business to stand alongside modern economies such as Israel, Turkey, and Botswana.

While India, China, Korea, and many other countries send business to places like Rwanda, the United States sends aid organizations. Some aid is certainly needed today, but US entrepreneurs are missing out on a tremendous opportunity to get in on the ground floor of a market that one day will make the people of Rwanda prosperous enough to afford their own medical care, their own water systems, and their own educational system.

But you cannot fault the young expats, American, Canadian,

UK, European, Aussie, Israeli, and many others, who come here with the aid programs to make a difference, which they certainly do.

Just as the businesspeople are doing deals at Bourbon, you will see the aid expats comparing notes and adding value to each other's work as they sit at the tables and long bar of Heaven, a few streets from Bourbon.

To get from Bourbon to Heaven, you walk down to the traffic circle, then along a main street until you get to Rue du Mont Juru. Halfway up to the president's house, there's a short driveway into Heaven's small parking courtyard. When the restaurant is busy, cars are parked along the street. All the taxi drivers know where Heaven is and most visitors know about it—travel sites have ranked it in the top three restaurants in the country since its opening. We're usually number one, in fact, and when it slips down for a month, Alissa goes into a nervous overdrive to make sure every customer goes away happy.

The steel doors to Heaven swing open for dinner at five o'clock. The doors close when the last members of the staff leave, a bit after midnight. The guard, Charles, stays on duty until morning. That is the case with most buildings and businesses in Africa. This is driving a boom in security. You see guards outside residences, but given Rwanda's low crime rate, they function like the helpful doormen of Manhattan.

Entering Heaven from the parking area, you pass a small, raised square of an herb garden, then walk under the spread of the huge trees, then into a thatched hut entryway, where, if all goes well, you are cordially greeted. From there, it's straight ahead to the long, curved, open-air bar, made from the wood that was accidentally cut too narrow for the deck. You will see young and old expats at the bar, often taking advantage of the wireless Internet. Between email messages, they strike up conversations with each other about their week's adventures and share information useful in improving each other's programs. Romances are sometimes begun around the curves of the bar. Expat men are in short supply and have an easy time of it—ten to one, by some counts.

If, instead of going straight to the bar, you take two steps down to your right, you will be on the great dining deck that extends toward the view of Kigali. Above you, quite high, is the sharp-angled roof with its papyrus reed ceiling. Coming in from one side are the branches of the great Umuvumu trees. Over one hundred people can fit on the candle-lit deck for dinner. It is quite romantic. If it's not romantic enough for you, and it's a Friday, go back, two steps up, to the bar. There are boutique guest rooms, too, in the adjoining old house—just in case you'd like to stay with us.

Here are some real people at the bar:

Chantal Ruta, Kigali's only female taxi driver and owner of a thriving tourism business, is sipping on a Coke, greeting the regulars and drumming up business. Most of her livelihood comes from our customers. She is sitting near Steve Jones, a horticulturist. He founded a company that uses a tissue culture process to extract pieces of healthy plants chosen by natural selection and reproduces them by the thousands, allowing farmers to get up to ten times more production out of their land, all without genetic modification. He lives in Rwanda most of the year, though his wife, Cheryl, and his kids are in Tennessee. His clients are the Rwandan government, farmers and co-ops. He is always finding partners for new agriculture projects. He has a thick black beard, broad shoulders, and a strong, planter's handshake—you can't miss him. He comes often enough to have his own "Steve's discount" button on the cash register, and he likes to refer to himself as Norm from *Cheers,* though he is no slouch.

Steve is talking to Ken Bialek, who keeps coming back to hatch good projects. He is presently developing affordable housing. Living about half the year here now, he came originally with his kids to try to understand the genocide. Their family had fled the pogroms of Eastern Europe in the first years of the twentieth century, and Rwanda seemed the fresher laboratory to find some understanding of the unimaginable. In addition to wisdom, what he has found here are great friends— *abazungu* and Rwandan. They all share—we all share—a sense of mystery about the impossible thought of genocide in so kind a country.

For Westerners generally (and, so notably, Joseph Conrad), Equatorial Africa is held in the mind as a metaphor for the darkest unknowns of life and for our fears and challenges— mostly our fears about ourselves. I think many people come here to study the genocide propelled by the unsettling knowledge that we are all capable of much that we don't want to imagine.

Here in the upper reach of the Nile is another darkness to be studied: this is where the worst diseases spring forth from animals into the blood of humans. Although we feel safe where we are nestled in Kigali, we are not far from the jungles where the virus that causes AIDS moved from monkey to human. There are still outbreaks of the Ebola virus, which melts the flesh most monstrously. Those diseases, of course, pale in their cruelty compared to the capacities of men. But it is all the same, somehow, and maybe that is why such bright and caring people come here to explore and offer themselves and their talents.

To say it in simple terms, people come here to find meaningful lives, which means to find themselves, as if their own lives were lost in these swampy labyrinths. There is something to that. This place works for that. When people leave here they perhaps want some sushi and Ben & Jerry's first, but then they want to continue with meaningful endeavors. You cannot leave Africa and then expect to be satisfied in ordinary living. You will have to continue doing extraordinary things, because you know what can be done in the world, and you know what you are capable of doing, and you know that, wherever you go, many lives will depend on your willingness to exercise your privileges and skills on their behalf.

Anyway, this is ground zero for all that, and it gets intense. It is good to wash down the day with a good drink with a friend who understands.

I often see Steve or Ken talking with Claude Mansell, a European who, after a successful career as a business consultant, first came here after he came across the Kiva microlending website and decided to volunteer as their man in Rwanda. He recently took a stake in an underutilized maize milling plant, which he has made profitable.

Allie Huttinger is often Skyping home from the bar. She was hired through the GE Foundation to get their state-of-the-art water filtration technology implemented at health facilities. Rwanda is small enough that it can't afford to become a dumping ground for every old machine a company wants to send over here as a tax write-off. Rwanda says, we need your help, yes, but we will accept only brand-new, state-of-the-art machines, and please send the people to set them up properly and train us. In response, the companies do exactly that. The biggest companies are actually like countries with their own foreign aid budgets, and they tend to make good use of those dollars—much better than Washington. The discounted copies of QuickBooks that we use in our health centers, for example, have pushed those centers forward with amazing speed. So, when you think of American foreign aid, you have to think of the young expats who come over here, and you must also think of the companies that come. It's amazing and makes you very proud.

If I haven't found someone yet that interests you, let me keep looking.

Eric Reynolds often comes in from Gisenyi on Lake Kivu and orders a Mutzig, his favorite local beer. He makes and sells energy-efficient stoves, and seeks to make Rwanda the world's first carbon-neutral nation while eliminating the chronic lung diseases caused by indoor cooking. He founded a major outdoor gear company in the States. He married a Rwandan woman, had a kid, and has raised millions for his project, "Inyenyeri—A Rwandan Social Benefit Company." He put a prototype stove up on the bar at Heaven not long ago to show everyone how it works with its energy pellets, culled from common farm waste and eucalyptus leaves. The bar smelled like a Swedish spa for a week and staff queued up to buy one.

Some nights you will see Soozi McGill and maybe Shal Foster, the founders of Rwanda Girls Initiative. Both are very fit young mothers from Seattle who started a girls' leadership school next to our Gashora Health Center. They like guacamole and chips, with a few Mojitos. Soozi and Shal are among the group we call "the educators," which includes a contingent from Boston who built a terrific school for girls not far from

Mayange, and Anne Heyman, who replicated an Israeli youth village concept called Agahozo-Shalom in a district where Health Builders operates.

At one big table will often be a group of Rwandan restaurateurs, tour leaders, and training specialists. Our good friends Jackie and Colin Kakiza are likely to be there. Jackie began her career as an interior designer but quickly developed a keen interest in the hospitality industry after working on some unique hotel design projects. She grew up in Kenya and later worked for the Four Seasons Los Angeles. She and her family are Rwandan, though often when she's giving a training class in English, everyone assumes that she doesn't speak Kinyarwanda. She's made many a student blush upon learning that she's fluent. When we talk about the diaspora's return, we think of Jackie. She convinced her husband, Colin, a Ugandan, that Rwanda is the next big thing. He worked at the prestigious Beverly Wilshire Hotel for many years but spends these days improving Rwanda's hotel industry.

If it is a hopping night at Heaven, Dr. Blaise will invariably walk in. He orders a Heineken and a sausage quesadilla with guacamole. He demanded we put goat and beef brochettes on the menu to keep the locals happy.

Before Dr. Blaise joined Health Builders, he worked for a project funded by the big gorilla of aid programs, USAID. He quit it in disgust because they asked him to write a report on how much money was spent on each child in the project area. He wanted to count only the money that actually got to the kids in the village, not the salaries of consultants in Washington and Boston, the plane tickets and hotel rooms of staff, the meetings in Geneva of contractors. In other words, he wanted to exclude over ninety percent of the money. Pennies were reaching each child—never enough to end poverty for them, but just enough to keep them alive so the "beltway bandits," as they are called, can have their lavish lifestyles and their homes and big salaries, and so the world's poor can be their justification, just as the world's poor are sometimes the toy train of the wealthy, who sometimes also do not give enough to actually solve problems.

Big aid people come to Heaven, too. Their money is welcome at the bar, and we hope that the influence of our gaggle of entrepreneurs helps to steer their efforts in better directions.

CHAPTER 32

〜〜

Your Age in Rwanda Years: Double

In spite of everyone's best efforts, the average Rwandan's life expectancy is still shy of sixty—that's a short life in the twenty-first century. The two rainy seasons and two harvests per year are perhaps offered as compensation, but they also bring twice the work: each year is like two. Even though Mayange's great harvest celebration still lingered in our conversations, and the ruts of the dignitaries' cars were still visible in the little-used corners of Mayange's soccer field, and photos of villagers standing beside high government ministers were still being proudly passed around, it was already time to plant the next crop.

The rains, however, were even slower coming this time than before. Little seedlings of maize popped up, but then managed only pale, short stalks—a crop of hollow, dry back-scratchers. Each morning they should have been a few inches higher, brighter green, racing against each other for the best light. But, still, they were pale and listless. A few short rains came, but never enough to do more than prolong the seedlings' suffering. In biblical fashion, those plants that beat the odds and shot up were destroyed by a plague of leafhoppers, which transmitted a deadly maize leaf virus. There would be a crop, but it wouldn't be much. The farmers thought that it might qualify as a "seed crop"—that the production would be exactly equal to the seed needed for the next season's planting. That meant maybe one anemic ear of corn for every few plants.

Donald was constantly visiting the fields and coming back to the office with dirt and burrs on his trousers and a deflated face; he had lost the defiant optimism of the first season.

"We may have been lucky with the first harvest," he finally said, admitting that things were not going to turn around. In Rwanda, one does not offer bad news freely to a boss, so he had delayed this harsh verdict for as long as possible.

A bad harvest could break the confidence of the community and undermine our credibility. Would they do anything more that we asked of them now? The community had set aside crop surpluses as per government mandate, so famine was not an immediate risk, though hunger loomed. But what about next year?

There was another problem: In order to get all the families into Mutuelle, the new national health care system that costs each person several dollars a year, we had encouraged the farmers to borrow from us, secured by the next harvest. To allay their fears of not being able to pay the money back, we agreed that if the crop failed, the little loans for the medical premiums would be forgiven. It seemed like a good idea at the time, and it did quickly improve health conditions. But now the crop was failing, and the full cost of the program would fall on our little organization. It was my fault. I had tried to make things happen too quickly. But you do things like that when you see sick children and mothers.

Because the government pays the nurses in the clinic, the government expects people to have the government insurance. Based on a community group discussion process, the poorest families were identified and their insurance premiums were covered by various government safety net mechanisms. Those diagnosed with HIV received free health care, but others—maybe a middle-aged man with a chronic health problem—could, in violation of government policy, be denied service at that time. We advocated for fewer cracks in the health insurance system, and improvements were made. Today, anyone entering a facility must be given care, with or without insurance. Patients do have a copayment to make per consultation of about thirty-five cents. In some districts over ninety percent of the population is insured—that's a sign of prosperity as well as of valuing the health system's services. Yes, a country as historically divided as Rwanda is much further along than the United States in figuring out universal medical coverage. That is in part why Rwanda is one of the few countries on earth projected to achieve the health-related Millennium Development Goals. Other nations should take that as an inspiration and a challenge.

The failing crop meant I had to go raise some money to cover all the health insurance premiums, but that's the kind of thing I can do. The more serious problem was that word was spreading in official circles that our early success was perhaps a flash in the pan. Maybe we were just another bunch of do-gooders who would pull up stakes and leave only disappointment behind.

But Donald and I knew that there was a bit of a silver lining in the disastrous harvest: we'd gotten people who had been locked out of the health system to use it and, by zeroing out everyone's debt and showing good faith, we'd earned the trust of the whole community, who were used to unscrupulous lenders who took houses away from late payers.

Word on the street shifted in its tenor, and people started sharing their sympathies with the team: "We know it's not your fault, it was the lack of rain. God sleeps in Mayange." We were deeply concerned that by forgiving the loans, we might break our cardinal rule and make adults feel like dependent children. But for the time being, there was nothing else to do.

CHAPTER 33

—◈—

Beginner's Luck

Through many of these days and nights I operated with some guilt for our crop failure; I was off at dawn, bumping through the smoky hills and muddy bogs with Op-ed, hearing his bright stories and planning my vigorous day—the leader must always be full of energy and optimism, for it flows out from the head of an organization, losing a bit at each pass. I had to maintain this even in the face of our first big project disaster.

So I planned and pumped myself up for each day with considerable focus to that responsibility. By evening I would be exhausted, having done perhaps a dozen things that I hoped might make a big difference in the lives of many families. Nonetheless, those satisfactions fed my spirit and gave me the energy to leave Alissa sleeping a bit later each morning while I played with baby Maya. Alissa's routine was usually deadening by comparison, and I knew it.

She was trying to move Heaven from its gala opening to an ongoing success, but she was having countless difficulties in that first year. Cooks and chefs and managers would come and go, often leaving disappointed customers and an ornery staff behind them. At one point, she hired a Kenyan national with a résumé that looked built for Heaven. He made us comfortable enough to take Maya on her first ninety-day-rule vacation in exotic Zanzibar. While there, we started to watch negative reviews piling up online. On our return Alissa investigated and found that the manager was spending service hours having a lovely time at the bar on our tab, while the customers were suffering the consequences. The short-term prescription was clear: we had to be hands-on with everything, always.

I was working closely with the kitchen trying to put systems in place—not unlike the systems in our health centers. Alissa would tell me the kinds of dishes she was excited about—Afro-Mexican goat brochettes, for example—and I'd whip something up. While I enjoyed creating new dishes, ensuring that our cooks maintained quality and consistency was going to take more than photos on the wall of how the final product should look. Plus, finding fresh tender goat isn't easy when the local goats are a hardy but bony variety. At one point, one of our chefs asked for "fresh" goat, and in the midst of service for eighty customers, a live goat was delivered to the kitchen. He made it known that that wasn't exactly what he had in mind.

Alissa and I dreamed of a self-sufficient kitchen in which an expat chef wouldn't be essential, and we tried giving the kitchen staff opportunity to show off. On President Obama's first election night, we projected the results on our huge screen and had two hundred people in the crowd. Alissa is never one for an all-nighter—even for that election—and went home around midnight. Thinking I had a great idea, I asked our chef de patisserie to do a wonderful morning treat for everyone. At four o'clock in the morning he pulled me from behind the bar where I was trying to keep up with drink orders to show off his creation. Hundreds of glistening, perfectly crusty croissants awaited me. I smiled and asked what was inside. "A special creation" he proudly announced, "vanilla custard with creamed spinach." My grimace upon taking the smallest of bites told him everything. I gathered the exhausted staff: "So who knows how to make pancakes?" Until well after sunrise I was on the griddle. We had enjoyed our initial victories, both with Heaven and Mayange, but perhaps these were little jokes played on us by Fate or whatever old tricksters roam these upper reaches of the Nile.

We had had a lovely dose of beginner's luck, and the real life of Africa was settling in hard on us. Alissa was usually up a four o'clock in the morning to nurse Maya. Constantly working at Heaven and coordinating motherhood and breastfeeding was a physical and emotional drain on her. The stress of the restaurant had given her a tic in her left eye and a strained smile. When I returned from the field, at a time of evening when most couples would finally relax and recharge, we instead put Maya down for the night and then headed to Heaven to manage things for the dinner crowd; thankfully dinnertime arrives early in Africa. Knowing that one bad customer impression would impact us enormously, we didn't feel comfortable taking a night off for many months.

When there was an illness with any of the staff or their families, it was an illness in our family, and Alissa was sending countless people in our network to the clinic and reminding them to vaccinate their kids and their younger brothers and sisters.

The fellow who was doing our maintenance at the restaurant told us of his ill daughter one evening. At our expense we made an appointment with a pediatrician we knew. The man didn't show up with his daughter for the appointment, telling us later that she was better. But soon after that the little girl—a lovely three-year-old—died. He claimed that the pediatrician could have not helped her, as she was suffering from a poison spell put on her by an enemy of the family—black magic. It was hard—it remains hard—to understand why people sometimes will not do the things that we Westerners believe with all our certainty to be the necessary things. But new ways take great energy; change is difficult for everyone, everywhere, though most especially so in the deep grooves of traditional lands.

On most evenings after getting home, I would clean the mud off my boots, change into my good clothes, and head up the hill with Alissa to Heaven. That may sound lovely in concept, but seven nights a week? Alissa was crying about that little girl when I came home one evening. I tried to console her with Op-Ed's axiom du jour: "If you share nothing, you will accuse each other of being greedy." After sharing a laugh, we pulled ourselves together and headed out. Playing host at Heaven is a lot like acting: regardless of the day's tragedies and challenges, our job was to make everyone feel that they were in the best restaurant in Africa that evening.

It would be the third trip to the restaurant that day for Alissa. She was deep in the daily grind of trying to scrape together a profit or at least break even after accounting for the rent and salaries. She would sit down with the staff when, for example, she noticed in the previous day's receipts that the coming week's olive oil was purchased by the quart yesterday instead of by the gallon. Had they not talked about this, that it is cheaper to get the bigger containers? Yes, but someone would explain there was a problem about that—there always seemed to be some problem.

As she worked, Alissa would be carrying Maya in the sling. It was not long before Maya was looking out at the world and forming opinions and attitudes and making demands. We knew we had a strong character on our hands—newborns can have such fully formed personalities.

The way Maya commands with compassionate confidence— except on the red clay tennis court where she's now renowned for being the strongest young hitter anyone has ever seen— reminds me of Katharine Hepburn in *The African Queen*. Ms. Hepburn traveled the back-lot version of these jungles with the same well-formed and demanding self-assurance. If Maya arrived as the Queen of Africa, she has remained so, with her penchant now for sparkly outfits and ballet poses.

In any case, Maya, given a few more years, would have no trouble on such an expedition, pouring the captain's rum overboard without a blink to keep everyone on mission. And while Alissa was trying to be a good and sometimes necessarily stern restaurant manager, it was occasionally the serious looks coming from the even tougher little person in the sling that straightened out the crewmembers.

She had a maturity, right from the start, of a wise old soul. It wouldn't be until a couple of years later, when her baby sister demonstrated the technique, that she would learn to cry.

Each evening we would take our turns in the kitchen and at the bar, training and retraining and retraining again, as these were new things and strange foods for the team to learn.

When things were under control, Alissa and I would visit the tables to greet the customers, as we still do, and then taste-test everything to make sure that it tasted as it should. We'd have a glass or two of wine to numb the pain of being on our feet for hours which also helped us smile more cordially against the wave of constructive criticism that invariably bubbles up in table-to-table conversations.

When we were just the two of us dining, Alissa seemed to know whether to ask me about my day in Mayange. She knew we were going through a very rough patch with the second season, and I might not want to relive it over dinner. There would be enough for us to talk about regarding the house, or the nanny, or something mundane, but my mind was always on scaling up Health Builders' work and how our efforts in Mayange might prove a house of cards—we needed success stories to raise money and get cooperation from the government. We needed triumphs if the people were to prosper and be healthy. Silly of us to have taken the weather for granted, when no one else did. Silly of us to count on luck in a luckless region. Even on an evening when rain might be pounding down on the great roof above the candle-lit dining tables, I knew that only an hour south, it would be dry. I had come to believe in the bad luck of Mayange. God sleeps in Mayange indeed.

Still, the wine and company would help, and often there would be some remarkable new soup that Solange had concocted, like her cream of mushroom soup, which somehow contains little cream yet maintains a sublime mushroom flavor and richness.

Solange started at Heaven as a cleaning steward. After Adam returned to New York, Alissa hired a manager from Kenya with a fine reputation and an ego to go with it. He took up residency in the old house on the property and insisted we hire someone to fetch his tea and do his laundry. Nineteen-year-old Solange was hired for that, and also to wash dishes for the restaurant. To Alissa's eyes, Solange seemed strong enough to stand up to this young manager if he ever dared ask too much of her.

She is slim, small, quiet, and conscientious. One afternoon, Alissa overheard the staff talking about Solange. She was so industrious with her cleaning duties that she had time left over to prepare the staff meal once weekly, and everyone loved her cooking best. So Alissa moved her into the kitchen to help with food prep—the sauces and all the chopped and mixed ingredients that are set in bowls for the chef like paints before an artist. After several months Solange had shown a mastery of basic skills, exceeding nearly everyone in the kitchen.

When I was having a bad day in the field, or when Alissa was having a bad day in Heaven, and we were wondering if our African adventure was even worthwhile, seeing Solange darting in or out of the kitchen would make Alissa and me glance at each other and smile. Solange had become the symbol of the good things that could happen here, given a little opportunity and sticking with it.

CHAPTER 34

✦

Postcolonial Patience

Joshua Poveda, our first, very serious chef, promoted Solange to sous-chef, and she became the leading Rwandan cook in the kitchen, capable of knocking out fifty plates of food in less time than anyone besides Joshua himself.

Joshua had come from Spain to explore Africa. Alissa met him as a customer in the restaurant and quickly talked him into staying as chef. The Heaven menu took a creative and delicious turn immediately. It also freed us up to imagine having another child, and before long we didn't need to imagine, as Alissa was pregnant again.

For Joshua, Heaven was not an easy transition. "Sometimes I walk in and there is shit everywhere. They are jumping over each other—dirty plates everywhere. It is a nightmare!" he complained to us when he first started.

He had cooked for a top New York restaurant and a Michelin-rated restaurant in Spain, so his standards were serious. The "back of the house" kitchen staff and the "front of the house" servers tried very hard to make him happy. They wanted to be proud of Heaven, and they knew Joshua was the man who could help make that happen. Because most restaurants in Rwanda were, at that time, very rough storefronts or mud shack affairs, it was degrading to tell your friends or family that you worked for a restaurant—unless it might be a famous restaurant. So they tried to make it that.

"Well, they've learned to keep clean and stay organized," he told Alissa a week later. "They really do try their best! One is as slow as can be and the way his brain is wired, he can get out starters but not desserts—it still makes no sense to me. But Solange comes to me every day with what she is learning— I want her to do her own specials now."

In New York, Joshua had been comfortable cooking great food for four hundred customers per night on twelve stoves— he could broil sixty steaks at a time—and he understood how crucial communication and timing are. Both were extremely foreign concepts in a Rwandan kitchen, ours included. An eggplant stack—a delicious concoction of fried eggplant in a homemade green curry sauce with a touch of sweet potato— that took two minutes to prepare would sit in loneliness losing its crispness under Heaven's heat lamps before it joined the grilled chicken twenty minutes later. Joshua taught the kitchen staff to coordinate so all the food was ready at the same time. In a place where time is treated casually or even as if it does not exist, that is not easy to learn.

"They do want to please me," he said over a cold Sprite at the bar one evening (he'd long before given up drinking booze). "I'm so sad we had to take the coconut-crusted fish *boulettes* [little balls] off the menu, but they just can't do it. It's not really that complex, because there's a recipe for it, but, if they don't have an ingredient, they'll omit it instead of finding something that will work as a substitute. If I don't have cilantro, I ask myself what can I use instead. They don't have that ability yet.

They don't have the taste buds; that's normal. And we've introduced so many Asian spices they've never heard of."

He made sure that every member of the staff, especially the servers, had the chance to taste whatever new item he added to the menu. He said that everyone should really be sent abroad for a few years so they could learn to love other foods. That, in fact, is what some well-financed African hotels do to improve their restaurant staff—or they just hire Kenyans and South Africans, who have been around tourist tastes for generations and have it down.

Before Joshua, the cooks had been decorating every plate with the same chopped parsley and tomatoes. No more: he was intent on teaching them new cooking skills, from the ground up. Most of them knew "old Belgian" cooking— boiled potatoes, buttery sauces, and overcooked meats. Joshua started from there, turning the "old Belgian" into "new Belgian," and then introducing them to new recipes with local ingredients, and creating tastes and presentations that astonished them. You could hear them cheering in the kitchen sometimes, as if he were David Copperfield and had just materialized a Thanksgiving feast with the whisk of a tablecloth. He worked with each person, getting them to stop and think and smell and taste.

Solange was the teacher's pet. By the time Joshua moved back to Spain, which he had to do for family reasons, he had raised Heaven's reputation—in no small part due to his wildly successful paella nights—and left behind a well-trained staff, especially Solange. But, in some ways, that only made Alissa's job harder, as high standards and high reputation require far more maintenance. Our core customer base had come to expect exceptional food. We had become a favorite stop for the tour companies, in fact. You can spot their Toyota Land Cruisers all around town, ferrying tourists in their safari gear up to see the gorillas or down to the sparkling new lodge in Nyungwe Rainforest down south.

"The tour drivers are angry at us," Alissa said one evening, over a virgin mojito. The men who drive tourists around, mainly up to see the gorillas, have tremendous power to bring in business, and it is normal to pay them a commission, much like a travel agent's commission. We were happy to do so.

"They want more, but they're already getting fifteen percent."

"That's enough. They're just being greedy, and they'll pit one restaurant against another. Don't give in," I advised.

"I wasn't going to. They came for a meeting this morning. They also want to eat for free at the bar while their customers eat on the deck."

"Maybe that could work."

"I told them we would consider it. But they also said they wanted to drink some beer."

"What did you say?"

"I said they should not be drinking and driving, and we would have no part of it. We would not serve alcohol to the drivers."

"Bravo. What did they say?"

"They said of course I was right, and that they would think about it."

"They have to think about that? Think about what?"

"They were probably just negotiating for more money, I'm sure. But knowing them, they'll want to go somewhere else where they can drink their fill. I'll call some of them tomorrow and thank them for coming. Also, they told me I should not be working at a job when I was pregnant. I should be home. I didn't get angry. Not openly."

Dramas like this filled our conversation nearly every evening.

A week later we were dining when I noticed that the little retail area in the opposite corner of the deck seemed dark. There are some craft groups in Mayange that make baskets and beautiful scarves, and we had given up a corner so the customers could support them and go home with something special. But the corner was very dark.

"You're looking at how dark it is on the merchandise," Alissa said between sips of Solange's best soup to date, a squash-peanut blend that reminded us of fall in New England.

"I'm only noticing you," I said.

"The lightbulb in the corner is out. I'm aware of it."

"Do you want me to change it?"

"The team is on it," she interrupted.

"It takes a team to change a lightbulb?"

"I asked the office manager today what his plan was for replacing all the lightbulbs."

"Plan? And?"

"He said he is planning to call in a technician," she said.

I had to laugh. Sometimes these things sounded like the punch lines of jokes. Brimming with frustration she said: "If they want to call in a technician every time a bulb burns out or the toilet clogs up, we'll never..."

"It's all right," I told her.

She loosened a bit. "I think they were scared to change it because it's a halogen bulb, which they don't have at home."

"Of course. They wouldn't want to do it wrong."

I giggled a little into my dwindling glass of South African

pinotage, a personal favorite from one of our best ninety-day-rule getaways.

"I told him I shouldn't always have to be the one to notice when a lightbulb goes out. They should just do some things on their own, without being told. I can hardly wait for the day when someone—security, kitchen staff, a server—sees something that's wrong and just fixes it," she said.

"They don't notice the dark," I replied. "When the staff in Mayange works into the evening, everybody on their computers, they just end up in the dark; no one turns on the lights. They grew up with just candles—the families who could afford candles—and they just seem to be able to see in the dark."

"I know. They promised to notice the next time one goes out. They're going to make a project of it."

"Do you think they will?"

"No, I don't think so."

"I would be happy to replace that lightbulb. Shall I do it right now, so we can think about something else?"

"No, there is no bulb. They have a plan for getting one tomorrow. They are getting the money from Honoline and are going to buy it. They got up on a ladder today and looked carefully. John or someone made a sketch of it. They'll take care of it."

Changing a lightbulb was one thing, but changing work culture was altogether different. We believed that tips should be divided up based on a point system—the better you performed, the more points you'd have and the higher percentage of tips you'd receive. We hoped that this would inspire learning and some constructive competition. The opposite occurred—the staff revolted. "We want to all be treated the same," they explained to us. Alissa and I shared one of our "we're not in the US anymore" moments when we heard that. It simply didn't make sense that even the hardest workers wouldn't want commensurate reward for their efforts.

The more complicated things were even harder to understand. Alissa would say that she sometimes felt as though she were in a city where she had to push each and every car down the road, one at a time. Nothing moved by itself. Everything needed precise orders.

We tried our best to concentrate on our dinner when it arrived, which was excellent. When Heaven was busiest, the kitchen and service were at their best. When slow, everyone shut down. This was a good night.

I had a starter as my main: chicken *boulettes* in a spicy peanut sauce. *Boulettes,* whether beef or chicken, were an early cornerstone of our starters menu. We wanted them to be a bit Asian, so Joshua had incorporated fresh ginger into the recipe.

Alissa ordered a dish that I'd been working on myself: honey-cumin pan-fried tilapia in a chapatti with coleslaw, pineapple chutney, and chipotle mayonnaise. She loved it but was distracted. There are always things she sees. She will notice my empty water glass; even if I do not want any more water, it's the point of it. Our waiter that night was a young woman who was trying very hard. Seeing as two parties of sixteen and twenty had just walked in without reservations, I moved my empty water glass behind the wine bottle so Alissa would not see it and would just enjoy her dinner.

"I still see it, you know," she said.

When the young waiter returned to see if everything was good, Alissa gently reminded her about the water. Keep the water glasses filled. Yes, of course. Even so, the water may not come for a long time, as if there might be a lengthy meeting by the bar about the empty water glass. Such things were a constant problem. The little cars had to be pushed each time.

I expect that if I had to serve food in the White House, I would get everything wrong for a long time. Indeed, Alissa still mocks my inability to consistently place silverware in its proper place on a table setting. But I am usually the bad cop when something difficult has to be said. I don't mind it, because I want to be able to recommend any of our staff to the best hotels and restaurants in Rwanda when they leave us.

Solange was close to that, already. She could work in fine restaurants, wherever French or Kinyarwanda might be spoken—a career that would guarantee her a good life.

Solange will often come out and sit with us before we go home. "And how are you, chef?" she will say to me. "How are your villages?" In this way, I am reminded that learning new things is very hard, and I should have some compassion. She knows very well how things are going in Mayange since it is not that far from where she grew up.

Maybe Solange would have prospered without Heaven, but probably not. People need opportunities, no matter how strong they are. Most of our cooks and servers, when they were first hired, could not pay for their most basic needs. Now they pay for their own health care, food, rent for their families, education for themselves and their siblings. Almost all are getting educations now. Four of the five servers, as we looked around, were already in university. This was worth something.

Look at Solange! She first arrived at Heaven in modest clothing to take the lowest position on staff, and now arrives in bright styles and dark glasses, perched on the back of a moto-taxi like Audrey Hepburn on a Vespa.

Yes we are colonists of a kind, bringing something new. It's a kind of hopeful and joyful living that Africa may have had before the days of colonization, but maybe not even then. At its best, it is a chance for life to be enjoyed in new and lovelier ways. We are missionaries of that. We are not shy about it. Everyone should get a great education. Everyone should be healthy. Everyone should be able to help the ones they love. Everyone should get to see something of this beautiful world, too, because life is too short, isn't it?

CHAPTER 35

—ᴗᴗ—

Solange's Africa

You cannot truly understand Africa until you have African friends and you know a great deal about them. You can perhaps picture Solange arriving for work, then tasting a new cook's sauce, then tossing her bag down in her little office surrounded by refrigerators and piled with recipes and notes and receipts. She doesn't sit there long, but long enough to think of how to make this evening's meal something people will think is amazing. Then she will enter the kitchen again and signal with her hands for people to gather around.

After her motivational huddle, she will work with the newest cook. I watched this, as I had many times before, through the breezeway that connects the kitchen to the bar and dining deck as I inventoried the bottles behind the bar.

"Taste it yourself," she told the new prep cook.

It was a beef mustard sauce that Solange loves and that is a new taste for most young Rwandans.

"It's good?"

The young cook's eyes popped. "It's strange!"

"Strange good, or strange bad?"

"It's strange good. Very different. It could be hotter."

"Don't make it too hot, or the *abazungu* can't eat it."

Solange was working hard to keep Joshua's culinary memory alive, and she had learned from the newer chefs who had come and gone since Joshua—it's hard to keep great chefs for long in this part of the world.

"This is good, but you still have something wrong," she was saying in French and Kinyarwanda, mixing vocabularies. "This needs cilantro, remember? *Vous souvenez?* It is no good without cilantro. Cilantro is everything for this sauce," she said. "Not the parsley. Taste the difference, you'll understand. The cilantro is like whisky; the parsley is only soda pop. It needs the stronger taste, because the other tastes in the sauce are also very strong. And not too much; you want them to balance. Don't use the parsley unless you don't have cilantro; then it's OK, but use more."

"I'm sorry, Solange—*je m'excuse*. I'll remember next time."

The apologetic young cook might or might not get it right the next time, as it is hard to learn about new foods and to remember thousands of things, especially if you can't read recipes or labels in French and English yet. Anyone would have a hard time of it, cooking foreign foods for foreign tastes and in a foreign language, and with an uncertain supply of ingredients.

The new cooks try very hard to learn the tastes of the customers who stream into Heaven each evening, including the professional class of Africans who own businesses or work for the government or are doctors or professors, the grandchildren of European colonists, the young Western expats who work for charities and generous corporations, the rich business visitors, and the tourists who are on their way to see the gorillas or on their way back.

The futures of the young cooks and their families depend on their jobs, so they try to please Solange and the chef by getting it right for the *abazungu*. She will remind them again and again, whenever they make mistakes. They will say "*Yego, yego*—yes, yes, I know," but they will get it wrong yet again and feel bad to have let her down. But Solange, who has many brothers and sisters, has learned to be patient.

She is not married, except to her dreams. She is not tall, but she looks tall, as she is thin and walks with dignity. Here is what seems to motivate her: One of her sisters, three years older, became pregnant at thirteen and is now condemned to poverty in her parents' fields. Solange brings her new beads and new clothing from time to time. Working in the fields, under the sun, wears a person out and ages them rapidly. Marriage at an early age is a kind of human sacrifice made to continue the race, where one's youth is given up forever, but the sacrifice is faster in poorer places. Seeing her sister's situation has been enough to put Solange off men until she can secure her success, which, to her, is a university degree in business management. She saves much of her earnings at Heaven for her tuition. In fact, she had already begun her first classes at the Université Libre de Kigali when Joshua returned to Spain. She was not going to let herself be discouraged by the loss of her great mentor.

Her tuition is about $700 per year, which is a small fortune here, but she is also putting some of her siblings through high school. That is the way it works for the lucky ones in Rwanda— your siblings will help you if they can. Perhaps they will interrupt their own studies to work in the fields so you can go another year, and then you will return the favor. Most young people are excited to get to a university if they possibly can.

This drive for achievement is tough in Rwanda—it struggles against a cultural inclination to blend into the crowd, and it can be hard to negotiate those opposing forces. The answer, for Rwanda anyway, must be the rise of the idea that the whole crowd is going to get educated and become prosperous. Then the crowd instinct will not conflict with the individual desire to excel. For example, when there is suddenly a big crowd of a hundred or more customers at Heaven, when everyone on staff must be at their best and remember everything, a miracle somehow happens. They move like dancers all night. They sometimes congratulate and thank Solange at the end of the evening: "Look at what we did, Solange!" Then they say to each other, "We were all professionals tonight!" It is always that they *all* were great, or *all* were not, as individual achievement or blame is an uncomfortable concept in Rwanda. The group, in such places, is always the safer place to be, and the dark middle of the group is safest yet. To stand out as leader or straggler is to be dangerously exposed. They have all seen that, and they know the danger of being the "other." They have many cousins or siblings or parents who are now but bones under a road somewhere or in the remarkable vaults.

Solange, however, never seems afraid to stand out. She was somehow born with that courage.

Now with a head chef du jour, we continue to recruit expat chefs to lead and train the kitchen, while Solange oversees the busy kitchen with cool and confident detachment. People are chopping, whipping, slicing. Things are boiling and baking. The great gas range and oven that was made from scrap iron is blazing and smoking. The heavy gas cylinders that fire it up are lugged in by laughing young cooks who are too small for the job, but they manage. There is no dolly to carry the cylinders, and no thought of one, as if wheels have not yet been invented, except for motos.

Water in the city is sometimes erratic, so there is a big storage tank above the restaurant and a special purification system to make it doubly safe for tourist sensibilities. There is no generator for when the lights go out, as people are comfortable with candles, the gas is enough for cooking the food, and all the chopping and stirring is done by hand. Doing all this without lights is no problem for young people who were raised by candlelight.

They listen to Solange most closely because she was raised in the same hills and fields as they. A few hours south of this restaurant, her parents and some of her siblings still scratch out a bare living in a small field. They are in a rural area in Butare. One of her siblings died at age six, and of the eight remaining children, only two have jobs: Solange, who is twenty-four, and her older sister, a married teacher, who helped put Solange through high school and gave her a room in the city. On her days off, Solange studies. She visits her brother and sister in town. She and her sister pay the school fees and expenses for the younger ones now. But she lives modestly in a rented room near Heaven that features electricity and water. She eats only once a day, which is the free staff meal at Heaven. In this way she saves every bit of money she can. Her brother, twenty-nine, lives in Kigali, too. He is married with a child but has no job, so she helps him. He did not go to high school at all, but may find his way back to school someday.

It is easier to see how to help developing nations when you understand this kind of striving and family cooperation. Very little from the outside is needed — beyond some decent jobs and good and affordable schools and universities.

"Not everything needs to be spicy," Solange told the new cooks as they gathered around her one afternoon when I was watching through the breezeway. She knows that cooks must learn to love the foods they prepare, or they will never get the flavors right, so she educates their palates as well as their minds. Today, it is a sauce for meats, tomorrow it is tilapia with mushroom sauce and cassava chimichurri—familiar, yet newly flavored, beautifully presented. At home in the villages, food will be in one small bowl per person, eaten quietly in a dark room. But this idea of food as a celebration, as a sensual delight, is very new.

In countries where your neighbor may be starving, food is eaten privately, ritualistically, and almost shamefully. So, something very new about food must be learned: that eating is nothing to be ashamed of, that making it beautiful and delicious is not some perverse sin, some gluttony, some cruel exhibition of wealth, but rather one of the great joys of life.

The food Solange prepares at Heaven includes meats and spices that were unknown in her household growing up. In that small mud home, all her sisters shared one room and all her brothers shared another, and her parents had the luxury of their own room. They ate what the land provided around their house. That was mostly cassava, which can be pounded into flour for baking or cut into chunks for cooking like potato or mashed into a porridge like a tapioca—indeed tapioca is made from cassava root and was often served with greens like kale or the cassava leaf itself. She also ate *patate,* which is the name for sweet potatoes, and beans. Growing up, she truly loved rice, especially with the sauces her mother would make for it, but they didn't grow rice, so it was usually beyond their means. Meat was reserved for one Sunday per month.

Her father attended school to the sixth grade; her mother only to the fourth. Their families had no money for them to continue, so their lives were set as poor farmers. But they had dreams for their children.

Solange's maternal grandparents and all the family on that side, also from the Lake Kivu area, were killed in 1959 when the genocide actually began. But Solange's grandfather on her father's side, also Tutsi, wisely moved his family where they were not known and somehow changed their legal identity to Hutu.

Solange was six when the worst of the killing began in 1994. Soldiers came to their door and knocked hard. They entered and took their food and looked at them with bloodshot eyes, but they did not drag them outside and kill them because their papers said Hutu, and their looks were mixed enough that they could get by. Some Tutsi are very tall and narrow of face, and such people did not survive by changing their papers. They were the "tall trees" that the Hutu were instructed to cut down. But it is very important to remember that the people did not even think of themselves as either Hutu or Tutsi until the Belgian colonists made them register as one thing or another, after which the Belgians abused the Hutu and elevated the Tutsi— divide and conquer. When the Belgians left in 1959, the retributions began. The Hutu had the numbers and the army to eliminate the Tutsi, who had been put over them and who sometimes had the better houses and farms, which now could be legally taken if there were no members of a family, young or old, left to claim it. So that work began.

With each passing year, the genocide is moving down the road from daily topic to history. Few speak of it much, except in the still remarkably heavy days of remembrance set aside each April.

All of Solange's younger siblings—three sisters and a brother—are in secondary school now, and the family looks only forward. As when Solange lived there, the family home has no running water, but there is a public water station nearby and it is easy enough to fetch water in the big yellow plastic jerry cans and make a shower in back of the house. There is now a lightbulb in each bedroom to help the children read and do their homework in the evenings. The electricity for the home's three bulbs costs a dollar a month, which is a big expense, but it is a good investment in their children's education.

When Solange was a young student, encouraged by her sister the teacher—who paid for her secondary school after her parents paid for her elementary years—she studied by candle for her first three years, then moved to Kigali to be with her sister. There, she learned to cook. She prepared rice, haricots verts (thin French green beans), carrots, and, each Sunday, some meat. On very special occasions, such as a birthday, both with her sister in Kigali and sometimes—in better years—at home in Butare, they would eat roasted goat meat kabobs, called *nyama choma,* with fries. That food, and salads, remain Solange's favorite foods. When she has the unusual pleasure of dining out, she will order modestly: fried potatoes, cassava, and *petits pois*—peas. When she goes home for Christmas, it is as it has always been: a feast of meat and rice and beans and cassava and perhaps something sweet brought from Kigali, plus soda pop for each person—Africa's guilty pleasure. More food than needed will be prepared so that some can be taken to the church for the poorest of the village—those too injured in the genocide to do farming, or too old, with no surviving children to help them.

There are more dreams than ghosts in today's Rwanda. Solange has her own dream: She has worked at Heaven for a Michelin-rated chef, and she intends to do so again. She intends that chef to be herself. She has a more proximate dream, as well: to bring her parents and all her family to Heaven for a family meal. They have never had a meal in a real restaurant, ever.

CHAPTER 36

———

Listening to Donald

People will not starve this time," Donald told me as we walked down a dusty road between fields of not much maize. It was a morning not long after Thanksgiving at Heaven, and I was amusing Donald with my narrative of how we had raised the turkeys in our backyard. One of them had tried to attack Maya one day, so I decided that it would be the first to be slaughtered. In spite of her fear of the bird, then two-year-old Maya was concerned about any pain that it might feel. In an effort to kill the first turkey humanely, we put up a killing cone, which lets you do the job quickly. In a scene of gore, however, the cone had fallen to the ground with the turkey. It was a mess, and Donald couldn't believe we'd gone through all that. We continued talking as Op-ed drove us back to the field office.

"We have some community food set aside. They still have money from the last harvest, and they always have a little cassava root. With their money, they can buy a little meat for the stew. That will be all right," Donald said as we bounced on a very rutted road. Cassava was the "safety" crop. The plants were not doing well, because of the mosaic blight, but it would be enough when added to what they could buy with their savings.

I looked at Donald differently now. Over the past year or more, I had relied on international agricultural experts to tell us what to do. They were smart and caring, but they did not control the rain, and their experience was no substitute for Donald's keen local knowledge and instincts. The weather was changing faster than the experts' almanacs knew; what was happening in Mayange was starting to look like permanent climate change.

I had been giving Donald short shrift. He was the better expert, and I needed to see him as that. He knew these hills, and he sensed the weather's changing patterns. Most of all, he knew this region was not a place to hope for luck with the weather or with anything. When there is no good luck, you have to think smarter and work harder.

We drove a long while in silence, the tires spinning up dust. We passed an orphanage that I thought might be the one Pierantonio saved. That gave me—as his stories often give me—a little kick in the pants to think as quickly and smartly as possible, as he did in those days of minute-by-minute crisis. When Pierantonio returned to Rwanda during the height of the genocide, he came across an orphanage full of children who would surely soon be murdered. He instructed the priests to drive their vehicles around the inside perimeter of the fenced property almost continuously through the night, so that the genocidaires would see it as a place that was under some kind of official guard. He even hired local genocidaires to guard the gate, as the job would make them attack that place last, he figured. That gave him time to speed south to Burundi to find buses to evacuate the children. He discovered that the officer in charge of the Rwandan Army in that district had a wife who was suspected of being Tutsi, so he offered that family a place on the bus. That officer would stand face to face with other army troops as the buses were leaving the orphanage, packed with children stacked in layers. The officer would ask the troops in the way to please either shoot or to please let the buses go, and so they stood aside. Even then, Pierantonio stopped the vehicles, walked back, and gave the soldiers some money and thanked them. He knew he would meet some of them, maybe just one of them, again.

How can you drive through these hills and not be inspired by his story, and the stories of so many other brave heroes? Not only bravery, but resourcefulness—Pierantonio was trying to cross from Rwanda to Burundi at one point with a truck full of orphans and other Tutsi hidden even underneath the truck, clinging to the frame. At the last checkpoint, which was red with blood, some children started playing around the truck as the officials double-checked Pierantonio's papers. He knew the children would see the men clinging below, so he tossed some hard candy that was on the dashboard out to the children, but as far as he could toss it, which purchased the ten more seconds they needed to get the green light and move across the border.

So what would Pierantonio do? It is always a good question in places like this. He had always used the natural tendencies of the people, the long traditions, to make the right things happen: men love jobs; children love candy. He never went against such simple wisdoms. I imagined him in our vehicle. He would not ask me what to do about the drought; he would ask Donald, who had always lived here.

"So what do you think we should do?" I asked Donald. Those were the best words I have ever spoken in Africa. They are the words Africa needs to hear from us more often.

He smiled as we bounced along. "You really want to know what I think."

"I do." I can never say those words without turning my wedding ring.

"There is a trial farm where I know they are cultivating cassava plants that are resistant to the mosaic blight," he said. "It is a government operation. They have a field growing with it. Perhaps we should talk to them. Perhaps we could grow mostly disease-resistant cassava here instead of maize, because the cassava grows with so little water. Our farmers could process it and sell it throughout the region as their cash crop, and then they could buy the other foods they need with the cash," Donald said. "Also, up in Uganda, there are nurseries I know where they graft fruit trees that don't need much water, really. We could sell all our remaining sacks of the fertilizer for maize and buy some fruit trees for everyone."

"You have been thinking about this," I replied.

"Yes, but these would be large projects, and very expensive, I think."

He proposed that we pull out the sick cassava plants from the entire region and replace them with cuttings from the mosaic-resistant plants. The labor would be intensive but it would be consistent with what people had been doing for generations. It was a big idea, and very creative. Would the farmers do it? Probably they would, partly on faith, and partly because we had earned their trust by forgiving their loans.

So I told Donald we should talk to the Ministry of Agriculture people working on the mosaic-resistant cassava. We could see if we could get hundreds of thousands of clippings—or a million.

"Truly?" he said. He laughed. He couldn't believe I was interested—that I would take his opinion over the sacred gospels of foreign experts whose maize, as good as it was, required more rain than we seemed to have coming. He couldn't believe I would bet a fortune and my own reputation on his idea.

By then, Annette had taken a UN position in Kigali and I had brought in a new crew of senior managers for the project who weren't exactly working out. Thus, I had another thing to say to him that he would find equally surprising:

"You must have known that the new managers of the Millennium Village have been cutting some corners."

He nodded. It was now public knowledge that I had fired a few people. They had been using our team vehicles to travel into Kigali to impress and visit their girlfriends. More importantly, their duties were being neglected. Any corruption, any family favoritism, can quickly destroy a community's joyful sense of itself.

"Yes, it was well known when you took action," he finally said.

"Why didn't you tell me they were screwing up?"

He wagged his head. "I was sure you would see it for yourself," he replied. There is simply no way to overstate how Rwandans avoid being the bearers of bad news to a boss.

A Kigali newspaper reporter had come to me after the firing and threatened to write a story about the firings if I did not sponsor a big advertising section in his paper. I tossed him out. He ran his story, but it did no harm. It certainly made me think twice when I heard critiques of government not being fair to the local press and the government shouting back, "You don't understand, they're not professional." Not professional indeed. Back in that day, expert extortionists. Nevertheless, the whole episode was deeply disturbing and depressing to me. Alissa thought I was ready to throw in the towel. Maybe I would have, had it been just me. But there was much more — Alissa, Heaven, a baby in hand and one on the way, and Health Builders.

"If you were in charge of the Millennium Village, Donald, if you were the head guy, and if there were another problem like that with the staff, do you think you would come to me and tell me about it?"

"Yes, it would be my duty to do so, under those circumstances."

"Then I would like you to take over the management of the village," I said.

We were driving through a field of blighted cassava. The sun was nearing the end of its run for the day. Donald didn't reply.

"Will you do it?"

"Of course," he replied.

I was in the front seat with Op-ed, whose big smile I noticed. He liked what was happening. So did I. Later, when Donald was not in the vehicle and we were headed back to Kigali, Op-ed said that I would see the real Donald now. "You have been impressed already, but you should wait and see him soon. There is a saying." Of course there is.

"Send someone where he truly wishes to go, and you will see his best pace."

Our fourth rule — the wedding ring finger, remember — is "don't marry it." You can't have a sustainable program unless local people are running it and caring deeply about it. This was a Rule Four moment, as if I were preparing to leave, which I always am.

And how would they survive without my fund-raising? Well, I wasn't leaving yet, but in the meantime there were things that could be put in place to generate revenue that would eventually replace fund-raising. A community-owned plant to clean and process cassava for regional export could generate good income. I could help them get that started, in addition to some other enterprises, before I left.

I started batting around ideas about how to raise money to do that, but I was beat down a little by Mayange's bad luck and I didn't want to count my cassavas before they sprouted.

Donald's idea about the cassava and the fruit trees? Within two years, the cassava crop was generating huge surpluses. The bumper crops in Mayange came at a time when drought hit hard in Burundi, just to the south. As the farmers of Mayange had a good deal more cassava than they needed for their own families, it was time to play out the original plan: export the excess crop.

The cassava cooperative, formed with our encouragement a little over a year before, had grown to four hundred farmers and now loaded up one hundred bicycles with cassava roots in great bundles and began their first foray into the export business. They would create, essentially, a bicycle conveyor belt to move the crop the two-hour ride south to the Burundi border.

Bicycles with a little flat seat on the back are the taxicabs of rural Rwanda. Early on, as I mentioned, we had asked the minister of infrastructure if planned road improvements in the area might be speeded up, as good roads were an important way to improve health delivery and commerce. It was done almost immediately. With the pavement came a new way to make a living: borrow money from everyone in your family, buy a bicycle, add a seat on the back at the blacksmith shop, and go into business as a taxi. The taxi drivers developed incredibly strong legs hauling people up and down the hills. These young men became the heroes of the Mayange international export caravan.

Donald and Jeannette and the team watched with optimistic fascination as the huge bundles were tied to the bicycles. We were bystanders now, as the community had come together and was running the show. Each bike was loaded with about two hundred pounds of dried cassava roots. Tires were checked and water bottles were tied to handlebars. Wives and children came out to watch the beginning of this historic new chapter. This would now be an export farming area, where, before, only banana moonshine had brought in a few extra Rwandan francs for the community.

The weather was perfect now for the bicycles. For once, the lack of rain was a blessing, as rain would only make the cassava loads heavier.

Off they went. They returned empty, and went off again with new loads, twice a day for nearly six weeks. No one made a fortune, but they made money. Each bicycle load was worth about forty dollars at the Burundi border. That added up. A farm family might make nearly $800, when the average income per person was, when we first got there, scarcely measurable and far below the global extreme poverty line of a dollar a day. But now, you could send a kid to school and fix up your house. You could install lightbulbs for school studies. You could have the best health care available this side of Kigali's two big hospitals. You could buy a cow, a pig, a goat, and put in a vegetable garden. I spoke with Felicien, one of our model farmers, about his new dreams: "Josh, when you first arrived I dreamed of having enough food for my family. Now I'm dreaming of purchasing a motorcycle—you can have a ride on it next year." Of course, the bike owners did well too, serving as middlemen and learning about business.

Jacqueline, who by now was really one of the leading voices of Mayange, put it best at the weekly farmers' meeting for her village. "Just a couple of years ago, all the bigwigs in Kigali thought that we were poor farmers who would always need food aid; now we are food exporters!" Everyone cheered. Many of these farmers and their families had little interest in life in the years after the genocide. They had suffered unimaginable horrors and losses. They had malaria epidemics that killed the young and the old. Before AIDS medications were available in the health center, people were dying of it. They were malnourished and clinically depressed. But now, all the health numbers were moving rapidly in the right direction. And it was in the middle of a drought—a drought that Donald's wisdom had rendered irrelevant.

The next step, in 2010, was for the cooperative to process excess cassava root into flour, which was a separate and profitable market.

The co-op borrowed $70,000 from our Millennium Village Project account for the machinery, and they began the management of the operation themselves. It was not as precisely managed as we might have liked, but it was their project, and that was far more important than perfection. It will go on and on, long after we've gone. The milling process requires a great deal of hand labor to peel and wash the roots, soak out the natural cyanide, press out the water, and then dry and mill it into a white flour. Some cassava tastes very bitter, in part because of residual cyanide left by improper processing, but Mayange's, handled so carefully, came out tasting almost sweet. It immediately became the favorite local product, replacing the imported brands and keeping money in the villages— and it sold for a premium over the other, low-quality flour. A thousand pounds of roots generated a bit over three hundred pounds of high-quality flour, so you see how much had to be cleaned away. Here was a high-quality product for local consumption and export. It also found a home in Heaven's kitchen.

For the farmers, it was easy to deliver big loads, instead of selling the roots in many different markets, some quite distant. For young people, the seasonal jobs at the flour mill offered a way to earn money for school and for better clothes—real clothes, and not rags. The community was looking good.

Other projects were also afoot. We introduced beekeeping, as the cassava plants and wild plants provide plentiful flowers. We loaned money for the wood to make hundreds of beehives, and trained the farmers to make them. They were an immediate success, and of course more bees means more pollination of the crops and more pollination means more productivity. Our investment of $2,700 for the bee program loan would generate tremendous new wealth in the community.

Jeannette wanted to build on local knowledge to make high-quality baskets. She put together five weaving groups and hired those who had trained top exporters to come to Mayange and provide lessons. During a visit to the women in Mbyo one day, I saw an elderly woman making what was, frankly, a horrible basket. I asked Jeannette what the co-op was going to do about it—she sheepishly said that the women would work it out. What they hadn't worked out was what to do with some of the men who had started showing up. "A man weaving a basket?!" they exclaimed. But indeed, when there's a job that creates income, even those sexist walls come down.

The Mbyo co-op named itself Imirasire—"lightening" or "luminosity"—and elected Jeanne d'Arc, a single mom without electricity or a concrete floor, to run it. After extensive training and investment, woven baskets and beautiful scarves were made and sent to the tourist market in Kigali. If you dine in Heaven, the woven placemats, coasters, and menu holders you use are their work.

As women and older people—Hutu and Tutsi alike—sat together to weave these products, old angers and severe depressions seemed to melt away. We all have a circle of family and acquaintances beyond which our empathy begins to break down. This kind of visiting while weaving widened those circles dramatically. They made massive baskets for Tommy Hilfiger stores around the globe. They helped produce the largest delivery of African products—handwoven scarves—ever sent to Anthropologie. To say that each scarf had an aspect of love and forgiveness included would not be an exaggeration, and one can only hope they brought good luck and good feelings to those who wore them.

Beyond reconciliation, there was a tangible rise in community spirit. I had been bringing visitors to see what was going on in Mayange, and it was not long before a little committee from the villages asked me if they might take over the tours and charge a little money for them. The committee formed a cooperative and set out hard rules for visitors, including: don't give out money or food to the kids or anyone who asked. That sort of thing is very damaging to the longer-term self-respect of the people and is damaging to the rise of community spirit, which requires pride. Ironically, one visitor went home and complained in a blog that the tour guides were acting like "don't feed the animals" zookeepers, but she simply didn't get the critical role of community pride and ownership. The tourism co-op tried to explain that more carefully to future visitors, who seemed to understand.

It was commonly said that the survivors of Mayange just wanted to die in the years after the genocide, and in the years of drought that followed. You could not say that now. The craft project would have been worth doing even if it didn't increase the prosperity of the families, but it did that, too, creating fifty jobs in each of the five villages of Mayange.

Crafts are not an easy business. When you deal with international buyers, the products you deliver must look like the products they ordered and perhaps they even advertised in their catalogs. Precision is not a usual thing in developing lands, so it is a good exercise in learning new ways, and it can carry over usefully to other parts of life. Anthropologie, in fact, sends people around developing country workshops to make sure the quality is right and the workers are indeed receiving the maximum benefit from their labors. It is typical for a woman craft worker to earn in four months what would take a year of backbreaking labor in someone else's fields. Now, in turn, that woman could afford to hire others, poorer than herself, to work in her fields. It's like Reaganomics' trickle-down theory in reality.

All these new things were adding up to real security for the people of Mayange. Security is the big word in the developing world. Ask someone from Darfur or Congo or Afghanistan or Guatemala or a thousand other places about the overriding necessity of their lives, and they will say it: *sécurité, Sicherheit, seguridad, usalama,* or here: *umutekano!*

They mean security from the cruelties of war and genocide, and they mean knowing they can feed their children not only tonight, but next month. For that reason, the villages began to store surplus beans and maize in great plastic cocoons provided by the Ministry of Agriculture. Just the sight of the great bags filling up—the biggest are big enough to park a truck inside and can hold over one hundred tons—was a joyful thing for everyone. With security, you could plan ahead. You could think about your children's education.

Jeanne d'Arc, the head of the Imirasire co-op, with the assurance of a regular income, starting sending her son, Jean de Dieu, to a good private high school. He went on to get a full scholarship to attend the Kigali Institute of Science and Technology. After he graduated, he became a top teacher at the International School of Kigali, where he earned enough to build his mother one of the biggest and nicest homes in Mayange.

The government effort was and remains a great force; it involved the crackdown on hate speech, the neighborhood justice courts where people could work out the truths of what had happened, the annual week of remembrance, and the last Saturday of each month, when people work together on community projects, regardless of ethnic identities. Already, the younger people, if you ask them if they are Hutu or Tutsi, will look at you sternly and answer, "Rwandan!" That is a remarkably important development. In the sharp-tooled kitchen of Heaven and on the machete fields of Mayange, the teams we assembled were people who had once identified themselves as Hutu or Tutsi.

With the co-ops now managing themselves—cassava, honey, crafts, and more—it was time for us to take a breath and step back and appreciate the changes that had swept over the area.

I brought stories home to Alissa—sometimes I was giddy with delight at what had happened that day. Sometimes I could not relate a particular story from the day without getting a little emotional. She was weathering her own difficulties with the restaurant, but she was happy for all of it.

There was also a bittersweet change in the atmosphere: Ranu was gone, back in the States to finish medical school. My time was now focused on daily improvement of the health clinic, expansion to a dozen more clinics in the district, and construction of four new 10,000-square-foot health centers where there were none. There was still a great deal to do, but the initial excitement had perhaps worn off, as the first days are always horribly scary and magically wonderful, and your heart is always racing. Mosquito netting was now over every bed. New malaria infections were down to a fraction of two years ago. Healthy births were way up. The AIDS epidemic was under control, with everyone being put quickly on the life-saving medications. The roadside clinics where AIDS victims had been coming just to die—sometimes two to a small bed—were now antiretroviral treatment centers that had people back on their feet and back on the farm. This was everything a Millennium Village was supposed to be. The reason for the success, I strongly believe, was that, at every turn, we applied strict management standards and demanded measurable results in the enterprise areas we were still hatching constantly. The craft cooperatives, because they came out of our enterprise operations, had improved management practices, even though we no longer had a direct role. The team had taught proper bookkeeping, which was essential because when a basket sold, ninety percent of the income went to the responsible artisan.

Mayange was exploding with advances—in business, health,

and agriculture. It had been a bare desert only a few years before. At first, you could see for miles through the bare fields and bare hills, all brown and yellow. Now, you needed to be on a hilltop or on a good rise of the road to see over the greenery. It was not the triple-canopy jungle it had been generations earlier, but it was a garden spot. The new cassava plants were a marvel. The old ones, a real danger to the new plants, were still being pulled out constantly, though not as energetically as Donald and I insisted should be done. Still, the imperfection was fine. If the old mosaic returned, areas could be stripped and replanted again. We knew—the farmers knew—how to do that. If it rained a lot, that was great. If it rained only a little, that was fine, too.

There was an ironic danger in our success in Mayange, particularly in the health center. We risked having the go-to spot for health in the region by delivering the health care that everyone needed. Blaise and I had a solution: we would use Health Builders to ensure that the same level of care would be available in every one of the district health facilities.

In addition to that work, I was thinking that there must be other low-water crops that could bring more wealth into the villages. By chance I met an organic plant specialist who visited the Mayange site. We walked up and down the valleys and hills, and he let the sandy soil run through his fingers. I was waiting for him to pronounce it the worst place to do anything, but he had something else in mind. "Sandy, unfertile soil, not much rain, harsh conditions—seems perfect for pomegranate trees." Then, when I saw the high price of pomegranates in Kigali markets, I thought this might be a good possibility, as there would be both a local and export market.

Donald wasn't so sure. It would be very new. We would be

asking farmers to invest their labor and some of their land in a crop they wouldn't see come to market for three or more years. And it was an unknown fruit to most of them. Why would you raise something you had never eaten or even heard of? It was some *umuzungu* fruit. People in Kigali ate it, but not country folk.

"Yes, but after you plant them, you just have to prune the trees once a year, and not during cassava harvest season. The labor component is almost nil. You pick the fruit and send it to market. No heavy cutting of roots or cleaning of product or replanting, and the trees will produce for twenty years or more."

I showed Donald the numbers. At the time, a single pomegranate could bring as much at market as ten pounds of cassava root.

He stared at my calculations: ten thousand trees, with one hundred fruit per tree (and that was just in year 3 or 4). He seemed slightly convinced. Not entirely. Then my friend the agronomist smuggled in a few pieces of fruit for the community to see and taste; they were sold on the idea.

I got in touch with POM Wonderful and visited their farm in Southern California, which was minting money in pomegranates, almonds, and pistachios. I got six hundred plants donated, moved them out to Mayange, and set up a nursery where I could keep an eye on them and where the constant stream of visitors could get used to them. The young trees grew lush and tall. This would be good. Donald worked with the community to get thirty farmers to each turn over a one-hectare piece of land to form a massive pomegranate cooperative. The notion was so exciting that it attracted investment from the US African Development Foundation.

One of my colleagues—who would later become the president of the World Bank—has quipped for years that there should be a journal of development failures, which are more instructive than success stories. The pomegranate experience would be one such story. The consultants hired by the US African Development Foundation in Kigali got deeply engaged with the pomegranate co-op while Alissa and I were in the states having our second child, baby Elodie. The lead consultant thought that the co-op workers should be paid for preparing the land, multiplying the stock, and overseeing the office. Instantly, the US funds became the harvest and the co-op's president took control of all financial transactions. Those who were not getting paid refused to help plant or prune. It became about the job and the money in hand, not about the future of the community. The co-op's president picked favorites, set up a phony procurement group, and started bleeding the funds. Anger doomed the project, and it was mostly abandoned, with about two hectares of perfectly planted trees becoming unproductive shrubs.

I took cuttings of each of the different varieties and asked my neighbor, Olivier, if he would plant them up on his small farm on Mount Kigali. He agreed. He now tends to them, and they flourish there and wait for a better day in Mayange, when the anger has been forgotten and the trees can return.

The lesson is this: Just like giving out money or giving away food without expecting something in return, the practice of hiring some people but not all people destroys the sense of community that real progress always, always requires. It is aid colonialism. This is the reason we insist on our sustainability rule, the wedding ring finger rule: a program cannot be too wedded to your brief stay; you must not start something that will go away when you go away, because it will divide the community, now or later, just as when the colonial powers divided the people into haves and have nots, and then left to let anger rise into whirlwinds. Yes, we paid farmers to learn about terracing and row planting, but we paid all who would come. There was no inside deal, no elite group established. There simply cannot be. They have been down that road before, and the world knows where it leads.

CHAPTER 37

—⁓—

A Mile Up

It is the elevation of Rwanda that makes it so lovely, that brings cool air into what would otherwise be a steamy, insufferable land. It is comfortable up here.

Alissa grew up in a home with a great view. And then she had this place called Heaven, overlooking Eden here. There was also another kind of elevation for me, which was the old kind that kept causing problems for me. It was the elevation of consulting work, which finally caught up with me so that I chucked it all and headed to Paris. It was the elevation of dealing with international experts when the best mind was Donald, already at my side. The more time that passed, I seemed to float up higher and higher until some moment when I would have to make that adjustment, or it would be made for me. While normally the adjustments came from circumstances right in front of my face, my next one would come in through an unlikely channel: Twitter.

The message read:

@Joshruxin: looking for urgent advice on moving badly burned girl Agnes from Heal Africa in Goma to hospital in Boston

Goma is the town on the north shore of Lake Kivu. It straddles the border between Rwanda and Congo and has been the site of recent rebel fights, but this young Agnes was not a casualty of war.

The message came from Children of Fire, a South African group committed to helping burn victims. While proximity to unprotected cooking areas accounts for most pediatric burns, witchcraft and ancient beliefs persist as elders attempt to drive evil spirits out of children. Baby Agnes, just ten months old, had been severely burned, under circumstances the family would not clarify to anyone's satisfaction.

Children of Fire didn't know anyone else in the area who might help get her to the States, where she might be saved, and I didn't know anyone else, either.

You have a choice, of course, when you get a message like that. I am very busy here, after all, and am almost daily getting requests from friends and strangers alike. It really would be OK to respond in a case like this, "Sorry, don't know of any. Try Red Cross," even if you suspect they cannot help in time. There is so much need that you can't let yourself drown in it. Maybe it was because I had been operating too high up lately, too distant from the on-the-ground realities, that I found myself unable to respond that way.

Two days later, Op-Ed shuttled Mitta Lebaka to our house from the airport. Mitta was a twenty-two-year-old burn survivor herself, sent by Children of Fire to solve the problem. Mitta had never been out of South Africa before, but she exuded worldly confidence and a sense of her mission—she reminded me of Ranu.

Alissa and I packed sandwiches for her and sent her toward Goma with Op-ed as her driver.

Hours later, Mitta called me, shaken, from Goma. The family was refusing to allow Agnes to go with her. They feared that this was an elaborate kidnapping. The grandmother, in particular, was extremely resistant. Six hours of discussions ensued, mostly over the phone with the mother, Mitta, Children of Fire, and me. Eventually, Mitta and Agnes were on the road to Kigali with the baby's mother, Princesse.

I was hoping for an immediate flight out to Boston's Shriners Hospital, one of the best places in the world for burn treatment and reconstruction, but knew the visa would take time. I didn't want the child to be exposed to the abundance of pathogens one finds in hospitals.

"Just bring her straight to Heaven's guest house," I told Op-ed. Mitta agreed.

We prepared one of the bedrooms in the old house on the property. I sent Apollo out on an emergency shopping run for sterile gauze bandages, diapers, baby clothes, formula, bottles, and toys—I had connected with an American doctor at the HEAL Africa hospital to better understand what we would need.

"Are you sure we want to do this?" Alissa asked.

I don't know why I insisted, but I did. Who knows what unresolved issues we have in our heads? If I could get her right on a plane, this really was the best idea. I had doctor friends who could help here, and they would give the child more attention than the overworked doctors at the hospital in Kigali. Our pediatrician, Dr. Philippe, confirmed the course of action.

Baby Agnes arrived. She did not appear to be in pain, which was strange as she was horribly burned. She was a little mummy in dirty bandages playing with toys donated by Maya from Elodie's collection. It took us two hours to carefully remove the bandages so they could be replaced with clean gauze. I ended up doing some of it; I'm still not sure how that happened, but her plight had somehow become something very personal to me. Maybe it was my need to help people up close that was again making an adjustment away from my higher perch. Maybe it was a chance to fix something I hadn't been able to fix before. I'm not sure.

I shouted at the office manager about the darkness of the bedroom. A lightbulb was burned out. I had him bring in more lamps. The bandages had become virtually part of her face, so Mitta and I applied solution to loosen them slowly.

The Heaven staff peeked in during the process to see what was going on. Several scrubbed up and helped, but most left the room and burst into tears—I could hear that outside the house. It was too hard for Alissa, and she couldn't bear to be in the room.

As we unwrapped Agnes's bandages, the severity of her situation was revealed: She had lost an arm, both her ears, her nose, probably the use of her eyes, and most of her face. She was a pink thing with not much besides a miraculous smile and the occasional giggle. She could eat, too. She was not giving up on a life.

The official family story was that a candle fell on a mattress. The grandmother was a self-trained mystical preacher. People like that have been accused of dousing children in boiling oil to cleanse them of bad spirits, usually with a fatal ending.

I had apprised the US embassy of the situation. They were on it, cutting every scrap of red tape that stood in the way. A call from Senator John Kerry's office followed: "The senator wants to assure you all that Agnes will be whisked through immigration and security on arrival in Boston with Mitta and we'll deliver her to the hospital." This is exactly our America, isn't it?

Princesse, Agnes's mother, dug into a Heaven burger with fries. She was very, very grateful. The flight was coming together.

The next morning, Agnes's grandmother and uncle appeared at Heaven. Mitta and I were nervous that they might try to take Agnes back to Goma, but Heaven's food and drink seemed to keep everyone calm and happy. It always helps to have a bar. We all went to the airport and saw Mitta and Agnes through customs. They were gone.

Thirty-six hours later, Mitta sent photos from Shriners, where the doctors and nurses were about to start treatment, including music therapy. All was going well. I started hatching a plan for keeping Agnes and her mother in Kigali when they returned.

I gave Mitta's daily updates to Princesse but also began the harder work of getting Princesse to Boston, as we knew the surgeries would take time—several months at least.

Then came the call from Mitta. She tried to assemble the words as best she could. "She's gone Josh. Sepsis post-op."

We both cried, then Mitta asked if I could call the family.

An hour after that horrible call, the doctor at Shriners called. "The family wants to see the body. They think she was just taken to Kigali and her organs were harvested there."

You have to deal with people's fears, or they will cause more problems. If we let this fear stand, it would be impossible for the burn volunteers to ever get another child out of the region.

It took my urgent arguments before Children of Fire's

director would agree to the cost of a little casket and the expense of the sad flight home. That expense would cost the ability to help another burn victim.

No one had ever seen such an ornate casket in Goma, but the funeral procession became a mob scene, with family members declaring their certainty that this was a Western conspiracy, that they had been wronged. Angry leaders within the crowd were preparing to storm the hospital after the burial ceremony, and some family members insisted that the casket be opened before it was lowered into the ground—they didn't believe Agnes was even inside.

What they found when they opened it, laid reverently on her little chest by the doctors and nurses of Shriners Hospital, were photos of all the loving nurses playing with her. There were pictures of her in music therapy, and a CD of the songs that she had responded to. On one of the photos, a nurse had written: "Agnes loved music." A silence passed over the family as they realized that these health workers really had known Agnes. Baby Agnes was put to rest under the earth, and everyone returned home.

—⊙—

"You should not have done it," one of the staff people at our office told me as we drove a long way out to a remote health center we were starting to help with our management methods. "The child was going to die, Josh. It is a mistake to get involved with issues like that." He was referring to the black magic fringes of life here.

"I know," I replied, "but you have to let me be a crazy American sometimes."

He laughed. "I suppose so."

I chuckled back, but it was the most heartbreaking moment I could remember since...perhaps since we came back to Africa without our own first child.

Privately, on a long road, I shared with Op-ed my impression that some people were being cold about the baby. I was in the backseat with papers laid out. He looked at me in the rear view mirror.

"If you live next to the cemetery you cannot cry for everyone," he said.

CHAPTER 38

The Eldest Daughter

Before we even moved here we had "adopted" the educational expenses of an orphan in Kenya—I mentioned Melsa earlier. Of course you never know what will happen when you do something like that. You see ads for adopt-a-child charities and wonder if it will really do something. Sometimes it does. We were dealing directly, which makes it easier to see what happens, but that is not always necessary.

We stayed in close touch with young Melsa. She soon was an engaging adult at our holiday tables. She was doing well in school and we were very proud of her.

In 1998, at the age of eleven, she had cared for her father; in 1999, at twelve, her mother; and in 2000, at thirteen, her baby sister. They all died of AIDS in her arms. She worried that she must have been infected, but she had never had the nerve to be tested. When she began spending time with us in Rwanda, where AIDS testing is very routine, she finally went to the clinic. She was OK. She almost couldn't believe it. It was a great relief to her, of course, and a surprise to us that she hadn't relieved herself of that worry years ago. Rwanda is quite different from most African countries in its routine AIDS testing, and the numbers here are therefore very good, by comparison. There may be reasons why we have better numbers here. Naturally, we like to think what we have done with the health clinics is a major factor. We appreciate the nuns in the Catholic health centers who, though they are prohibited from family planning activities, manage to let contraception distribution happen at little health posts just outside their gates. And there is the custom here of what is called drumming. Prior to the sex act here, it is expected that the man will do a little of what is called drumming to make sure the woman is excited and prepared for him. This helps assure not only pleasure for her, but less possibility of tissue harm, which would make disease transmission much easier. In fact, if a woman is not pleased in bed with her husband, that is grounds for divorce in Rwanda, and has always been so, I have been told.

One more story about AIDS before I tell you Melsa's second secret.

The first day I pulled up to the Soprano house with Ranu, who was proud to have found it, there was a young woman named Denyse standing by the gate. I learned that she had been standing there every day for the past two weeks, in anticipation of my arrival, or the arrival of someone like me. She had two kids and a faraway husband. She desperately needed a job to supplement her four-dollar weekly income, which came from washing the clothes of an expat.

Someone told her that some Americans were looking at the house; she didn't want to miss her chance. I asked her for character references, which she presented in writing the next day. We hired her.

When Alissa first arrived in Rwanda, she taught Denyse how to clean a bathroom, how to disconnect a clogged pipe, clean it out, and replace it. She quickly became the keeper of the house.

One morning we came downstairs to find Denyse in tears. Her husband was suddenly very ill and had been admitted to the hospital far away. I phoned the hospital director. "Josh, he's got end-stage AIDS. We could have saved him months ago, but not now."

Alissa and I broke the news to Denyse.

"He lied to me!" she said through sobs.

We asked Denyse if she wanted to be tested. She did. And she was infected. But in Rwanda the best medications are available, and they are free. We assured her she could lead a nearly normal life, and a cure will be found someday.

Then Alissa presented a terrifying notion: Denyse's children ought to be tested, too. The next Friday, Denyse arrived with her kids in their Easter best. Alissa took them all to the health center. The kids were fine. This news brought Denyse back to her old laughing self. She worked with us for seven years until she succumbed to illness.

———✦———

On to Melsa's other secret: It was something I discovered very late in her education.

She attended Strathmore College, Kenya's best accounting school. We paid the tuition. A year into her schooling there, I was in Nairobi and stopped by to check on her and to help her move into a decent apartment—her dorm was like a prison. She showed me her grades: straight A's. I told her how proud I was, and took her to a restaurant to celebrate with a pizza, her first ever.

She told me two things over that pizza: the first was her new idea for her life, and the second was her secret.

Her new idea was this: Despite her top grades, she didn't think being an accountant was what she wanted for her whole life. She said that when she was caring for her dying family, she wished she were a doctor so she could help them, as there was no doctor there. She had never seriously believed that she might be able to do that, but now, with her good grades, she thought perhaps she could do anything, even that. But could Alissa and I continue to help her? Would we be angry about the year of accounting school?

I said that she was our daughter and if medical school was her dream, then we would pay for it and very proudly and happily. She cried quietly into her napkin, getting tomato sauce on her nose.

"There is another thing," she said. I held my breath. I was so afraid of diseases, pregnancies, everything—Nairobi is a hard place.

"My eyes," she said as she made a gesture that said they were no good.

I held my hand out as far as I could get it from her. "How many fingers?"

"Three? Two, I think. I don't know."

From the restaurant we went to an ophthalmologist—an old German man who had settled in Kenya decades before. He cleaned the dot of sauce from her nose and examined her eyes. "So, vhat have you been doingk for eyevear?" he asked as he worked.

"Nothing—I didn't have money for glasses."

"Zen how do you read, child?"

She held up a pamphlet about six inches from her eyes. I could not imagine how she had not been hit by a car—Nairobi streets are like a mad computer game. I could not imagine how she did her schoolwork.

"Ve vill start light and over ze next nine months ve'll ease you through three prescriptions until you can zee."

She admitted that she had not properly seen a chalkboard since she was perhaps six.

You will never stop being amazed at how much misery comes to Africa for want of the cheapest thing. Glasses at an early age could have made her life so easy. A twenty-five-cent penicillin pill could have saved Samson, the young man we sent for two heart surgeries in South Africa and Israel, and avoided all that misery and cost.

Melsa finished up accounting school that year with flying colors, then went on to the University of Nairobi School of Medicine, where, of course, she did great. She's finishing up her internship in western Kenya now, and giving me weekly reports on the horrors she's seeing: like the woman waiting on a hard bench for fourteen hours after gynecological surgery without pain meds. It is all around her. She is on a mission.

She wrote most recently:

> We received a six-year-old boy from lower eastern Kenya who was weak, wasted, and had a distended abdomen. He had several episodes of nose bleeding. He was in need of emergency blood transfusion. I had to spend six hours in the blood transfusion unit to get the blood at the earliest opportunity. He was lucky I had finished my duties early. The boy was transfused in good time and was to be admitted thereafter but the mother could not raise the deposit needed prior to

admission. She did not have even the money to buy the boy some food. The doc on duty paid the amount and the boy was admitted. A diagnosis of visceral leishmaniasis was made, which had caused enlargement of the spleen and the liver. The hypersplenism was destroying his blood cells and that's the reason he was severely anemic. He had been receiving treatment for typhoid back home. It took two weeks for the boy to get to our hospital as the mother was trying to raise bus fare. The boy is the ninth in a family of ten. His father died five years ago. The mother washes clothes for people to earn a living. She's worried about her other children who have to take care of themselves while she's away. The woman is only thirty-four years old but looks fifty. The boy is doing well and might be going home any time now.

There are now a bunch of great programs for sponsoring African higher education (including Generation Rwanda) that are not scams, so there's little reason these days not to have a daughter like our Melsa.

CHAPTER 39

—∿—

In the Garden

We flew home to America for the delivery of our second child, Elodie, and again we came back with a caravan's worth of supplies for Heaven and our family. We have become good at such logistics, and Apollo and Op-Ed take such occurrences as routine. The baggage conveyor belt at the Kigali airport is now much improved and does not groan to see us come. I'm sure the government made the improvement without us entirely in mind, though we may have hastened things.

When we returned with Elodie Keza (Keza means beautiful in Kinyarwanda), we knew, as we always know, that there would be some picking up of pieces waiting for us at Heaven. In fact, it had gone south under the supervision of a professional expat team, so there was a customer base to rebuild again and a staff to reenergize. It has never been easy.

Elodie took to Africa like she was coming home. Maya was her guide and publicity agent and union representative, so it was now two of them making their demands that each day should be magical and loaded with adventure.

Life with our two girls was easier than we could have expected—it takes a village to raise a family, and that's exactly what we had: lots of caring and loving people like Joel and Denyse to help us on that journey. Where we had had to work hard to extract a smile or a giggle from Maya when she was a baby, Elodie was easy. We started to realize that our kids were bringing us incremental joy. Somewhere at the back of our minds, though, we wondered what it would be like to have a boy, and more than once we wondered whether that had been what we'd lost the first time around. Although Alissa treasured being in shape and was not a happy pregnant person, we went for a third baby, and it went easily for her, as did the delivery. The boy, Elias, came out smiling like Buddha and has been smiling ever since. He was a happy perfection we couldn't have imagined. He is happy to wake up with the birds and just listen. He waves as his sparkling sisters go off to school each morning—they have gone to old schools established by the Belgians and French in colonial times, and then moved to a Montessori school that seems to give them the kind of creative freedom American kids—or perhaps their parents—prefer. In any case, the schools are good here, it is safe, and the atmosphere for raising children is very conservative, very 1950s. The kids have good friends of every color and from all over the world.

I try to speak and read to the three of them only in French, while Alissa talks and reads to them in English. That is not appropriate in every instance, but it does give them both languages, which they will appreciate.

The doctors are wonderful, but you do worry that if something very serious happened, you would have to get your child at least to Nairobi, and that would take time. That is the big worry, really. There is no 911 to call, no paramedics in a fire station up the street.

Alissa and I are both public health trained, but that does

not mean we are doctors. As a result, we find ourselves a bit obsessive about planning. But I think, especially after our first loss, Alissa is the more careful one. Every trip back to the United States is an opportunity to bring back a little more insurance in the form of medical supplies.

It sometimes gets a little weird. We have CPR dummies to train everyone working in the house how to resuscitate a child or an adult. The dummies live not far from the epinephrine pens for severe allergic reactions. We have given out motorcycle helmets to everyone who works for us who might take a moto-taxi. Our medicine closet looks like a clinic: antibiotics, malaria test kits, allergic reaction syringes, painkillers, bandages, on and on.

Alissa winces when she sees other expats driving around with their kids literally hanging out of the windows.

The expat kids growing up here, including ours, seem very happy. It might be the last place you'd think would feel like a utopia, but it's just that.

We may not be here forever, but this will be a remarkable memory for our children. Beautiful, strange things will have shaped them, like our trips eastward into Tanzania where they can get out of their car seats and stand up through the open roofs of safari vehicles and see lions and giraffes and elephants and monkeys and scream with delight in two languages and feel at home. Heaven, of course, is currently their favorite destination, and now that we've got the best Sunday brunch in the city, it's our go-to place once weekly. I'm looking forward to the day when Maya is old enough to head out to Mayange and hang out with Donald and Jeannette and Jacqueline and pick some of the big, lush mangoes from trees we planted back in 2006.

CHAPTER 40

———

The Whole Operation

We've finally got a routine down. If it hasn't been a very long night at Heaven the evening before, we get up with the kids at dawn. Maya and Elodie still awaken with the birds at five thirty, but Elias waits until seven o'clock.

I go downstairs to make the coffee. I'm an experimenter, and lately I've been infusing our morning cup with Ugandan vanilla and fresh-ground cardamom. I head to our big coffee table in the living room, which is strewn with laptops and wires, and I read the news and emails from the States—it is an hour or two past midnight in New York when we are starting our morning.

Alissa joins me at the table and, on her laptop, starts going through the prior night's sales at Heaven. She wants to know if we made payroll and rent for the day; we usually do. She then looks at the requisition for supplies from the manager: ten kilos of avocados, twenty-five kilos of baking flour, six cans of cooking gas—a week's worth, five jerry cans of cooking oil—maybe two weeks' worth, twelve cases of South African wine—a big event has booked, bunches of cassava leaves for our chimichurri, a couple dozen violet artichokes from the Imbabazi orphanage, five kilos of Nile perch, three hundred rolls of toilet paper, two hundred organic eggs, and eight liters of fresh cream from Masaka Farms for our homemade ice cream.

Most of the items will come from the two big open-air farmers' markets in town, Kimisagara and Kimironko. Apollo will make the shopping trip after he drops the girls off at school. Alissa will stay with Elias and I will head for our office in town or out to the health centers.

Apollo rolls in at a quarter to eight. He looks over Alissa's shopping list and tells her how much money he will need, to the franc—he is an expert on market prices. She gives him the cash—everything is cash and everything must be obtained from the market and taken home in our vehicle, as there are no delivery trucks serving restaurants yet. We strap the girls into their car seats and kiss them goodbye.

After leaving the girls at school, Apollo will pull off the road across from one of the big markets. By his prior cell phone arrangement, two or three men will meet him at the road and follow him through the market, ferrying his rapid-fire purchases back to the big Land Cruiser and filling it completely. The vendors in the market, mostly small farmers, know Apollo very well. They call him the Boss, because he makes big purchases regularly. They know to give him the best quality and fair prices—you do not want him to pass by your stall without stopping next time. They will tell him if something good is coming next week, and he will tell Solange so that a special dish can be offered at Heaven.

Apollo moves through the clean and well-ordered market with a serious face, but gentle eyes that make people smile. There are rows and rows of fresh fruit—big, smelly, bizarrely shaped jackfruit, mangoes, guayava, and citron. Then there is the bean section—a rainbow of colors in gorgeous pyramids.

To do business in places like Rwanda, you will find people whom you will come to think of as irreplaceable. Apollo is just that.

When his shopping is complete, he will honk outside the gate of Heaven, which will then be danced open by Charles, always smiling, who will help unload the supplies.

Somewhere in the day, Alissa and I will work out together at the gym. We will, in any case, be back together to have early dinner with the kids. Then we'll run up the hill to Heaven to greet people and see how things are going. With our well-trained staff now, we don't have to go in every night, though in the high season, it's all hands on deck. The rush of a busy night is still intoxicating and must be the reason restaurateurs stay in the business. It can't be the margins or the hours.

We originally came to Rwanda for a couple of projects, but have produced a number of other initiatives since then. The Mayange Millennium Village Project is the nonprofit that has employed the community mobilizers and Donald the agronomist, and that has, in coordination with government, achieved incredible things. Most of Mayange now has electricity, and no family is more than five hundred meters from water, which now runs year-round. By 2013, the project had scaled back on staff because the key objectives had been met and a full exit was being planned for 2015. The project has been a participant in the government of Rwanda's rightful boast that it is on track for achieving many of the Millennium Development Goals, highlighted in its extraordinary achievement of lifting one million Rwandans out of poverty between 2007 and 2012.

Health Builders is the heart of my work in public health. It predates the Millennium Village, as it was the initiative I hatched on the Harvard campus with Jeff Sachs and hired

Dr. Blaise to run in Rwanda. Once Health Builders became a field operation, it soon operated in eighty-six health facilities serving about two million people. On Dr. Blaise's urging, we constructed five gleaming new health centers, thanks to donors as diverse as Garth Brooks and his wife, Trisha Yearwood, and Google's Eric Schmidt and family.

Celebrities, by the way, like Brooks, Bono, Scarlett Johansson, and others who believe in Rwanda's story, make more of a difference than you might expect. They reenergize everyone here to do even more, and they attract wider donor resources that help us expand our effective range. And it's fun to meet them, because it's wonderful to have someone to call when a kid needs a special, very expensive operation. That has happened more than once. I don't mind making the calls, and there are quite a few people who don't mind taking those calls and covering those costs.

A couple years ago, the Segal Family Foundation, financed by a former roofing magnate, became concerned about the plight of malnourished children in Rwanda. They financed the start-up of the country's first private dairy collection center. It has benefitted dozens of dairy farmers in the south, and we hope to expand it shortly.

That is the goal with Heaven, too. In 2012 Alissa resumed her role as general contractor, renovated the existing house, and introduced Inn Heaven, a boutique guesthouse. This new arm of the business allowed Alissa to expand training to housekeeping and other guesthouse services, including tour guiding. Emboldened by that success, a few months later, Alissa joined Jackie and Colin Kakiza, the Rwandan/Ugandan hospitality training duo, to launch the International Hospitality Academy of Rwanda, complete with tracks for culinary skills and front-of-house management. It was a dream she had tried to pursue three years before, but babies and management and staff turnover, as well as lack of funding support, prevented it from becoming a reality. Now, with renewed energy and five years of experience leading the top restaurant in the country, Alissa felt an urgency to launch. Seeing a Marriott, Hilton, and Sheraton being constructed before her eyes, knowing they were already poaching some of her best staff to send to Dubai for training, Alissa knew she had to introduce a local solution for ongoing hospitality training. Her goal was not just to teach lengthy multiyear theory-based curriculums as the existing schools do, but to introduce an accelerated practical training "boot camp" to groom future leaders for the hospitality industry.

These developments come at a time when our kids are beginning to have a very general understanding of what we do. Their principal interests, taking after their parents, are gastronomic. Every Sunday, Maya and Elodie run into Heaven's kitchen, grab a couple buttermilk biscuits, and tell Solange and the crew how much they love them. They are still young, but they have visited our new health centers and seen kids get their shots and newborn babies in sparkling clean maternity wards. Nothing is better in their world than going to Heaven on a Saturday night for a performance of traditional Rwandan dancers or for a movie. They are surrounded, every day, by a handful of interchangeable languages and by people from around the world who have committed to Rwanda with intention and with the vision of a better future. It is easy to imagine our children growing up in Rwanda. Maybe they will, or maybe we will have moved on. But here or elsewhere, I believe they will feel a special engagement with the needs and opportunities of the real world. I think they will take over wherever Alissa and I leave off.

CHAPTER 41

———◈◈◈———

Under the Umuvumu Tree

Just don't look at it," Alissa said. I had spotted another casualty of a power surge, a blown-out bulb, and our servers and staff seemed not to notice. We were dining in Heaven, under the Umuvumu tree. We were eating early, as it was Saturday movie night, when we clear the tables and show a good film from the States—the popcorn is free and the bar does a good business.

Actually, things at the restaurant are much better. That doesn't mean we don't remind people about a dozen things every day. We remind and remind and remind about things you wouldn't think necessary—Did the after-dinner drink cart appear after the customers' bill? Did you pick up the place setting when you saw that there was one less customer at the table? Did you repeat their order? Did all the tables receive their gazpacho amuse-bouche? Did you notice their Mojito was empty and offer another? Did you see the litter on the floor by their feet? Did you notice the music is turned off?— but it had become somehow different.

It could still get tiring and even upsetting, but is somehow less so these days. We are set on imposing high standards, for everyone's good. We were seeing it as a rhythm now. We were settling in.

"If we could do things all over again, do you think we should have started a restaurant?" I asked Alissa over dinner recently.

I was digging into my new favorite, pan-seared Nile perch over a bed of sautéed collard greens with a thick buttery lemon sauce. It was low-carb, leaving plenty of room for dessert, which I had my heart set on: a rhubarb macadamia nut bread pudding with rhubarb ice cream. My life, as I have said before, is very hard.

She argued with herself for just a second, shaking her head a little as she cast out the negative possibility.

"I would do it all again," she said. "It's what we came here to do, isn't it? Sort of?"

I told her that it was even more than we came here to do. We paused in the silence that followed.

Through all the stresses and losses, the snippy moments, the immense frustrations of dealing with the birth pangs of an emerging continent, our relationship had grown closer each year. Alissa's courage and her effort had not only given us a beautiful family, it had opened the way for all the things we want to do next. Maybe we will put a Heaven in some other heart of darkness. Maybe Jackie and Colin, our partners and cofounders of the International Hospitality Academy of Rwanda, who are wonderful managers and have great hearts, can take over this one—we are not married to it, after all. Maybe another Heaven, and another, will send some amazing people to school, and they will change the world. Maybe the modern management of clinics can be spread beyond Rwanda, so the numbers can start going in the right direction all over Africa and beyond. Maybe flour mills and dairies that bring jobs and end malnutrition should be started in other places, too. We are young, and so is today's Africa, so why not?

We think we can see the end to poverty and, yes, we may see mirages sometimes, but we are naturally hopeful. And, really, don't you see it, too? Isn't this thing possible? Why should we not live in the amazing time when poverty is cured on this little planet? Why should *we* not be the people who do that? Isn't life too short not to try? Isn't it the greatest thing we can do here?

This much I know: If there is an afterlife and we go there and there is a bar, I have already met many of the people I will see there. Dr. Blaise and Ranu and Jeannette and Apollo and Op-ed and so many, many others—and all the young, fresh college kids who have such beautiful hearts. Well, maybe they will come later, but there will be a place for them, too, because we all met here, doing what our hearts compelled us to do.

Is it getting to be time for our family to move on? There remains a great deal to do in Africa, but where should we be? What adventure? What new memories for our children? When you have success in a developing nation, it is wonderful when the government takes the programs as their own—it is what you want. But you also become something of an embarrassment to them if you stay too long, to receive too much credit.

I explained to Op-ed why he should keep his eyes open for other opportunities, as we might not stay much longer. I told him that I might be outstaying my welcome. He nodded.

"There is a saying for that," he said. Of course there is.

"The higher the monkey climbs up the tree, the more he exposes his you-know-whats."

I knew what.

So, who knows? Only the future knows what it will bring, is another saying here. The important thing is that whatever we do next, I know I want to do it with Alissa. We count each other as our best friends and most confidential advisers. We have gotten closer than when we were first married, which is amazing to me. How many times have we held each other on the deck of Heaven and danced a few steps in the dark corner under the Umuvumu tree or farther out, under the same stars we knew in Manhattan? Is there really such a thing as finding happiness, or yourself? Is it perhaps always shifting, like the source of the Nile? We feel close enough to finding ourselves while acknowledging that we will always be shifting — our little dance, I suppose.

Whatever happens, it seems we are having this dream together about Africa.

Epilogue

On a recent Saturday, Alissa asked me to lead the weekly training session at Heaven. On cue, moments after we began, the daily afternoon cloudburst descended upon us. The serving staff, gathered on the dining deck with me, waited for the roaring waterfall to subside, as it is impossible to hear anyone speak when the big rains come. The flood and mist, cascading from the high, tiki-angled roof above, closed in a silver curtain around us. The furniture rattled on the deck as thunderbolts moved closer. The staff were wide-eyed and quiet. I've found that people who have always lived with these rains, who were born and fell asleep to their familiar sound, still jump at the lightning strikes and watch, mesmerized, the sheer volume of water. They smile and raise their eyebrows at each other, acknowledging another awesome rain. Everything but memory seems to be washed clean again. In ten minutes the rain subsides.

The staff members know each other very well. Nevertheless, I asked them to take turns introducing themselves, just as they might to arriving customers. They introduced themselves in whispers. I held a cupped hand to my ear, but even with that prompting they were very shy and quiet in their introductions.

Angelo, however, always smiling, gave out his name in a confidently hearty voice. "I am Angelo! Welcome to Heaven! I will be your server tonight!"

"That's how to do it!" I projected as I strutted toward him. "Just like that! You see how he is taking charge of the customers' evening, so they will be able to relax and know that he is going to take care of them?" Everyone nodded and looked at Angelo with admiration, as if he had just arrived from another hilltop by tightrope.

"It is not dangerous to speak out, to stand out. No customer will beat you if you speak out and act like a world-class server."

They laughed a little, but my beating reference was not an idle one. "Seriously, many of you were taught to be quiet, to hold back your thoughts. Isn't that so?" They nodded. Angelo did not.

"Which of you was beaten in school?" They all laughed, except Angelo, who smiled. We talked about that for a while. Everyone said that they had been beaten except Angelo, who explained that he attended a progressive school where such things were not allowed.

"So, it's easier for Angelo to be confident and to introduce himself in a strong voice. The rest of you must work on that. Pump up your confidence. You should take pride in the fact that you survived, and that you have good jobs and are well-trained professionals. A proud man or woman speaks in a strong voice and smiles at everyone—a lion with no teeth has no bite. It's better to be loud and proactive than to be quiet and meek."

What is written deeply in our personalities from an early age is not easily altered. Those habits have to be eroded by time and patience. These words about confidence would have to be repeated often, so that little by little, they might smile more and try to be more outgoing.

For this training session, however, I had an important new thing to say that might reshape their thinking a bit faster:

"I want you to remember that your families are coming to dinner soon. I want you to make them proud of you, to see you full of confidence and professional charm." They brightened at the thought that their relatives would soon see them in a uniform, at a paying job, as part of this team. "Do you want them to think, oh, that Angelo was very good, but you were so weak and shy?" They looked toward Angelo, quiet. I could tell I was getting through. "So let's introduce ourselves again." This time, their voices could be heard from one end of Heaven's terrace to the other. Progress.

I noticed Solange watching from the kitchen doorway. She, too, was excited about her family coming. She will be the star of the evening, of course. We are all very excited.

Yes, it all takes time. Rwanda has been catching up fast and leaving other nations far behind. It has been putting up office towers and hotels at an accelerating rate and has been busy doing other things. It has been engaged in a great experiment in survival and forgiveness, one that is working. It has focused on the health and prosperity of its people, who are in many ways the models of Africa.

It's hard to describe how far Rwanda has come since we started living here; everyone who comes back after a few years away is stunned by its development. This little land that seemed bound for perennial horrors just two decades ago now seems destined for greatness. A recent Oxford study suggested that on its current course, Rwanda may eradicate poverty in the next twenty years. Such predictions will require an enormous, sustained effort, but progress is already visible. Worldwide poverty, which is the source of so much illness and violence, has cut its toll by hundreds of millions, particularly in China, since 1990. Sub-Saharan Africa continues to have the gloomiest outlook for poverty reduction, as few countries have the commitment and political leadership of Rwanda. Nonetheless, deaths in the region from AIDS, tuberculosis, and malaria have fallen tremendously, as have childhood and maternal deaths. The Global Fund has been an important reason for that—dodging the traditional aid system to deliver life-saving medicines to country-led programs. The personal efforts of so many people—young people mostly, from the Rwandan government ministers, permanent secretaries, mayors, and local leaders to the expats who sit at the Heaven bar—are the true heroes who make that new money actually save lives and build prosperity.

Yes, there have been many times when we felt we just wanted to be on the next plane out, but those feelings come rarely now. Our eyes are still opening to Africa. Maya and Elodie are starting to gauge what poverty means—they see children their own ages balancing impossibly large loads on their heads and they wince at how hard life is for them. Elias will see similar stories of struggle when he is a little older, too; for now he serves as the neighborhood Buddha, coaxing smiles from even the neighborhood's most reticent residents. In twenty years, our kids may live in a world where extreme poverty is a memory. If we can just get millions more engaged in the grueling and gratifying work to be done, we can make it a reality.

Our time here has taught us that the private sector, which we public health academics may have once looked down upon with slight disdain from our pedestals, is the crucial partner, and the most powerful force for the future health and happiness of Africa—and the world. Indeed, as we have seen the results of our public health work in addition to our modest effort in the private sector, we are rather astonished that more people are not jumping into business and business-guided initiatives that save lives and create jobs. Private sector investments can work for a fraction of the money that is otherwise wasted on international aid. Applying private sector approaches to not-for-profit programs gets results, too. Health Builders, for example, uses clear business interventions and metrics to improve community health outcomes and has seen extraordinary results in increased consultations, malaria treatment, family planning, and child health.

It is frustrating not to be operating on the widest scale with the programs that work. It is immensely important because when we end disease and poverty, over time we will also reduce terrorism and brutality. Then it becomes possible for every girl and boy to have a good and safe life. Imagine that for our little planet! We imagine it.

We do love going back to the States to see friends and family, and to luxuriate in the heaven of America. But after a few weeks stateside we get excited to return to the work in Rwanda. The pace and impact of activity continue to grow: The Health Builders team, continuing to hone our model, has generous support from the GE Foundation to launch a system with UNICEF that enables Rwanda's forty-five thousand community health workers to track every single pregnancy and birth using their cell phones. A couple months into a woman's pregnancy, her local village community health worker receives a text from a central database about her schedule for care: "Has Asina been to the health center for her prenatal checkup?" The community health workers can follow up to make sure she is properly cared for. The system allows the Ministry of Health and health providers to track potentially complicated births and get on the path to bringing down maternal and neonatal deaths to rich-country levels.

We get reports on rural health centers transformed as a result of the new sustainable management practices we have implemented. How do we know it's sustainable? We know it because we've started officially exiting many of our health facilities. They might need us once in a while to check in on a software glitch, but their systems are solid and their numbers—healthy births, immunizations, consultations, malaria treatments, HIV tests—are on par, or nearly so, with developed nations. As a result, they can provide excellent health care for about fifteen dollars a person. We get press releases about a new health center opening its doors to a community for the first time in its history. In 2013 we inaugurated our fifth new gleaming health center in Nyarugenge, Bugesera district. It was a grand affair with the minister of state for public health there to cut the ribbon. During its first two months of operation, the staff at Nyarugenge saw four thousand patients and delivered fifty-six newborns. There is no Health Builders' plaque on the wall, of course—it's a Rwandan health center, and the Rwandans will care for it and ensure that it thrives. Our core donors tell us that for the price, they've never come across a better, more sustainable intervention anywhere in the world.

And Heaven, too, is a model we will expand where and when we can. Can Heaven pull together the critical components of a serious East African business—gourmet restaurant, training facility, and boutique bed and breakfast? We hope so. Imagine Heaven Kampala, Heaven Nairobi, Heaven Dar es Salaam. Although you would think that those more developed nations would be awash in restaurants like ours, we're constantly reminded that they need a piece of Heaven, too.

At the end of the day, with the equatorial sun setting on this beautiful land, it is the businesspeople, donors, investors, and activists who, like us, really can see the end of poverty on our beautiful planet. It is within reach now. There is no reason for cynicism or negativity, which only slows down what might be done. There is every reason to share in the joy that comes from optimism and from action, from every one of us.

Recipes

A Meal at Heaven

We've had many of the best meals of our lives at Heaven and are pleased that so many of our customers have experienced the same. The following meal will, we hope, bring the flavors of Heaven to your home.

The Cocktail

South of the Equator

3 ounces vodka
3 ounces black pepper syrup (recipe follows)
1½ ounces lemongrass syrup (recipe follows)
1½ ounces freshly squeezed lemon juice

Combine all of the ingredients in a cocktail shaker, add ice, and shake well. Serve the mixture in two short cocktail glasses on the rocks.

Black pepper syrup

½ cup whole black peppercorns
2 cups sugar
2 cups water

Pulse the peppercorns in a spice grinder to break them down, but not until they are a fine powder. Combine the pepper, sugar, and water in a medium-size saucepan and bring to a boil over medium-high heat, stirring occasionally to dissolve the sugar. Reduce the heat and simmer for 30 minutes. Store overnight in the refrigerator, then strain through a fine-mesh sieve.

Lemongrass syrup

2 cups sugar
2 cups water
1 bunch (a handful) lemongrass, roughly chopped

Combine the sugar, water, and lemongrass in a medium-size saucepan and bring to a boil over medium-high heat, stirring occasionally to dissolve the sugar. Reduce the heat and simmer for 30 minutes. Strain the mixture through a fine-mesh sieve. Store in a closed jar for up to one week in the refrigerator.

Makes about 16 South of the Equators

First Course

Heavenly Peanut-Squash (Pumpkin) Soup

4 tablespoons (½ stick) unsalted butter
1 medium-size white onion, finely chopped
4 cups chopped pumpkin or squash of your choice
2 cups pureed cooked sweet potatoes (from about 3
    medium-size sweet potatoes)
6 cups chicken or vegetable stock
1 teaspoon freshly ground black pepper
1 teaspoon salt
1 cup smooth peanut butter
1 cup whole milk, or to taste

Melt the butter in a large stockpot over medium heat. Sauté the onion until lightly browned, then stir in the chopped pumpkin and sweet potatoes.

Add the stock, pepper, and salt and stir well. Stir in the peanut butter and milk to taste and blend the mixture with an immersion blender or in a blender. Bring to a boil, then reduce the heat and simmer for 20 minutes.

Serves 6

Main Course

Heaven's Signature Cassava
Chimichurri Filet Mignon

Serve the filet mignon with grilled corn and potatoes, any style.

Beef Filet

½ cup soy sauce
⅓ cup dry red wine
¼ cup honey
¼ cup balsamic vinegar
2 tablespoons chopped ginger
2 tablespoons chopped garlic
2 tablespoons freshly ground black pepper
2 pounds filet mignon

Cassava Chimichurri Sauce

½ cup cooked cassava leaf puree (or substitute a mix of
    parsley and cilantro leaves)
1 small red onion, cut into quarters
15 garlic cloves
2 bunches fresh cilantro
1 bunch fresh flat-leaf parsley

Pinch of dried oregano
2 teaspoons dried red pepper flakes
Juice of 1 lime
1 teaspoon salt
Freshly ground black pepper, to taste
2 tablespoons olive oil, or as needed

For the beef, whisk together all of the marinade ingredients in a large bowl. Add the filet mignon and turn to coat it thoroughly. Cover the bowl and refrigerate overnight, turning the meat occasionally in the marinade.

To make the sauce, puree all of the ingredients in a blender, adding olive oil as necessary to make a smooth puree.

Preheat your grill or broiler. Remove the beef from the marinade and cook to your liking. Slather chimichurri on top and serve.

Serves 6-8

After the Main Course

Watermelon-Chili Granita

1 large watermelon
4 cups lemongrass syrup (recipe on page 292)
1 teaspoon salt
1 habanero pepper, halved, or your favorite chili sauce
    to taste

Cut the watermelon flesh into chunks. Put the chunks in a low-powered blender and pulse until broken down into juice, but be careful not to puree the seeds.

Strain the watermelon juice through a coarse strainer to remove the seeds but keep the small pieces of flesh. One watermelon should yield about 8 cups of juice—adjust the other ingredients if your amount of juice is significantly different.

Combine the watermelon juice with the lemongrass syrup, salt, and pepper. Let the mixture sit for 10 minutes and taste. You want a hint of heat from the pepper, but not a lot. Let it sit a little longer to get more heat, or add another pepper.

Transfer the mixture to an ice cream maker and process according to the manufacturer's instructions.

Serves 8

Dessert

A Spice Tour

Serve the nutmeg cake drizzled with the cardamom syrup beside a few pieces of sesame brittle and ideally with your homemade ice cream of choice—we recommend coconut!

Nutmeg Cake

½ cup butter (1 stick), at room temperature
1½ cups sugar
3 large eggs, at room temperature
2 teaspoons ground nutmeg
1 teaspoon pure vanilla extract
1 teaspoon baking powder
1 teaspoon baking soda
¼ teaspoon salt
2 cups all-purpose flour
1 cup buttermilk

Preheat the oven to 350°F (175°C). Butter a 9-inch round cake pan.

In the bowl of an electric mixer, beat the butter and sugar until fluffy and noticeably lighter in color. Add the eggs one at a time, blending each into the butter mixture fully. Mix in the nutmeg, vanilla, baking powder, baking soda, and salt.

Add one-third of the flour to the bowl; mix just until incorporated. Stir in half of the buttermilk, mixing gently. Continue adding the flour alternately with the buttermilk, mixing until combined. Spread the batter into the prepared pan.

Bake in the preheated oven until a toothpick inserted in the center of the cake comes out clean, about 45 minutes. Let the cake cool in the pan for 10 minutes, then invert onto a wire rack to cool completely.

Cardamom Syrup

4 cups sugar
4 cups water
½ cup whole cardamom pods

Combine the sugar, water, and cardamom in a large saucepan and bring to a boil over medium-high heat, stirring occasionally to dissolve the sugar. Reduce the heat and simmer for 30 minutes. Store in the refrigerator, leaving the cardamom in the syrup. Keeps well for one week.

Sesame Brittle

1 cup sesame seeds
½ cup water
½ cup sugar
¼ cup honey
¼ teaspoon salt

Combine all of the ingredients in a small saucepan over medium heat. Cook, stirring continuously, until the mixture is a deep caramel color. Pour the mixture onto a sheet tray lined with a silicone baking mat or parchment paper, and smooth with a spatula to an even thickness. Allow to cool, then break into pieces.

Enough for 8-12 Spice Tours

Acknowledgments

Adequately thanking a country, its people, and its leaders for their many thousands of acts of kindness and generosity, large and small, year after year, is, in any real sense, an impossible task. Instead, I offer this book as a long-form thank-you note for the privilege of living and working in Rwanda.

Above all, my thanks to Alissa, whose willingness to join me on these unlikely adventures is the best thing that's ever happened to me. Without Alissa, there would be no Heaven, no kids, and no book. Our children—Maya, Elodie, and Elias—provided inspiration for all that's in these pages. Our respective crews of parents and siblings helped enable what is here through their support—financial, logistical, and otherwise. Now deceased, Joseph Cice and Rabbi Charles Lippman, of blessed memory, have one way or another influenced these pages.

The genesis of the book came from my discussions with my fabulous agent and friend Gail Ross. It was Gail who introduced me to my latest mentor, Dennis Burke. Dennis's contribution to all elements of this book was enormous, and he proved an incredible writing instructor and collaborator. Along similar lines, I will always be grateful to my writing teachers at Yale, Tom Perrotta and Fred Strebeigh. John Parsley, my editor, listened, tweaked, polished, and ultimately chaperoned this work through its sometimes punishing series of deadlines.

The generosity of the Truman Foundation, the Fulbright Foundation, and the Marshall Commission allowed me for years to cultivate my interests in development without having to drown in student loans. I owe an enormous debt of gratitude to the advocates and funders, small and large, who have supported the work in Rwanda over the past decade. They include: the Glaser Progress Foundation (with a shout-out to Martin Collier, Mitchell Fox, and Melessa Rogers), the Schmidt Family Foundation, the Segal Family Foundation, David Bonderman, the Pace Family Foundation, the Pfizer Global Health Fellows, Global Health Corps, the Maia Foundation, the Garth and Tricia Brooks Teammates for Kids Foundation, the J & T Meyer Family Foundation, the GE Foundation, the Deerfield Foundation, the Stephen Lewis Foundation, Millennium Promise, the MAC AIDS Fund, the Chernin family, and Venture Dairy.

This book stands in loving memory to the late Denyse Niyonsaba, whose personal battle against the forces of poverty left an indelible mark on my family. Support on the ground — consisting of Apollo Gakuba, Damascene Hategekimana, Asna Nkundumukiza, Paul Mugaragu, Joel Rwakayiro, Sylvain Rutikanga, and Claudia Shimwa — has allowed Alissa and me to free up the time necessary to do our work. There were many extraordinary volunteers from abroad in the Millennium Village's early days, including Susan Doll, Max Fraden, Maria Claudia Escobar, Ranvir Dhillon, and Shawn Johnson. Similarly we're grateful to more staff and other helpers than we can list here. We thank the many Heaven's "Angels": Solange Murekatete, John Mugabo, Charles Gacamabuye, Alex Sorenson, Shane Bartlett, Daisy Freund, Joshua Poveda, and Meg McLaughlin. Grace Lesser served as my COO for the last few years and in that capacity did wonders for our project work while serving as my go-to editor. Jenn Lee now tackles that role with gusto and joined in time to make many important edits. Karen Schmidt, Lauren Margulies, Merry Stricker, and Katie Kampf provided assistance in all aspects of the work, both in New York and in Rwanda. Ross Kornberg freed up huge amounts of management time by serving as an extremely capable leader for our dairy work. Josh Bress was the key doctor involved in Baby Agnes's early care and has since proven a tremendous colleague and resource for activities in eastern Congo. Felix Kayigamba has ably served as head of Health Builders in Rwanda, and I appreciate our amazing team's stellar results. David Zapol and Andrew McLaughlin provided vital last-minute and late-night modifications to the text. Finally, I thank my dear friend and colleague Bruce Rabb and the other board members of Health Builders who have served Rwanda generously over the years.

Index

Index

Index

Index

Index

Index

Ministry of Health, 93, 122, 133, 171,
    287–88
moto-polo, 58, 61–62, 64
mountain gorillas, 6–7, 36, 46
Mukabalisa, Jeannette, 141–42, 143,
    144–45, 167, 179–80, 187, 247
    basket weaving and, 249–50
Musanze, Bugesera District, 175
Museveni, Yoweri, 147–48
music, Rwandan, 191
Mutuelle de Santé, 133–34, 140–41,
    212–14
Mutzig beer, 56–57

N

Nairobi, Kenya, 56
Ndahiro, Donald, 112, 115, 140, 141,
    143, 167, 174, 181, 182, 187, 258,
    276
    background of, 94
    cassava crop and, 107, 240–41,
        243–44, 246–47, 254, 255
    damage to Heaven's Umuvumu trees
        and, 173–74
    failure of second crop and, 212, 214
    hiring of, 94
    listening to advice of, 240–41,
        242–47, 248
    management of Mayange Millennium
        Village turned over to, 245
    pomegranate project and, 254–55
    terracing of hillsides and, 98, 109,
        139
NGOs (non-governmental
    organizations):
    Alissa's search for job with, 66,
        72–73, 78
    critiques of, 170–71
    employees of. See expats
    sustainability issue and, 174–75
Nigeria, 132
Nile, 12, 85, 96–97, 98, 185
    source of, 84
9/11 attacks, 32, 33, 34
Ntakirutimana, Jean-Baptiste, 197–98
Nutmeg Cake, 295–96
Nyamata Catholic Church, 97, 98–102
Nyamata Hospital, 134–35
Nyarugenge, Bugesera District, 288
Nzangwa, Bugesera District: health
    center in, 130–31, 136–37

O

Obama, Barack, 216
ONE Campaign, 81
Op-ed. See Abed

P

Paris, Ruxin's sojourns in, 31–33
Passover story, 18–19
Peanut-Squash (Pumpkin) Soup,
    Heavenly, 292–93
Philippe, Dr. (pediatrician), 260
pomegranate trees, 254–57
POM Wonderful, 255
Poveda, Joshua, 222–24, 228, 232, 233
poverty:
    private sector investments as force
        for eradication of, 286–87
    stubbornness of, 119–20
    worldwide trends in, 285–86
pregnancy, health workers' tracking of,
    287–88
profit model, 29, 105, 201–2

Q

QuickBooks, 117, 133, 208

R

Ranu. See Dhillon, Ranu
recipes:
    Black Pepper Syrup, 291–92
    Cardamom Syrup, 296
    Filet Mignon, Heaven's Signature
        Cassava Chimichurri, 293–94
    Lemongrass Syrup, 292
    Nutmeg Cake, 295–96
    Peanut-Squash (Pumpkin) Soup,
        Heavenly, 292–93
    Sesame Brittle, 296
    South of the Equator, 291–92
    Spice Tour, A, 295–96
    Watermelon-Chili Granita, 294–95
Reynolds, Eric, 208
road improvements, 182, 246–47
Rucyahana, Bishop John, 190
Rugengamanzi, Epafrodite, 15
Rule One: feed starving people, 103,
    115
Rule Two: demand high standards,
    122–24, 279–80
Rule Three: don't give aid to corrupt
    nations, 154–56

Index

Index

About the Author

Josh Ruxin is on the faculty at Columbia University, directs Health Builders, and contributes to the *New York Times, Forbes,* and other outlets. He lives in Rwanda with his wife, Alissa, and their three children and is frequently seen bartending and tweaking recipes at Heaven.